The Republic of Hunger and Other Essays

The Republic of Hunger
and Other Essays

Utsa Patnaik

MERLIN PRESS

© Three Essays, 2007

First published 2007 by Three Essays Collective, India

First UK edition published 2007 by
The Merlin Press
96 Monnow Street
Monmouth
NP25 3EQ
Wales

www.merlinpress.co.uk

ISBN. 9780850366068

British Library Cataloguing in Publication Data
is available from the British Library

Printed in the UK by Lightning Source, Milton Keynes

CONTENTS

INTRODUCTION

The present selection contains five of my longer papers, of which all except the last have been published in *Social Scientist* between 2000 and 2005. It also contains seven of the many short pieces written at various times during the last decade and carried in *People's Democracy*. All these papers have been written with the idea that they should be easily comprehended by the non-economist reader, so I have avoided the use of jargon as much as possible. The unifying theme of these papers is the impact on the third world of the new imperialism in the present era, which takes the form of deflationary neo-liberal 'economic reforms' and a thrust towards free trade. The focus is on the impact of these policies on the agrarian question and in particular, the food security and livelihoods of the rural populations of developing countries including India. It is clear by now that these policies have led to absolute decline in purchasing power and a comprehensive crisis of livelihoods and food insecurity for the mass of the population, even as ruling elites enjoy a consumption boom fuelled by rising income.

The perspective on trade and development in relation to the agrarian sector, which I have acquired over the last fifteen years, is radically different from the standard approach to these questions by economists in developing countries, and owes much to my experience of teaching a course on comparative economic history to students for three decades. I realized quite soon that the pure theory of trade advocating the benefits of free trade for developed and developing countries alike, was logically incorrect for it rested on a material fallacy, of assuming that different countries could produce the same primary goods. In reality today's developing countries, located in warm climes, are highly bio-diverse and can produce a range of primary products which today's advanced countries cannot produce at all (the tropical crops), or cannot produce all the year round (the temperate crops). A brief critique of the Ricardian theory of comparative advantage and the conclusion that mutual benefit does not necessarily result from trade, may be found in "The Costs of Free Trade" in this volume, but a fuller treatment is available in Patnaik 2005a.

Acquiring control over tropical lands with their superior and unique productive capacity, was a major plank of traditional colonial systems, and it invariably led to a surge in exports from plantations and from peasant agriculture, but always at the expense of falling foodgrains output and availability for colonized populations, reducing their nutritional standard and leading even to the extreme outcome of famine. The exports were financed out of taxes raised from the local populations, which depressed their purchasing power and ensured that their need for basic nutrition could not be fully expressed as market demand. This was also true in a temperate colony like Ireland which ultimately saw famine owing to heavy rent burdens, taxation and the mandatory exports of primary products. This phenomenon of increase in primary exports to metropolitan countries leading to falling domestic nutrition, is observed in every single historical case – Java under the Netherlands, Korea under Japan, British India under Britain, to give a few examples. A fuller treatment of the historical cases may be found in Patnaik 2003 and 2005b.

Why there is necessarily an observed *inverse relation* between primary exports and domestic food grains availability is not difficult to understand if we remember that the earth is the cradle of all life and the arena of human productive activity, and that *land is a non-reproducible means of production*. There is a limited supply of tropical lands and if heavy external demands are made on its productive capacity while insufficient investment is put in, then history demonstrates that the satisfaction of domestic needs is not possible and local populations are plunged into undernutrition and poverty. In short, there has always been a *global asymmetry of primary productive capacities relative to demands on them* – poor developing countries have the capacity to produce a qualitatively different and quantitatively more extensive vector of outputs, and their very richness of land resources have made them targets of the greed of less well-endowed peoples who have in the past acquired forcible control over them. The advanced countries are, to this day, even more heavily import dependent than in the past on the superior productive capacity of tropical lands and the living standards of their populations are crucially dependent on ensuring a continuous flow of cheap primary products. They call for full opening up to trade by the developing countries so that they can once more re-structure cropping patterns towards the exports they want in order to sustain their high standards of life. Agriculture is included under GATT for the first time in 1994 and the entire policy regime is geared to make poor countries export more primary products. Whether this process leaves more people in hunger or dead in these countries does not appear to concern the advanced countries today any more than it did in the past.

We cannot increase the physical extent of our lands when called upon to supply external demands, emanating from those advanced countries which, no matter how technologically advanced they are, can never produce the crops that our lands can, or cannot produce certain crops all round the year. At most we can increase the yields of our lands, so that exports do not lead to falling domestic supplies. But, under colonial systems the question of raising productivity enough so that local populations did not face declining nutrition, was never given any importance by the colonial rulers, who on the contrary made sure that taxation was heavy enough to reduce internal purchasing power (deflate mass incomes) thus releasing land resources for more exports. Moreover the export surplus earnings were siphoned off by the rulers to settle their own external trade deficits with sovereign lands: so no stimulus came from export production for colonized peoples. Increased hunger, in many cases famine, was the result. In present times, the deeply disturbing fact is that the deflationary agenda of finance capital imposed on developing countries, is producing exactly the same result of lowering investment and growth in agriculture. The possibility of more exports without lowering local food availability becomes even more remote than a century ago, for in the meantime cultivable wastes have disappeared so lateral expansion is no longer possible.

For a few brief decades after decolonisation, the developing countries succeeded in protecting their agrarian sector from rapacious external demands of the advanced world and turned their attention towards raising internal purchasing power and satisfying internal mass demand, so that nutritional and health standards rose albeit slowly. For an even briefer period in the early 1970s, their primary exports commanded adequately high international prices.

All this changed from the end of the 1970s, with the new era of dominance of global finance capital which started imposing its retrogressive agenda through loan 'conditionalities' via the Bretton Woods Institutions. A new drive for implementing deflationary policies in the material productive sectors of third world countries was seen, combined with a drive for once again promoting one-way free trade from the late 1970s. There was mandatorily greater trade openness for developing countries culminating in the WTO discipline, while advanced countries retained intact their non-trade barriers, even imposed new tariffs and subsidized output of their primary products heavily.

Given knowledge of the historical trends, it was alarming indeed to find that in Sub-Saharan Africa, in the course of the 1980s, under structural adjustment programmes advised by the IMF, high rates of export volume growth had been associated with steeply falling per head food grains and food staples availability. In the summer of 1992 I spent some time analyzing the UNDP (1992) data which had just become available, for 46 sub-Saharan African countries, on output of export crops and of domestically consumed food staples, expressed per head of total population. The results showed a faster rate of decline of per capita food output over the single decade of the

1980s than we had seen in the inter-War period in colonial India. Next year my study of the Mexican experience of reforms and free trade up to the late 1980s showed a similar trend of declining food grains availability for the Mexican peasants as export volumes grew fast, and additionally fodder crops for the livestock-raising *latifundia* (which exported to the US market) rose to one-third of cereal output compared to one-twentieth a mere two decades earlier.

In all these countries deflationary policies at the macroeconomic level had been followed under Fund-Bank advice while opening up the economy to free trade. It was clear that these modern deflationary economic reforms and free trade package was leading to a replication of all the structural features of the colonial era. Mass incomes were being cut – mainly rural incomes in Asia but also urban incomes in Latin America – and rapid cropping pattern shifts were observed away from domestically needed crops towards export crops.

Standard economic theory would say there is nothing wrong with this for a developing country should specialize and it can always import any food grains it might need out of increased foreign exchange earnings from its exports. Standard economic theory however ignores the actual working of the political economy of the new imperialism, which ensures that no matter how fast primary export volumes increase, there is no net increase in food availability for the masses through imports (although grain imports may go up to produce livestock products for the local elites). This reduction of the nutrition level of the masses happens through a three-fold policy mechanism: First and most important, deflationary policies of reduction in state expenditures on rural investment and development mean that unemployment grows, internal mass incomes are cut and mass purchasing power thereby reduced. In short the aggregate market demand of the poor majority itself is made to fall although their needs are being satisfied even less than before. The mainly urban elites on the other hand raise their incomes since reform policies favour expansion of this segment of the market to which the more advanced countries can export their consumer durables.

Second, also an important factor, increasing volume exports by dozens of third world countries all urged to export more and compete with each other, simply depresses the unit dollar prices of their primary exports and this is further aggravated by the incessant pressure to devalue their currencies. Very heavy subsidies by Northern countries to their farm sector to enable them to dominate global markets, also play a role in depressing global primary prices. The net result is that high rates of volume growth of primary exports bring little or no growth in foreign exchange earnings from this source. Free trade leaves poor farmers unprotected from price volatility and subjects them to the long-term decline in their terms of trade. The crashing global prices from the mid 1990s to which farmers have been exposed in India for the first time since Independence owing to removal of effective protection through quantitative restrictions, has plunged millions of farmers in the morass of cumulating debt and led to more than nine thousand officially recorded farmer suicides since 1998, the bulk in Andhra Pradesh. Suicides continue at present every day in Vidarbha, Kerala and Punjab, with not an iota of official action being taken to address the causes.

Third, even if foreign exchange earnings are growing from other sources (in India remittances by workers abroad and other invisible earnings have been large) the policy makers do not import food grains but let the masses go hungry by making the callous claim that there is voluntary reduction in their intake, even though grain intake has been actually made to fall involuntarily through the deflationary, income reducing policies. The first episode of stocks build-up in the early 1990s in India was discussed in a brief paper titled 'Mass Income Deflation, Burgeoning Foodstocks' in 1996. The second episode of stocks build-up, far more dramatic, started from 1997-98. Thus by July 2002 public grain stocks of 64 million tonnes had built up, or a massive 40 million tonnes in excess of the normal stocks, because sales from the ration shops had fallen owing to the loss of purchasing power year after year. This steeper decline was because in addition to the already operating cuts in public expenditure, farmers were also exposed from mid-decade to steeply falling global primary product prices as protection was dismantled, the buffer of official commodity boards was destroyed and the TNCs came to dominate purchase of major export crops, and the food subsidy was targeted cutting out many millions of the actually poor from access to affordable foodgrains. The falsity of the official interpretation that high food stocks are the result of voluntary diversification of expenditure away from food grains is discussed in an extract in the volume from a longer paper, 'Food Stocks and Hunger'.

With the false official claim of the build-up of stocks being the outcome of 'voluntary' demand reduction, 22 million tonnes of grain were exported out of stocks at a low subsidized price by the government during 2002 and 2003 – the largest exports ever since Independence – despite a severe drought starting from the second half of 2002. These grains went to feed European cattle and Japanese pigs while Indians were going hungry.

Some of the results of agrarian crisis induced by neo-liberalism in other developing countries have been briefly discussed in the shorter pieces included here, as in the case of the Philippines and Mexico. The severe economic and demographic collapse in the former Soviet Union has been largely ignored by Indian economists - a brief piece on Russia is also included here. The bulk of the discussion however centres on developments in India since the inception of the neo-liberal policies from 1991. The severely adverse impact of this on the agrarian sector, especially as regards the undermining of food security, was predicted by me in a paper written in 1992 on the basis of our own historical experience and the experience of other developing countries which had already implemented such policies.

But I could not have anticipated the extent to which official economic policy in the 1990s would become systematically anti-farmer and serve pro-imperialist interests, the extent to which successive governments, drunk on the mirage of growth through IT-enabled services alone, would wilfully ignore all warning signs of impending agrarian crisis repeatedly pointed out to them. Nor could I have anticipated the extent to which Indian intellectuals and policy makers would abandon the pursuit of logic and rational economic discourse, for the mindless dogmas which pass as economic theory, peddled by the international financial institutions, and which consist in essence of the long discredited pre-Keynesian idea that the supply of savings in the economy is fixed no matter how high unemployment might be. We continue to hear the absurd view 'Public spending leading to high fiscal deficits, crowds out private investment' – the same logically incorrect view which, because it induced the wrong policies of expenditure cuts to balance budgets, had plunged the world into the Great Depression seventy years ago.

The paper titled 'The Republic of Hunger' was presented as a public lecture in April 2004 just before the general elections to give readers some idea of the utter falsity of the 'shining India' campaign of the National Democratic Alliance (NDA). With the new United Progressive Alliance (UPA) government however we see no change in the official analysis as regards agriculture: the problem of output growth is now recognized but not the basic problem of demand deflation and deepening hunger. Indeed it is shocking that the deflationary hammer was once again brought down on the peasantry in the very first fiscal year 2004-05 of the new government, as pointed out in the short piece 'It is Time for Kumbhakarna to Wake Up'. While the passing of the National Rural Employment Guarantee Act is important, its implementation is bound to be sought to be sabotaged by the powerful neo-liberals controlling key portfolios in the present government, who are all deflationists in subservience to the pre-Keynesian deflationist dogmas of the Bretton Woods Institutions.

The official 'solution' being put forward – the corporatization of India's agriculture – is yet another major step towards the breaking by the government, of the implicit social contract with the peasantry with which our post-Independence development had started. It is a recipe for the subjugation of our farmers through high-technology debt, to the giant transnational corporations, which pursue profit alone and which in other third world countries have already ground down producers to the level of paupers.

The claim of the Planning Commission and of many individual economists that rural poverty has declined during the 1990s is completely inconsistent with observed rising unemployment, deepening of hunger and widening agrarian distress. A closer investigation of the method officially used for estimating poverty shows us that it is an illogical method, where the current National Sample Survey (NSS) data on the actual cost of nutrition are not consulted at all, but a poverty line based on the quantities people consumed 33 years ago is brought forward through a price index. The implication of using this price-index method with a far distant base year is that the official poverty line becomes a gross underestimate of the actual cost of accessing even a bare minimum nutrition level. Indeed it is amazing that anyone is found to survive.at all on less than Rs.12 per day (the official poverty line in 2004) for meeting all expenses. No defence can be acceptable for the bizarre result of the official method, that in states like Andhra Pradesh and Kerala the official poverty line for year 2000 was so low that it allowed at most 1590 and 1440 calories per day respectively to be accessed, over 800 to nearly 1000 calories below the required daily allowance. In short the alleged poverty 'reduction' is arising only because of the trick of lowering continuously over time the consumption standard with respect to which poverty is being measured. The paper on 'Theorizing Food Security and Poverty' explains these issues to the interested non- specialist. It is a basic right to information that every citizen should have, how and in what manner data are being manipulated by the specialists they trust, to present a false picture of reality, to show decline in poverty when the reality is precisely the opposite.

We are today on the threshold of a major revival of peasant resistance to the iniquitous process of globalisation, which is nothing less than a new phase of imperialism characterized by primitive accumulation vis a vis the third world. This phase of imperialism involves the blatant corporate grabbing of peasant land and forest resources, the undermining and pauperization of the peasantry and the domination of third world agriculture by the giant corporations under contract farming. The last lecture delivered in July 2005 analyses some of these issues from the perspective of the imperative need for peasant mobilization to resist and reverse these processes.

Utsa Patnaik

THE IDEOLOGY OF 'OVER-POPULATION'

China and India, as everyone knows, have the largest nominal populations in the world: 1205 million and 897 million respectively in 1994, adding up to 2.1 billion or nearly one third of the entire total of world's inhabitants. Both countries are habituated to being told, especially by experts from northern countries, that it is highly irresponsible of them to have let their populations grow to such large figures and that there is an imperative need to restrain this rate of growth. China and India are considered to be 'over-populated' countries and apocalyptic pictures are painted of the worsening situation in future. On present trends, it is expected that China's population (which is growing faster than before in the last fifteen years of Dengist reforms) will be 1540 million by the year 2025 and India's nearly 1400 million (these projections are by the United Nations Population Fund).

Population figures are freely used in talking of economics; yet unlike all other variables where real as well as nominal concepts are used, in the case of population variable only nominal numbers are usually ever talked about. This is in fact highly misleading and it plays an ideological function of masking certain important exploitative aspects of international economic relations. Looking at nominal population the most populous countries in the world are India and China. *If the concept of real or effective population is used, the most populous countries in the world would turn out to be located in North America, followed by Western Europe and Japan.*

By real or effective population is meant the population figure adjusted with respect to its demand on resources. This is the only rational sense in which one can talk of 'pressure of population'. When the government of the Soviet Union had instituted rewards for motherhood and encouraged large families after the Second World War, it was reacting to a converse situation where its nominal population was the fourth largest in the world (despite the loss of 20 million lives in fighting fascism), but nevertheless was not large enough relative to the need for employing available resources.

We are all quite used to adjusting the nominal earnings of a person by the change in the index of prices in order to get an accurate idea of the real income, or the actual purchasing power of the nominal income. This is necessary not only because of the question of what happens to a given person's income over time, but also because it affects the extent of the gap between the person's income and others' income. The same rise in food prices for example will lower workers' income more than an employer's income, affecting income distribution. Income earners are so familiar with all this as part of their own experience that they hardly need an economist to point it out. But when it comes to the question of 'population pressure' the discussion even with trained economists nearly always assumes a strange level of naïveté, becomes extremely simplistic in that real or effective population concepts are never used.

The very term 'population pressure' implies that population is so large as to make excessive demands on available resources. But is the problem of 'excessive demand on resources' a function of nominal population alone? Clearly not. We can have a situation where two populations are exactly the same in nominal terms and with the same resources; but if one has twice the per head income of the other, its demand for resources will be twice as large and we would be correct to think of it as a larger population in real or effective terms, exercising greater 'pressure' on resources. This is precisely the characteristic of world population problem: *the greatest 'real population pressure' emanates not from China or India, but from the advanced countries.*

Let us take the most important resource, commercially produced energy which is also the most problematic because most of it is directly or indirectly from non-renewable fossil fuels (coal, oil, thermal part of electricity and natural gas). At the time of the Earth Summit in July 1992, it was estimated that in the previous year the total commercial energy consumption per capita in coal equivalents in North America (USA and Canada) was 10,737 units compared to 5,218 units in Western European countries. In India it was by contrast around 100 units and in China less than 230. Thus the per capita commercial energy use in North America was about 47.5 times higher compared to China and over 100 times higher compared to India. The difference between Indian and Chinese per head use of energy in turn is of the same order as the difference in their per head incomes: Chinese average income at present is slightly more than double the Indian level.

With less than 4 per cent world nominal population, the USA alone accounts for some 40 per cent of the world consumption of commercial energy. With almost one-third of the world nominal population, the two Asian giants together account for less than 5 per cent of world commercial energy use. Yet they are termed countries which are so 'overpopulated' as to exercise pressure on resources!

The grotesque inaccuracy of the description is clear. But the charge of 'overpopulation' heaped on the poor countries is very useful for those rich countries who through their life-styles actually exercise immense pressure on global resources. It serves not only to divert attention from the very high levels of effective or real population pressure they exercise, but also to secure for them an agenda of actually trying to reduce the meagre consumption of the poorer countries.

We can construct a simple country-wise index of per head demand on energy resources taking the Chinese per head demand as the base level, then adjust the nominal population of each country by this index, to obtain real population.

- The Chinese real population is equal to its nominal population of 1.2 billon.
- The adjusted or real population of North America is 47.5 times its estimated 1994 population of around 285 million, which works out to 13.5 billion (compared to standard population of China—1.2 billion).
- Western Europe and Japan with its total of 435 million population works out to at least 10 billion real population.
- India with its nearly 900 million nominal population in 1994, has a real population of 0.40 billion.

The two Asian giants of population taken together thus account for a mere 1.6 billion real population, compared to a real population of as much as 23.5 billion, or nearly fifteen times higher, in the advanced world.

Incidentally it must not be imagined that energy consumption is 'bound' to be high because of cold climate of the northern countries. That factor does not take account of the wasteful life-style: huge public buildings and offices are kept centrally heated around the clock even when not occupied at night; with bright sunshine everyone still uses automatic clothes dryers. Petrol pricing policies ensure that a litre of petrol costs in the US, even at the present devalued rate of exchange, a mere nine rupees, or much less than a bottle of mineral water in India or in the US. Expressed as a fraction of the daily income of the average person in the USA, the cost of one litre of petrol is one part in two hundred only (0.05 percent), while in India it is a little over one half (50.0 percent) of the average Indian's daily income.

In short, adjusting for incomes, the US prices its petrol at a hundredth of our price; its consumers pay, as it were, only 18 paise per litre. This gross under-pricing has encouraged the location of large suburban family homes in the US which are up to a 100 miles from their place of work, mandated the universal use of the private automobile, and reduced public transport to a joke. This irresponsible North American life-style has been declared to be 'not negotiable' by the then US President and even the outcry by the local environmentalists against the gross under-pricing of petrol has produced little substantive result.

It is to sustain this 'non negotiable' life-style that an assured supply of oil has to be kept flowing from the Arab states, and the US has shown during the Gulf War of 1991 and after, to what lengths it is prepared to go to ensure the continuation of a political set-up that in turn will maintain a smooth and uninterrupted flow of oil. (Though it has large oil reserves of its own, the US follows a policy of not stepping up domestic extraction in order to keep its own exclusive 'strategic reserve' in case of war and therefore relies heavily on imports).

Energy is not the only resource guzzled by the huge effective populations of the advanced countries. A vast volume of imports from tropical lands (which their temperate lands cannot produce at all, or can do so only seasonally) are sucked out to underpin their high living standards. There is, therefore, continuous pressure on the developing world to export more even at the expense of lowering their own consumption, and to devalue their currencies again and again to keep their exports cheap.

A small minority of thinking and progressive people in northern countries themselves understand the injustice of the situation and explicitly advocate both a cut-back in northern consumption and themselves practice alternative life-styles; but they remain a tiny minority.

The leaders of the advanced world are greatly disturbed over both nominal population increase and per capita income rise in the developing countries because it will necessarily mean that these countries will absorb a slightly higher share of the scarce or non-renewable resources whose world supply has been successfully hogged by the advanced countries so far. They are not prepared to give up an iota of their privileges. China in particular gives them nightmares because the Chinese growth rate of income is high, and its economic policies are not amenable to their pressures, unlike India whose growth rate can and is being curbed through the imposition of debt-conditional structural adjustment policies, thus curbing the growth of its real population.

People's Democracy, April 7, 1996

THE COSTS OF FREE TRADE
THE WTO REGIME AND THE INDIAN ECONOMY

It is indeed a privilege to have been asked to deliver the EMS Namboodiripad memorial lecture and I thank the organisers for it. Two years ago, after EMS (as he was referred to affectionately by everybody) passed away in March 1998, there was a memorial seminar held in June at Perintalamana in Malabar, the town which is within a short distance of EMS's ancestral home. I read a paper on this occasion, which was specifically on EMS's writings on the agrarian question – in particular how his famous Minute of Dissent to the Commission Malabar Tenancy Reforms, was informed by the Marxist theory of ground rent. This has been published in a recent issue of *Social Scientist* (Patnaik, 1999). In that paper the concern was with the contradiction within the agrarian economy between those who monopolise landed property and those who derive a livelihood from the land.

In today's lecture I propose to talk about another very important contradiction which is fast maturing – that initiated by the liberalised trade and investment regime under the earlier loan-conditional structural adjustment programmes from the late 1970's as applied to the developing

The First EMS Namboodiripad Memorial Lecture organised by the Students Federation of India, delivered on February 16, 2000.

nations, and strengthened further with the current WTO discipline imposed after the signing of GATT in 1994. All of this, I would proceed to argue, is part of a new onslaught by the advanced capitalist countries (following their own economic interests), on the third world countries' attempts to follow growth trajectories best serving their peoples' development and welfare. In talking of this emerging new contradiction I would like first to discuss briefly the historical experience of trade-liberalized regimes, and refer to the theoretical underpinnings of analysis relating to these trade liberalized systems. Then we will discuss, again briefly, the costs paid by the other developing countries which in the last two decades have followed a liberal trade and investment regime, and finally look at the specific results and future implications for the Indian economy of the current 'free trade' regime.

It is often accepted as an unquestioned truism by economists, including economists from developing ex-colonized countries, that the freest possible international trade is necessarily a good thing for everyone participating in that trade. For over two centuries now the ideology of free trade has been so thoroughly dinned into the heads of students, via the textbooks and in today's world also via the conventional wisdom filtering through the print and electronic media, that any systematic alternative viewpoint which stresses the costs of 'free trade' is hardly ever encountered. The ideology of free trade dates back to Adam Smith and David Ricardo, and it is no accident that both theorists should be from Britain and have written at a time when that country was in the process of grasping the land and resources of other civilizations, and launching on the world's first Industrial Revolution after creating a conducive economic environment for it by forbidding its colonies to manufacture anything and forcing them to specialize in producing the wage goods and raw materials its own industry needed. Neither theorist was English, for Smith was a Scotsman while Ricardo's forebears came originally from Spain. Yet both were the quintessential theorists of the emerging manufacturing bourgeoisie in Britain in the last quarter of the 18th century and the first quarter of the 19th century respectively. The free trade that they advocated has been much misunderstood; it was the freeing of British trade from its own monopoly trading companies, but very much while retaining control of subjugated colonies; hence the freedom to Britain to continue to industrialize at the expense of other nations and peoples, and definitely not a general freedom for any potential rival to do likewise. Thus Adam Smith, in a passage in *The Wealth of Nations* which is seldom if ever quoted, strongly opposed the idea of North America developing its own manufactures rather than relying on importing manufactures from Europe:

> It has been the principal cause of the rapid progress of our American colonies towards wealth and greatness that almost their whole capitals have been employed in agriculture. They have no manufactures, those household and coarser manufactures excepted which....are the work of the women and the children in every private family. The greater part both of the exportation and the coasting trade of America is carried on by... merchants who reside in Great Britain. Were the Americans, either by combination or by any other sort of violence, to stop the importation of European manufactures, and, by thus giving a monopoly to such of their own countrymen as could manufacture the like goods, divert any considerable part of their capital into this employment, they would retard instead of accelerating the further increase in the value of their annual produce, and would obstruct instead of promoting the progress of their country towards real wealth and greatness.(Smith [1776], reprint 1986, p.466)

Here was the first clear articulation by a metropolitan economist, of the now familiar and self-serving argument that the colony's best interests lay in remaining an agricultural exporter, leaving the manufacturing and trade to be done by the metropolis.

These words, published in 1776 were famous last words, for after winning Independence less than a decade later, from 1783 North America's European settlers went on precisely to do the opposite of Adam Smith's advice, namely they erected protective barriers against the inflow of manufactures from Britain and Europe and built up their own industry in a process of import substitution. Because they did so the USA is today the world's leading capitalist country: had they listened to Adam Smith's version of 'free trade' it would have been at most an Argentina. As the leading capitalist and imperialist country in the world the USA follows today in turn policies to encourage its own growth at the expense of the third world's freedom to industrialize, a question I propose to discuss later.

Of course, the modern theory of international trade is associated above all with David Ricardo and is an elaboration and development of Ricardo's theory of comparative advantage (Ricardo [1815], 1986, Ch. VII on Foreign Trade). The essence of the ideology of international free trade can be said to reside in this theory, for it says that specialization and trade is necessarily of mutual benefit to both parties entering into trade as long as relative cost differences in producing goods exist, even where one country may produce all goods at a lower absolute cost than does the other. The theory has been immensely influential and has been used to explain not only the trade between countries of equal economic strength, e.g. intra-European trade, but also the pattern of international trade in which the colonies and subjugated areas came to specialize in agriculture while the European countries specialized in manufactures; and to argue that not only the colonizer but the colonized too benefited from this pattern of specialization and trade. Comparative advantage is the reason given, for example, by Professor K N Chaudhuri in the *Cambridge Economic History of India* to explain why from being the world's largest exporter of cotton textiles in the pre-colonial era, India turned into an importer of cotton manufactures from Britain and an exporter of agricultural products like raw cotton, jute, opium, indigo and so on (Chaudhuri, 1985).

No argument can be more fallacious than Ricardo's theory. Why it should have been necessary to use military force to induce countries like Portugal, China or India to trade if it was so beneficial for them, is not explained. Even more important, the theory is internally logically fallacious. A fallacy in a theory can arise either because the premise is not true, or because the process of inference from the premise to the conclusion is not correct. In the case of the comparative advantage theory, the premise itself is not true. The premise is that in the pre-trade situation (assuming the standard two-country two-commodity model) both countries can produce both goods. Given this premise, then it can be shown that both the countries gain by specializing in that good which it can produce at relatively lower cost compared to the other country, and trading that good for the other good: for compared to the pre-trade situation, for a given level of consumption of one good a higher level of consumption of the other good results in each country. This mutual benefit arising from comparative advantage is adduced as both the reason for and the actual outcome of specialization and trade.

The reality was that the tropical or sub-tropical regions with which Britain, Netherlands, France, etc., initiated forced trade using military power were bio-diverse and could, and did, produce a much larger range of goods than the North European countries could, including tropical crops which could never be produced under field conditions in the temperate regions. In tropical regions crops can be grown all the year round and multi-cropping of the same physical unit of land is possible. Not only is the output vector much larger but it is a qualitatively different output vector, for it contains elements which are not present in cool temperate lands at all. Moreover since it is agriculture which provides not only food for subsistence but raw materials for manufacture, fibres for clothing and traditional materials for housing, the better resource base and lower costs of subsistence in a bio-diverse tropical region lead to abundant supply and lower costs of all these elements vital for the standard of life.

While Portugal, which is a warm temperate land, could produce both cloth and grape-based wine on a large scale, Britain could produce only cloth but not grapes under field cultivation, for the latter requires land within a mean July isotherm of at least 19 degrees Celsius or 66 degrees Fahrenheit, which no part of Britain (except perhaps Cornwall) possessed. Similarly while India, Burma, Vietnam or Indonesia could produce both cotton cloth as well as raw cotton/sugarcane/ indigo/tea/coffee/jute/ rubber etc., Britain, Netherlands, Germany and France could produce only cloth and none of the other crops, and so on. The cost of production of raw cotton, indigo, tea, coffee, jute, rubber etc thus cannot even be defined for cool temperate Britain, Germany, or Canada. If absolute cost is not definable, then *ipso facto* relative cost is not definable. The premise of the theory is not true, namely that both countries can produce both goods, hence the conclusion does not hold, that specialization and trade is necessarily mutually beneficial. Certainly the country with the poorer output vector benefits by acquiring goods it cannot produce; but the country with the superior output vector does not necessarily benefit: specialisation and enforced trade can lead to very adverse welfare outcomes such as falling mass nutrition levels, as we will show below.

Yet economists have continued to make logically untenable, hence nonsensical statements like the following: Britain exported cloth and imported tea/indigo/cotton from India because it had a comparative advantage in cloth production while India had a comparative advantage in the crops specified. How does one at all talk of production, or cost of production of tea and indigo in Britain? This absurd fairy tale masquerading as serious theory continues to hold sway in trade theory to this day, modified only to say – the labour-abundant country produces labour intensive (primary or simple manufactured) goods while the capital abundant country produces capital intensive (advanced manufactured) goods.

The lack of the basic and crucial premise – homogeneous productive capacities across countries – in history was itself the positive real reason for this important segment of trade: thus adopting the premise amounts to assuming away the real reason for this trade. The basic motive of forced trade was for the temperate lands to gain access to tropical bio-diversity and to inexpensive manufactures like textiles of mass appeal and mass consumption which were based on using the unique and cheap resources of these regions. In the course of the three centuries since 1700 the consumption basket and standard of living of the Northern populations has altered beyond recognition. It is based on importing goods from all over the world, the major part being goods not producible at all in the temperate lands.

While Ricardo's explanation was superficially extremely clever, he did a signal disservice to the cause of objectivity and science, by pretending in effect that all trade including forced trade, was freely chosen trade determined by technologically determined, neutral cost factors. Trade patterns which had been in reality the outcome of trade wars, genocide, slavery and political subjugation, were discussed in such a way as to ignore this historical reality of 'capitalism's blustering violence' (to use a memorable phrase first employed by Rosa Luxemburg, 1963); and by focusing only on value-neutral cost factors – necessarily in a fallacious manner – Ricardo provided an intellectual justification for, and hence an apologetic for forced trade. 'Capitalism's blustering violence' was neatly sanitized into the theory of relative costs. All subsequent mainstream trade theory has been similarly fallacious and apologetic in character, and has talked of mutual gains from trade as the necessary cause and result of all observed patterns of specialization – not simply that between countries of similar economic strength.[1] 'Factor endowments' are talked of while completely ignoring the real differences in productive capacities in the same 'factor', land, in different countries. Many generations of third world economists have been fooled into believing that somehow being involved in a particular pattern of primary sector specialization was unavoidable in terms of pure cost-of - production logic and was to the ultimate benefit of their countries.

But why blame Ricardo alone? It is only to be expected that the leading economist of a country which built its empire on slavery and on the principle of grabbing others' resources, should provide a theoretical apologia for its trade. It does not explain why the theory should have enjoyed currency for two centuries and why third world economists should subscribe to it. As regards the first the answer lies in hegemony of Northern universities in academic life, the fact that mainstream economists find it expedient to push an incorrect theory because it continues to play the ideological role, in today's world as well, of justifying trade which is not of benefit to developing countries but does benefit advanced countries. As regards the second question, we in the third world remain mentally and intellectually colonised even when we are politically independent: we do not dare to question the most nonsensical of theories as long as they come from the centres of academic hegemony and power, we do not dare to point out that the Emperor is naked. This is not accidental: as long it is not the search for objective truth which guides us, as long as it is professional publications and professional recognition in metropolitan centres which remain our implicit aim, in short as long as third world academics continue to suborn themselves, intellectually infantile and dishonest theorizing will continue to hold sway.

What was the historical cost to countries like ours of being involved in 'free trade' as defined and implemented by the colonizing powers? I am here not talking of the well known costs by way of the genocide and decimation of entire peoples, their numbers running into millions, involved in colonial conquests. I would like to focus on the mechanisms of free trade in more recent times.

There have been two very important types of cost historically, which have again come to the forefront in the present era of loan-conditional liberalization and WTO discipline: the first is the re-emergence of an inverse relation between agricultural exports and domestic food availability, and the second is de-industrialisation. To understand the first type of cost we have to conceptualise tropical land as akin to a non-renewable resource. Usually it is the fossil fuels alone and the minerals which are thought of as being non-renewable. But we have to recognise that land is not homogeneous in productive capacity, and that the earth's bio-diversity and botanic diversity is concentrated in the tropical lands. It is clear that there is a limited supply of these lands, for unlike in the 19th century when ample cultivable wastes existed, by now there are no open frontiers, the limits of physical expansion have been reached and only the vast tropical rainforests remain whose ongoing destruction carries serious adverse environmental implications. In big countries like India and China total cultivated area is no longer expanding, in fact it is shrinking. Our land now is virtually like a non-renewable resource. It is not completely non-renewable: sown area can still be expanded if enough investment is pumped in, especially into irrigation. But the regime of neo-liberalism is precisely one of macro-economic contraction, 'withdrawal of the state' and falling rates of public investment, and in this context tropical land must be conceptualized as non-renewable.

But the global asymmetry of demand, established over two centuries ago, continues: the world's rich countries which account for over 80% of global income although they have hardly 16% of world population,[2] cannot produce in their own countries anything but a small fraction of the highly diversified consumption basket on which their populations have come to depend, and they want access to our more productive, bio-diverse but limited lands on the one hand, and on the other hand access to our markets for the few primary goods they can succeed in producing (notably food and feed grains), and for their manufactures. Their high living standards are crucially dependent on the physical availability of our products. A typical Northern supermarket in W. Europe or USA carries on average 12,000 items of food alone in raw and processed form (Friedman 1990) and at least 60-70 percent of the items have a wholly or partly tropical to subtropical import content. If these goods were to disappear from the supermarket shelves the standard of life of Northern populations would plunge to a near-medieval level, that prevalent three hundred years ago.

The solution developed earlier under colonial and imperial systems where there was direct political control was simple: first, protect metropolitan industry through trade barriers to the inflow of cheaper manufactures based on ample supply of raw materials from countries like ours; second, promote in the colonies the export of the raw materials, wage-goods and luxuries required for running metropolitan industries and sustaining an improving standard of life; third, keep the colonial markets completely open to the flooding in of manufactures from the metropolis; and fourth, monopolize invisible incomes (at that time, from shipping and financial services). This remains the basic agenda of the advanced imperialist countries today as well, although the economic mechanism has changed to debt-conditional policies and a trade discipline operating through international organizations (while invisible incomes have changed to modern forms of financial and communication services, the electronic entertainment industry, and returns to research in pirated bio-resources). Advanced countries continue to protect their own producers, continue to demand that we export tropical primary products or at most simple labour-intensive manufactures and continue to seek market access for their manufactures, their surplus temperate crops and continue to try to monopolise invisible incomes.

As regards the costs of these policies, in particular the second one, to the subjugated nations then (and the developing nations today), the single most important in my view, is the fact that nutrition levels of our people were lowered and in extreme cases mass starvation resulted. An inverse relation necessarily developed between primary product exports and food availability for the colonized populations. While demanding an increasing supply of the products of tropical lands, the foreign rulers did not put in adequate investment to raise productivity; hence increasing primary exports could only take place by diverting land and resources away from producing the necessary food consumption of the people. In every single case of export of primary products to advanced countries the per head food consumption of local producers fell. This applied also to the only temperate area which remained a colony in the 19th century: Ireland. There are two complementary aspects to this fall: on the supply side the diversion of resources to export crops led to reduced growth rates of foodgrains supply for local populations, while on the demand side these local populations' purchasing power and hence aggregate demand was curtailed through heavy taxation (or land rent extraction), and the use of a large part of taxes by the colonial government to finance the export of goods of benefit to the metropole.

As Britain's first colony, from the mid-18th century Ireland was obliged to export grain and livestock products to an increasingly food-deficit Britain, at the expense of the local population's own consumption. After the ruthless 17th century Williamite conquest the local Irish had been turned into rack-rented tenants of English settler landlords. These Irish tenants, who were "pauperized beyond belief" (Hobsbawm, 1969 in *Industry and Empire*, p.96), were obliged to export wheat and livestock products to Britain in order to pay high rents to their English landlords, while they themselves lived on cheaper potatoes, introduced from the New World and developed as a staple food crop for the labouring poor. In the great 1846-7 potato blight famine one million Irish died out of the 8 million total population.

B.H. Slicher van Bath details the harsh actions of Britain during the famine years:

> The measures passed by the British government drove the tenant farmers to emigration. Outstanding rents and taxes could be collected by law. Tenants who could not pay were evicted, and their dwellings broken up or burnt. The intention was to destroy small landownership and tenant farms. (*The Agrarian History of Western Europe*, p.270)

Wheat and livestock exports to England continued while the famine raged.[3] The Irish famine is by far the biggest famine in the last two centuries, carrying away over one-eighth of an entire population, larger even than the Bengal famine of 1770 in which one-tenth of the population reportedly died. Yet we find no mention of the great famine in a general reference source, the *Encyclopaedia Britannica,* under the history of Ireland: a brief mention of the famine is relegated to the entry under "potato"! A massive famine resulting from Britain's colonial exploitation – the more intense and implacable given the proximity of the colony and the ease of military control – is to this day, re-invented as a characteristic of a tuber! Why the Irish had to live on potatoes alone when they grew wheat, is not a question which is raised in these ideologically biased sources. So traumatic was the famine that, Ireland, the only colony in Europe, is also the only European country whose population was steadily declining (owing to out-migration exceeding population growth) until by 1911 it was a mere 4.4 million, compared to 8.2 million in 1841.

Looking at the data for Java under the Netherlands we find that per capita foodgrains output fell by about 20% from 199 kg. annually to only 162 kg. between 1885 and 1940, while sugarcane and rubber production rose 762 percent and 332 percent respectively. On a per capita basis the two crops rose by 380 percent and 166 percent. The volume of exports rose 3.7 times in the half century after 1890 (Table 1).

Table 1
Population, Output of Paddy Rice and Export Crops, Java 1885-1938

Year	Population mn.	Paddy Rice mn.t.	Rice per head kg.	Period	Rubber output index	Sugarcane output index
1885	19.92	3.650	199	...	...	...
1890	21.97	4.155	189	1890-99	...	100
1895	23.67	4.210	178	1900-09	...	263
1900	26.15	4.470	171	1910-19	100	382
1905	27.39	4.410	161	1921-25	251	491
1920	34.98	6.110	175	1926-30	504	668*
1930	40.89	6.500	159	1931-35	600	402
1940	48.42	7.840	162	1936-40	762	332
Annual growth	**1.6**	1.4	-0.3		8.8	8.6*(-7.3)

Source: Calculated from various tables, *Agricultural Development in Indonesia* by Anne Booth 1988. For sugarcane the first growth rate is for the period up to peak output, 1926-30, and the second rate gives the decline thereafter.

Japan like Britain was food-deficit during its period of industrialization, and it increasingly relied on rice imports, amounting to over one-fifth of its own domestic output before World War II, with the share of its colonies, Taiwan and Korea, in total rice imports rising vertiginously (Table 2a, Schumpeter 1940). Korea was a more important source than Taiwan; Korean peasants were heavily taxed, and the tax-financed rice exports to Japan grew to account for over half of its domestic output, while Koreans were forced to eat millets and suffered a one-sixth decline in per capita calorie intake starting from an already low level, over a mere quarter century (Table 2b, Grabowski 1985). According to Hayami and Ruttan (1970), poorer Korean peasants were driven down to starvation levels and were obliged to subsist on wild grasses for a part of the year.

Colonised India, in the half century preceding Independence, had a growth rate of exportable commercial crops which was over ten times higher than the growth rate of foodgrains, which almost stagnated. The per capita

Table 2a
Annual Production and Imports of Rice, Japan 1915 to 1937

PERIOD	Domestic Output Q m. koku	Net Imports Korea and Formosa m. koku	Colonial . Imports/ Q %	Total Rice Imports m.koku	Colonial Imports/ Total M %
1915-19	56.13	2.65	4.7	4.73	56.0
1920-24	59.07	3.96	6.7	6.02	65.8
1925-29	58.97	7.49	12.7	10.38	72.2
1930-34	62.57	10.83	17.3	11.68	92.7
1935-37	60.74	12.69	20.9	12.94	98.1

Source: Annual series in E Penrose 1940, Tables 22, 23. Five-year averages calculated from annual series, except last row which is three-year average.   1 koku = 4.96 bushels

Table 2b
Daily Per Capita Energy Intake in Calories, Korea 1913-1935

Period	Percent of Rice Export to Output of Rice	Rice	Barley	Millet	All	Total Calories from all Sources	Index of Total Calories
1912-15	11.3	877	490	274	1641	2133	100.0
1916-20	17.3	842	526	329	1697	2206	103.4
1921-25	30.2	731	468	365	1564	2033	95.3
1926-30	41.9	650	449	381	1480	1924	90.2
1931-35	51.4	630	468	296	1394	1812	85.0

Source: Shuh 1977 as quoted in R Grabowski 1985

food production fell by nearly 29% in the inter-war period in British India, and by as much as 38% in Eastern India (termed 'Greater Bengal' in the source); since there were little or no net imports the availability declined also to the same degree (Table 3). While quantitative estimates for earlier periods at the all-India level are not available, we have enough arguments and evidence – starting from the writings of Dadabhai Naoroji and R.C.Dutt – of severe regional famines being precipitated in the 19th century owing

Table 3
Decline in per head Foodgrains Output by Regions, British India

Region	Period of Change	Total Percent Change	Annual Rate of Change
BRITISH INDIA	1901-1941	-29	-1.14
Greater Bengal	1901-1941	-38	-1.18
Madras	1916-1941	-30	-1.40
Bombay-Sind	1916-1941	-26	-1.21
United Provinces	1921-1941	-24	-1.36
Central Provinces	1921-1941	-19	-1.05
Greater Punjab	1921-1941	-18	-1.00

Source : G Blyn 1966

to the displacement of the non-traded part of food crops by traded export crops (including the export of food crops like wheat), a process which was economically coerced by imposing heavy rent and revenue burdens on the peasantry.

As Table 3 shows there was a steady decline in per capita foodgrain production and availability in British India, and the situation reached a nadir during World War II. In a critique of Amartya Sen's theory I have argued that he defines 'food availability decline' too narrowly, to refer only to the short term effects of droughts, cyclones and the like, ignoring completely the *long-term structural changes* brought about in the cropping pattern and output pattern by colonial export policy, which led to foodgrains availability decline as is so clear from Table 3. It was the increased vulnerability resulting from lowered nutrition, as a direct result of secularly falling per capita food output arising in turn from colonial export policy, which accounts for the *extent* of the toll – over 3 million dead – in the great Bengal famine of 1943, although the proximate *cause* of the toll itself was the huge burden of wartime deficit financing unjustly placed on India.[4]

Nothing can be more immoral than the fact that the North sustained its own high consumption and low-inflation growth literally at the expense of squeezing the living standards of millions of subjugated people, to the extent of precipitating mass famine in many cases.[5] I may add that all this was not possible without the willing collaboration of comprador elements within the third world populations, those who identified their interests with the powerful rulers and in the way they lived their lives, betrayed their own countrymen. That element too remains unchanged today: power will always attract the opportunists and the servile persons who have no scruples in identifying themselves with what they consider to be the 'winning side' and by their servility hope to gain, and do indeed gain very materially. In the charge of intellectual servility I would include all those globalized Indian academics today, who are intelligent enough to know very well what the real economic mechanisms are, but who find it impolitic to ever mention it in their writings, because their objective is to be acceptable to and to be lionized by the powerful North-dominated academic establishment.

I would argue that the costs of the 'free trade' instituted under loan conditional trade liberalisation in India from 1991 and accelerated after the signing of GATT 94, are exactly the same as in colonial times. They are the same because the agenda of imperialism is the same although conditions are so different. *Plus ça change, plus c'est la même chose* as the French say: the more things change the more they remain the same. For, the dependence of Northern populations on Southern bio-diversity has increased, not declined, despite sporadic attempts to find laboratory substitutes for natural tropical products; hence the present WTO regime insists on the prising open of third world land in order to alter cropping patterns and increase exports of those primary products which advanced countries cannot produce themselves,[6] and prise open third world markets to free imports of the wheat and processed dairy products of which they have a glut.

The second great historical cost of 'free trade' to our economies has been de-industrialization. Forcibly open and trade liberalized economies like ours and other subjugated countries too, underwent a destruction of their traditional manufactures and the occupational structure moved towards higher dependence on the primary and tertiary sectors. This resulted from one-way free trade, viz. a situation where the North protected its own industry by various means and opened up the subjugated markets of the third world countries. To use a memorable phrase that Keynes had once used, describing a situation where a country insists on exporting to another the good that the second country also produces, thereby the North 'exported its unemployment' to other countries.[7] That agenda too remains unchanged: non-agricultural market access is a prime objective of the earlier and ongoing loan conditional liberalization and of the present WTO regime which is its continuation. Although on paper the provisions on market access are to be applicable to all countries, in practice steps are taken to ensure differential market access, viz., opening the advanced country door a very little to third world exports of manufactures but forcing open the third worlds' doors wide to unrestricted inflow of advanced country manufactures. This has already resulted in substantial de-industrialization in many Latin American and SSA countries in the last two decades and the process is now underway in India as well.

Trade and Declining Food Security in Present Times

Let me, to begin with, take up the first great cost of present-day one-way free trade namely, falling food output per head and falling nutrition levels in developing countries, and then go on to discuss de-industrialization briefly. As we know agriculture was included for the first time in the Uruguay Round of negotiations leading up to the signing of GATT 1994. The trade-related intellectual property rights and trade-related investment measures also carry important implications for primary sector trade. What was the basic objective of including agriculture whereas it had never been included earlier?

The reason does not have to do only with intra-Northern trade, despite the wrangles between USA and the European Union over subsidizing agriculture, which have been much publicized. All Northern countries made sure that they did not have to reduce subsidies at all (by using a trick brought out by Table 5, which we discuss a little later). I believe that the most important impetus lay in two developments: first, the loss of export markets for food and feed grains by the advanced countries of N.America and W.Europe owing to the economic collapse of Russia and Ukraine as well as Eastern Europe, and hence their desperate desire to seize new Asian markets; and second, the rapid growth of monopoly in the already concentrated structure of the big transnational agro-business corporations. The first, the loss of East European and Soviet markets in the early nineties was very substantial, amounting to around 28 m.t. of grain exports in the early nineties, and gave an urgency to the targeting of Asian markets – first the S.E.Asian markets and now India. For this it was necessary for the advanced countries that all independent systems of domestic food grains procurement and maintenance of buffer stocks by third world governments should be dismantled and they should turn into food importers from the global market. The Philippines provides a case study of the success of this strategy: its public procurement and distribution system was wound down in the early nineties under loan-conditional pressure and it turned into a substantial net grain importer.

Some 85% of the global trade in foodgrains was accounted for by the advanced countries organised in the OECD on the eve of GATT 94. Both the specific provisions of loan-conditional liberalisation, and the provisions relating to agriculture in GATT 94, have been tailor made and designed for this purpose: it attacks input subsidies, attacks subsidies for stock holding and general subsidies to the consumer. The Agreement on Agriculture mentions food security as a non-trade concern at the behest of the developing countries and most magnanimously 'permits' stock holding activities for food security reasons. But the conditions attached have serious implications: countries are 'allowed' to undertake public stockholding of foodgrains provided "the difference between acquisition price and external reference price (i.e. the ruling international price) is accounted for in the Aggregate Measure of Support" where the AMS is subject to reduction commitments. This did not matter for years when the domestic procurement price in India was below world price, but now that the world grain price has fallen in the course of the last two years, and is below the current per tonne production cost in India, the pressure to give up procurement at a fair price to our farmers is bound to mount. Indeed with the current reduction of import duty to a flat across the board 35% in the 2000 budget, Indian farmers are already subject to unfair competition, since the world grain price itself is not related to production cost abroad but is the result of massive subsidy used for capturing markets.

The small print of the Agreement has been written in such a way (allowing cash to be paid directly out of the nation's budget to farmers under 'green box' and other provisions) and such prior measures have been taken that advanced country subsidies have remained almost unchanged while third world subsidies have declined (Table 5).

The second development was the growth of monopoly through mergers and take-overs in the already oligopolistic sphere of global agro-business corporations in the course of the late seventies and the decade of the eighties. These are now giant vertically integrated companies each with a wide range of interests ranging from pesticides, fertilisers, genetically engineered seeds, farm machinery, plantation production for export, exportable crops acquisition through contracts, and operation of agro-processing and livestock industries. The existing international agreements on plant-breeders' rights have been found to be inadequate by these corporations, which have their eye on the immense gene pool which tropical bio-diversity represents, which though located in developing countries, they see as providing the free raw material for their laboratory research leading to highly profitable potential applications in the sphere not only of agriculture and pest control but also medicines, cosmetics, health foods and so on. Companies like Monsanto took a very active part in mobilising other TNC executives, formulating the TRIPS provisions and lobbying the US government to incorporate the precise provisions they wanted.

A paper titled "GATT Intellectual Property Code" presented to the Licensing Executive Society USA/Canada Annual Meeting in October 1989, by James R Eynart, Director, International Affairs, Monsanto Agricultural Company, describes the successful efforts of the Company along with like interest groups in pushing the IPR provisions they wanted: "A country cannot exclude drugs, chemicals, biotechnology and the like from patentability; a reasonable term must be provided with 20 years from filing suggested. Compulsory licenses are to be tightly limited." The paper is interesting for its fulminations against developing countries, which are accused of seeking "magic ways to shortcut the development process", and against the UN system "where high flown rhetoric and crackpot ideas are taken seriously" even by many developed country academics who "took this New World Economic Order stuff seriously".

The provisions of the TRIPS agreement in relation to bio-resources are tailor made and designed to introduce into new regions and strengthen elsewhere the monopoly control of these giant TNCs, over drugs, chemicals, and bio-technology comprising new varieties of plants including genetically modified varieties, and over genetically modified organisms in general.[8]

The traditional rights of local plant breeders are not the issue at all; modification of the existing patent laws are sought solely to extend the period of monopoly that a patent confers, and to restrict the ease with which others can at present reproduce the patented product. Given that the entire process of research by the TNCs is based upon the pirated genetic materials from third world countries over which then a monopoly is instituted, and is to be enforced by international policing organisations like the WTO which is answerable to no general body of nations, the authoritarian implications are clear. These are dangerous developments for the third world countries given the background of the already existing trend of falling per head food output in such a large part of it, owing to an enormous primary export thrust under loan-conditional trade liberalisation.

The Latin American and Sub-Saharan African countries had been implementing structural adjustment programmes and trade liberalisation for a decade and half before India did and the results have been plain to see. Mexico which had pioneered high-yielding wheat varieties turned into a net foodgrains importer by the eighties and has been experiencing falling per head output of maize and beans at the same time as it has turned into a tropical agricultural annexe for supplying beef products, fruits and vegetables to supermarkets in the USA. The effects of cattle-raising for supplying the US market has been devastating for the Central American countries like El Salvador and Honduras.

The Sub-Saharan African countries engaged in a primary exports thrust in the eighties very successfully – the exports have been growing at minimum rates of 6 to 14 percent annually- but at what cost? The per head foodgrains output has fallen all through the eighties and continues to stagnate in the nineties. In 1992 I carried out a fairly painstaking calculation using the UN data for all 46 countries of SSA, defining 'food crops' generously, to include not only cereals but also tubers and plantains (pulses, important in India, are negligible in SSA). This showed that in the six most populous countries, accounting for over three-fifths of the population, per capita cereals output had fallen by 33 percent in the second half of the 80s and the per capita food crops output had fallen by one-fifth. For the entire region cereals per capita had declined by 16.4 percent and food crops per capita had declined by nearly 12 percent. This is a faster rate of fall than we had in the half century before Independence. Since the initial per head cereal and food crops output was already low by Indian standards – only 159 kg. gross annually per head – the level after falling, was only 141 kg. by 1990, and the situation has not improved since. It is no wonder that large areas of SSA are on the verge of famine.

It is often argued that the inverse relation does not matter for exchange earnings from primary exports can be used to import food. But whether this is so, depends on the terms of trade. The absolute unit dollar price of primary exports declined by nearly half in the 1980s alone owing to the fact that dozens of developing countries were made to competitively devalue and deflate their economies while engaging in a competitive export thrust, under loan-conditional programmes overseen by the Fund-Bank. After a brief two years of improvement the decline continued in the second half of the nineties at a slower pace.

A subsequent calculation of availability by adding on food aid and imports shows that it was insufficient to maintain nutrition levels, for calorie intake per head has declined for four out of six most populous countries and is stagnant for one, showing a rise only for Nigeria which is exceptional

Table 4
Change in nutrition level in the six most populous countries in
sub-Saharan Africa

Country	Cereal imports (000 T) 1,000 tonnes		Food aid (cereals) (000 T)		Change in imports* (000T.)	Per cent change in calories per head
	1.	2.	3.	4.	5.	6.
	1980	1990	1979-80	1989-90	1980-901	1979-81 to 89-91
Tanzania	399	73	89	22	−259	−2.17
Ethiopia	397	687	111	538	−137	−9.92
Uganda	52	7	17	35	−63	−6.00
Nigeria	1,828	502	—	—	−1,326	15.45
Kenya	387	188	86	62	−175	−9.86
Zaire	538	336	77	107	−232	1.54

Source: P. Patnaik 1999b:174. For first four columns, various issues of *World Development Report*; fifth column derived from earlier ones. For last column, see FAO 1996. Note that calorie intake refers to total calories from all food.

* Imports are net of food aid. Units are one thousand tonnes.

Note: Column 5= (2–4) – (1–3). Import figures refer to calendar years while food aid figures refer to crop years (July–June) so that their comparison gives an approximate picture only. Since aid data are from foreign donors, July–June is compared with the following January– December to take care of lags in aid arrival.

in being an oil exporter (Table 4). These four are precisely the countries which had gone in for two to three loans and had a successful export thrust under intensive adjustment programmes. Their primary exports have been growing at between 8 to 14 percent annually. The inverse relation between their primary exports and domestic food production was pointed out in an earlier article of mine (Patnaik 1996). Since the unit dollar value of their exports has been declining however their foreign exchange earnings hardly rose at all. It is little wonder that it was some of the African countries who, given their long and bitter experience of liberalization, were at the forefront of the anger against the WTO regime at the Seattle meet.

On the basis of some knowledge of this alarming experience of the Latin American and SSA countries under liberalisation and adjustment I had written in December 1992, 18 months after India went in for a \$4.8 billion loan and started implementing SAP, that with trade liberalisation and export thrust we in India too could expect a decline in per head food output, as the powerful magnet of the advanced countries' demand start to restructure our own cropping patterns away from the foodgrains our population needs and towards exports, just as it had done in colonial times.[8] It gives me no pleasure to say that my prediction has been fully borne out. For the first time in 30 years, in the nineties the food grains growth rate in India has fallen to a mere 1.66 percent, well below the population growth rate (even though this itself is slowly declining) whereas it had averaged 2.6 percent in the preceding two decades, well above the population growth rate. Furthermore this is against the background of a sharp rise in the rural poverty percentage to 44% from around 33% between 1990 and 1992; while poverty moderated subsequently as more expansionary policies were followed, the latest estimates by an economist in the Planning Commission, shows a rise again to 45% in 1998 admittedly on the basis of the thin sample data. (When this paper was written I was not aware that both official and individual estimates were substantial underestimates of the actual extent of poverty, because the method followed is an indirect one totally de-linked from any nutrition norm – for a critique, see 'Theorizing Food Security and Poverty' in this book).

It is to be noted that the data given on foodgrains availability in the Annual Economic Survey, which do not seem to show a fall, is subtly doctored. If we look at the population figures used to calculate the per capita availability and given in the relevant Table S-44 every year, we see that the same absolute number, 16 million (1.6 crores) is being added to the population year after year; the base is enlarging but the assumed addition to population remains the same, so that by 1998 the implicit growth rate is only 1.66 percent, doctored to be exactly equal to the declining foodgrain growth rate.[9] In fact with Indian population crossing the one billion mark in 1999, the compound growth rate from 1990 to 1999 works out to near 2 percent, well above the sharply lowered foodgrains growth rate over the same period.

The per capita expenditure on cereals in real terms has been declining in India as a number of analysts of the NSS consumption data have pointed out, at the same time that the per head production is declining, and per head availability is stagnating.[10] It is only those illiterate in economics who can argue that this reflects an Engel effect *in toto*, i.e. more diversified consumption for everyone as per head income improves. There is indeed such an effect for the top 15-20 % of the population, who concentrate anything between 70 to 80 percent of national income, depending on the estimate of black money we adopt. But the remainder, especially the poorest, are paying for it with a decline in their consumption of basic staples, given the overall stagnation of per head availability of cereals in physical terms.

A little explanation is in order, since there appears to be a widespread misconception not only among students of economics but also among many senior teachers, that with rise in income, the absorption per head of the staple cereals, falls. Exactly the opposite is the case: per capita cereals absorption rises, and rises quite a lot, owing to indirect cereal consumption in the form of animal products. The USA produces over 300 million tonnes of foodgrains, for a population a quarter our size; even after a substantial fraction is deducted on account of exports, the average US citizen absorbs annually nearly 900 kg. of foodgrains, or over four times the average Indian annual absorption of 200 kg. (we are taking throughout the gross figures viz., gross foodgrain output retained within the country, divided by population). Even the Soviet Union in the late eighties when its agriculture was supposed to be in crisis, was producing and absorbing 760 kg. foodgrains per head of its population, nearly four times India's level. (The situation in the former Soviet Union changed radically in the 1990s and grain absorption fell owing to the drastic decline of aggregate demand- see 'The Economic and Demographic Collapse of Russia' in this volume). Of course, North Americans do not, and the Soviet citizens did not, directly consume all grain as grain: they ate about 200 kg. directly as bread etc, with the remainder being converted to animal products by being used as feed, while grain is also used in industry (commercial starch, alcohol, etc.). The reason that this process leads to such a high absorption of grains per capita is because as is well known, at even the most efficient technologies of conversion, animal production – especially beef and mutton favoured by Northern populations- is highly grain intensive and therefore wasteful from a social point of view. The grain which could feed directly six to eight poor families in a year, goes to providing milk, meat etc for one well-to-do family (Yotopoulos 1971). The income elasticity of demand for animal products is high and has been estimated at 1.6 taking a large number of developing countries. As the per capita income rises, so therefore does the average absorption of the food grains which double as feed grains, rise, and this has been also true of India where animal products have been growing at between 8 to 12 percent annually.

In the light of this, it may be judged how serious is the situation today in India given that – despite rise in the average per capita income both in nominal and in real terms for the country as a whole – the per head foodgrain availability for the population has been registering decline. This is a highly unusual scenario and cannot happen if the distribution of income remains unchanged. We know that the top two decile or so of the population is absorbing grain per head to a much greater extent than before owing to the fast growth in their demand for animal products, which implies that there must necessarily be a greater than average decline in availability of grain for direct consumption by the poor. This can only happen if income distribution is worsening, with absolute income decline for the mass of the population.

The situation is not entirely hopeless; many organisations have become aware of the threat to food security faced by third world countries and that nothing less than an economic recolonization is being attempted by the advanced countries through WTO. Within India the many womens' organisations have come together with NGOs to form the Alliance for the Protection of Food Rights. Similar organizations are active in a number of Asian countries. At Seattle the African nations in particular were at the forefront of the opposition mounted against the advanced countries for obvious reasons, for they know from their direct experience of the last 15 years the sinister outcome of the designs of the advanced countries. What is urgently required is unity among the developing nations to work out a common minimum strategy to protect their interests against the onslaught on their land and bio-resources.

Removal of Quantitative Restrictions on Trade

Many of you must be aware that India had put forward a nine-year phase - out plan of giving up the prevailing Quantitative Restrictions or QRs on imports starting from 1997 and ending in 2006; but this was not acceptable to the group of six advanced countries wishing to access our markets, who argued that India's foreign exchange reserves position was comfortable and India could no longer invoke article XVIII (b) which specifies that QRs can be retained by countries facing possible balance of payments problems. Subsequently even though five out of six countries accepted a reduced period of six years phase-out, the USA remained obdurate and took India to the dispute settlement board which ruled against India. As a result all QRs are to go by fiscal year 2000-01 which is already upon us. Now, in anticipation of converting QRs to tariffs the advanced countries had announced very high tariffs ranging from over 200% for wheat to over 150% for other cereals. India's tariff bindings on the other hand are only 150% for wheat and amazingly, zero percent for rice and sorghum. Why and how the rice farmers and sorghum farmers of this country are to face the onslaught of competition without any protection whatsoever is not clear. Who were the incompetent officials who gave this anomalous structure of tariff bindings and is this a conspiracy against the farmers of this country, are questions which need to be answered. Japan which produces highly subsidized rice declared tariff bindings for all crops except rice and has thereby kept its options open while we seem to have closed ours quite inexplicably.[11]

There is not only mere absence of a level playing field, but indeed the field is steeply inclined towards the developed countries owing to the trickery they have employed. Let me illustrate this from the subsidies data on agriculture. GATT 94 specified that the AMS or aggregate measure of support to agriculture was to be reduced by all countries compared to the base-level support in 1986-88; but reduction was to be to a greater proportionate extent by advanced countries compared to developing countries.

This looked good, on paper, for developing countries: but what is the reality? The advanced countries, facing falling global primary prices in the early 1980s, without exception scrambled to raise their subsidies to agriculture phenomenally between 1981 and 1986. In the early 1990s when the Uruguay Round negotiations were going on, in anticipation of future subsidy reduction commitments, they declared the 'base period' from which reduction is to be calculated as 1986-88. As may be seen from Table 5 the USA had raised its Producer Subsidy Equivalent which is part only of its total transfers to farmers, from only 9% of value of crop production under such subsidies in 1980, to as high as 45% by 1986, namely a 500% rise in the relative share alone, representing a much higher rise in the absolute sums involved. It is this highly inflated transfer which then became the base for reduction, so that after reduction the transfers still remain a multiple of what they were in 1980.

The story is the same for the other high-income primary exporters; even Japan in which PSEs already amounted to 71% of output value in 1980, raised it further to 93% by 1986. Ten countries of the EC raised the share from 25% in 1980 to 66% by 1986. Even full compliance with the reduction commitments by advanced countries from these inflated base period levels would leave them with an absolutely dominating position; and full compliance has not taken place. Developing countries on the other hand, not only did not raise their meagre subsidies at all but sincerely – and foolishly- tried to comply with WTO reduction commitments, thus steeply tilting the field against themselves. It is this kind of manipulation and dishonesty, which makes the demand by advanced countries that developing countries should reduce their already meagre subsidies, such a hypocritical demand.

As global primary products prices have been falling from 1996, the advanced countries have been once more increasing the transfer to their farming sector, as the OECD data summarized in Table 6 shows clearly. These

Table 5
Percentage of producer subsidy equivalents to agricultural production
by selected countries

Year	Australia	Canada	European Commission (10 countries)	United States	Japan
1980	5	15	25	9	71
1981	8	16	30	12	65
1982	15	20	42	14	77
1983	8	19	26	34	79
1984	9	25	24	21	81
1985	13	39	44	26	86
1986	19	54	66	45	93

Source: Ingersen et al. 1994.

are budgetary transfers, under green box and blue box provisions, which they have been careful to write into the Agreement on Agriculture. Since these are rich industrial countries where the farm sector employs less than 5 percent of full time workers and correspondingly contributes 4 percent or less to GDP, they can easily afford to give budgetary support to the extent of 2 to 3 percent of GDP, which amounts to half or more of the total value of agricultural output. In India where agriculture employs two-thirds of the workers and contributes over a quarter of GDP, a similar order of support would not be possible even if every single rupee of central government revenues went to agriculture alone.

This leads us logically to the question of de-industrialisation. Let us briefly take up this other very important result of the trade-liberalisation discipline of the WTO, namely the de-industrialisation of developing countries. Again the WTO is merely codifying and implementing the provisions which were already a part of loan-conditional liberalisation earlier. We have ample documentation on the way that the free inflow of capital has served to de-industrialise the Latin American and SSA economies from the works of many economists, and not necessarily those

Table 6
Estimates of support to agriculture in 24 OECD countries (text says 2624 is correct)and the United States (in million US dollars)

	1986–1988	*1997*	*1998*	*1999*
OECD 24				
Total value of production (at farm gate)	500,752	624,164	585,034	548,527
Total support estimate (TSE)	275,630	291,268	323,962	325,997
Percentage of TSE of total value of production	*55.04*	*46.5*	*55.4*	*59.4*
United States				
Total value of production (at farmgate)	143,624	208,673	194,174	189,245
Total support estimate	68,254	71,628	88,150	96,530
Percentage of TSE to total value of production	*47.5*	*34.3*	*45.4*	*51.0*

Source: OECD (2000:161, 249).

Note: The OECD 24 Group excludes the recent members namely, Czech Republic, Hungary, Korea, Mexico and Poland.

of radical persuasion alone (Seperi, 1994; Lall 1992, Stein 1992). In India too it is becoming clear that even while the entire economic policy regime is geared to a servile wooing of foreign DFI, the total actual inflow has been not more that 10-12 billion dollars over the entire last decade and a substantial part of it has gone into mergers and acquisitions.

At the same time that they forcibly prise open our markets for their goods the advanced countries blatantly mount non-tariff barriers against us. The question of using labour-standards as a weapon against the competition of cheaper goods is not new and is familiar to students of inter-war history. From the late 1920s when Japanese textiles invaded Indian markets ousting Lancashire textiles there was an outcry from Britain that Japanese labour was super-exploited. All these crocodile tears shed on behalf of Japanese labour had only one objective, to exclude Japanese competition and continue the British monopoly of the Indian market. Similarly the same countries which are bombing others and denying medicines to children in Iraq, are today shedding crocodile tears on behalf of Indian child labour, with the sole objective of erecting non-trade barriers to our cheaper imports.

Unfortunately the awareness of these tactics and the opposition to it has come rather late, at a time when our markets have been already substantially opened up and penetrated, for the developing countries have been bullied into lowering their average tariffs to a much greater extent, which is nearly double the meagre extent to which developed countries have lowered tariffs. The time phase of QR removal and tariff reduction has been shortened for developing countries whereas important barriers to their exports to advanced countries like the Multi-fibre Agreement which is a system of quotas, have been given a much longer lease of life; and by the time it is dismantled other non-tariff barriers will have been put in place which will effectively close their markets to our textile exports.

Perhaps the saddest and most disturbing aspect of the present neo-liberal regime is the speed with which our industrial structure in the public sector is sought to be dismantled through discrimination in favour of foreign companies. Our governments in their eagerness to woo foreign capital are ready to underwrite private foreign profits and get the risk to be borne by the Indian people by giving sovereign guarantees to companies like Enron and Cogentrix. This is no different from the way that the colonial governments gave guaranteed returns to private foreign companies to build railways in the last century – a process which Daniel Thorner had described as "private profits at public risk". It has been estimated that not only will the power supplied by these projects have substantially higher cost per unit owing to inflation of the capital costs, than power supplied by the plants set up using domestically produced power equipment, a staggering additional burden will be put on the government exchequers by way of guaranteed returns. For example a decision in March 1993 was taken by

Government of Karnataka that the KSEB should buy all power from Cogentrix. This decision involved guaranteed payments totalling over 2000 crores a year for a period of 30 years, namely a guaranteed purchase order of Rs. 75,000 crores to a company whose total equity was only Rs. 45 lakhs! Economic unreason appears to hold sway. Despite a severely critical report from a team of experts, a power purchase agreement was signed again in 1995 with a power company whose sole promoter was Cogentrix. Public outcry and a writ petition led to a ruling by the Karnataka High Court for a CBI enquiry (Mehta 1999, 130-133). Again recently despite the success of this public interest petition and High Court ruling which led to Cogentrix announcing a welcome pull-out, the Supreme Court was induced to overturn the High Court verdict, and the Central government has come forward with fresh guarantees. It is a difficult situation indeed when comprador thinking and comprador elements pervade the intelligentsia and the administration, when many bureaucrats and academics alike in positions of power, are prepared to sell their birthright for a mess of pottage.

The solution to the attempted recolonisation is to fight back. This fighting back has to be at many different levels: through mass organisations of workers like trade unions, through the womens' movement, through the indispensable political parties, and through theoretical analysis and exposure of the agenda of neo-imperialism. Never has the discipline of economics in particular become more of a battlefield than it is today – as the other disciplines like history and politics have always been. This is not a time for continuing intellectual servility to the self-serving ideas generated in the mainstream of theorising in the Northern universities: the real issues must be understood and young people in particular must come forward to provide the badly-needed theoretical competence and moral commitment for a renewed resistance to economic recolonisation.

Notes

[1] Joan Robinson is an exception. In her 'Reflections on the Theory of International Trade' (1975) she points out that "In Ricardo's example Portugal was to gain as much from exporting wine as England from exporting cloth, but in real life Portugal was dependent on British naval support, and it was for this reason that she was obliged to accept conditions of trade which wiped out her production of textiles and inhibited industrial development, so as to make her more dependent than ever."

[2] These figures relate to the USA, Canada, EEC and Japan taken together.

[3] For the importance of imports of livestock products from Ireland in meeting 12 to 18 percent of the actual consumption in England-Wales during the Industrial Revolution, see E L Jones 1981.

[4] For India see estimates by George Blyn, *Agricultural Trends in India, 1897-1947* (Philadelphia: 1966). For a critique of Amartya Sen see my 'Food Availability and Famine: a Longer View' in *Journal of Peasant Studies*, 1991, also reprinted in U Patnaik, *The Long Transition – Essays on Political Economy* (New Delhi: Tulika 1999).

[5] For a theoretical discussion of the way that coupling their economies to the subjugated economies enabled non-inflationary expansion in advanced countries see P. Patnaik, *Accumulation and Stability under Capitalism* (Oxford: Clarendon Press 1997).

[6] This includes those fruits and vegetables which can grow in cold temperate lands only in summer, but whose supply is maintained all the year in the supermarkets through imports in winter from distant subtropical to tropical countries.

[7] This is not altered by the fact that some industrial re-location of production of textiles and other consumer goods destined for Northern markets has been done by Northern TNCs seeking to profit from the much lower wages in third world countries; these too face tariff and non-trade barriers.

[8] Utsa Patnaik, 'The Likely Impact of Economic Liberalisation and Structural Adjustment on Food Security in India' (Workshop organised by ILO and National Commission for Women , New Delhi, January 1993).

[9] See the *1998-99 Economic Survey*. By mid-1999 it was clear that the 1998-99 foodgrain output had again reached its earlier peak at 203 mn.tonnes, so the latest *1999-2000 Economic Survey* released in February 2000 suddenly adds an

annual increment of 22 million persons quite arbitrarily, to obtain the 1998 population figure, and then has reverted to adding 16 million to that to obtain the 1999 provisional population. Nevertheless this remains at only 986 million owing to the earlier window-dressing, whereas we have been informed with great fanfare that India's population crossed the one billion mark by October 1999! According to independent demographers, there is no reason to believe that the population growth rate is less than 1.9 to 2 percent. By the time authentic estimates of the nineties population growth from the 2001 Census are available, people will have forgotten the doctored figures of the *Economic Survey*.

[10] Availability per head is defined as production plus net imports minus change in stocks, all three taken per head of population. Even when production per head declines, as has been the case in the nineties, availability can be maintained through net imports and buffer stock changes. Net imports can be minimized if the strategy is to cut the purchasing power of the poor and reduce their effective demand for foodgrains; I argue this has been and continues to be the strategy under the demand-deflation policies guided by the Fund-Bank for developing countries. See Patnaik 1996.

[11] Some time after this was written the tariff bindings for rice and sorghum were re-negotiated.

References

Blyn, G. 1966. *Agricultural Trends in India 1891-1947* (University of Philadelphia Press).

Booth, A. 1988. *Agricultural Development in Indonesia* (Allen and Unwin).

Chaudhuri, K.N. 1985. 'Foreign Trade and the Balance of Payments', in D. Kumar and M. Desai (Eds.), *The Cambridge Economic History of India Vol.11* (Orient Longman in association with Cambridge University Press).

Davis, R. 1979. *The Industrial Revolution and British Overseas Trade* (Leicester University Press).

Deane, P. and W.A. Cole. 1969. *British Economic Growth 1688-1959 – Trends and Structure* (Cambridge University Press).

Drescher, S. and S.B. Engerman. 1998. *A Historical Guide to World Slavery* (New York: Oxford University Press).

Dutt, R.C. 1960. *Economic History of India* Vol.1 – *Under Early British Rule 1757-1837*; Vol.2 – *In the Victorian Age, 1837-1900* (Delhi: Publications Division, Government of India).

FAO (Food and Agriculture Organization). *Food Balance Sheets 1992-94* (Rome).

Friedman, H. 1990. 'The Origins of Third World Food Dependence' in H. Bernstein, M. Crow, M. Mackintosh and C. Martin (Eds.), *The Food Question – Profits versus People?* (London: Earthscan Publications).

Grabowski, R. 1985. 'A Historical Reassessment of Early Japanese Industrialisation', *Development and Change*, 16.

Hayami Y. and V.W. Ruttan. 1970. 'Korean Rice, Formosan Rice and Japanese Agricultural Stagnation', *Quarterly Journal of Economics*, November.

Habib, I. 1995. 'The Colonialization of the Indian Economy', in *Essays in History – Towards a Marxist Perception* (Delhi: Tulika).

Hobsbawm, E.J. 1969. *Industry and Empire* (Penguin Books).

Jones, E.L. 1981. 'Agriculture 1700-80', in R. Floud and D. McCloskey (Eds.), *The Economic History of Britain since 1700*, Vol.1 – *1799-1860* (Cambridge University Press).

Lal, Sanjay. 1992. 'Structural Problems of African Industry' in F. Stewart, S. Lal and S. Wangwe (Eds.), *Alternative Development Strategies in Sub-Saharan Africa* (London: MacMillan 1992).

Luxembourg, Rosa. 1963. *The Accumulation of Capital* (London).

Mehta, Abhay. 1999. *Power Play*, pp.130-133 (Delhi: Orient Longman).

Naoroji, D. 1962. *Poverty and Un-British Rule in India* (London, 1901 reprint Delhi).

Patnaik, P. 1999. 'On the Pitfalls of Bourgeois Internationalism', in R.M. Chilcote, ed., *The Political Economy of Imperialism – Critical Appraisals* (Massachusetts, Kluwer Academic Press).

Patnaik P. 2000. 'The Humbug of Finance', Chintan Memorial Lecture delivered on Jan. 8, 2000 at Chennai. Available on website (www.macroscan.com); also included in P.Patnaik, 2002. *The Retreat to Unfreedom* (Delhi: Tulika).

Patnaik, U. 1991. 'Food Availability and Famine: a Longer View', *Journal of Peasant Studies* XIX, 1. Reprinted in Patnaik 1999.

——. 1996. 'Export Oriented Agriculture and Food Security in Developing Countries and in India', *Economic and Political Weekly*, XXXI, 35-37 (Special Number) August. Reprinted in Patnaik 1999.

——. 1999. 'E.M.S. and the Agrarian Question: Ground Rent and its Implications', *Social Scientist*, Vol.29, No.9-10 Sept.-Oct.

——. 1999. *The Long Transition: Essays on Political Economy* (Delhi: Tulika).

Penrose, E. 1940. 'Rice Culture in the Japanese Economy', in E.B. Schumpeter (ed.) *The Industrialization of Japan and Manchukuo* (New York: Macmillan).

Ricardo, D. 1986. *On the Principles of Political Economy and Taxation*, Vol.1 of *The Works and Correspondence of David Ricardo* edited by Pierro Sraffa with the collaboration of M.H. Dobb (Cambridge: Cambridge University Press).

Robinson, Joan V. 1975. 'Reflections on the Theory of International Trade', *Collected Economic Papers*, Vol.V (Oxford: 1975).

Schumpeter, E.B. 1940. *The Industrialization of Japan and Manchukuo* (New York: Macmillan).

Seperi, Ardeshir. 1994. 'Back to the Future? A Critical Review of (the World Bank Report) "Adjustment in Africa: Reform, Results and the Road Ahead"', *Review of African Political Economy*, No.62.

Slicher Van Bath, B.H. 1963. *The Agrarian History of Western Europe 500-1850* (London: Edward Arnold).

Smith, Adam [1776] 1986. *The Wealth of Nations Books 1-111*, Penguin Books, (ed.) Andrew Skinner.

Stein, H. 1992. 'De-industrialisation, Adjustment, the World Bank and the IMF in Africa', *World Development*, Vol.21 No.1.

UNDP (United Nations Development Programme). 1992. *African Development Indicators* (World Bank, New York and Washington).

THE ECONOMIC AND DEMOGRAPHIC
COLLAPSE IN RUSSIA

In the course of 1991 the Soviet Union experienced a deepening political crisis in which the forces opposed to socialism gained strength to the extent that the agenda of the reform of the socialist system through *perestroika* (restructuring) was supplanted entirely by the replacement of socialism itself by capitalism, viz., by a counter-revolutionary agenda. By December 1991, the Soviet Union had ceased to exist and had fractured into fifteen states loosely termed the CIS, or Confederation of Independent States, which as one western scholar has put it, was an event which was "unexpected and generally undesired by most of the population". The term CIS is also seldom used now because there is no effective 'confederation' and analysts prefer to talk of the 'former Soviet Union'.

The analysis of the causes leading up to the situation where the majority of Soviet citizens found themselves, without consultation, becoming citizens of individual countries oriented to the establishment of capitalism, lies beyond the scope of this comment. Certainly this was an event of historic and tragic significance; immediately the capitalists of advanced countries and their international financial institutions descended on the dismembered corpse of the former Soviet Union, like so many vultures, joining the domestic counter-revolutionaries feeding off that corpse. The rich natural resources and the productive capital built up through such great collective effort under the socialist system, were once again available for grabbing by a minority within the country for its private enrichment, who have for the same motive sold collective assets to foreigners at throw-away prices. (Russia has the world's largest deposits of oil and gas and is also a major source of gold, other minerals and raw materials including timber.) The advanced capitalist countries sent advisers who advocated 'shock therapy' for the transition (read: regression) to capitalism: the lifting of price controls, immediate privatization of all state-owned enterprises, a sharp reduction of state expenditures, unimaginable macro-economic contraction, and a dismantling of the impressive welfare system built under socialism. (Incidentally, the same 'advisers', headed by a young North American economist, Jeffrey Sachs, have now been invited to 'advise' the Indian government, which shows the economic policy direction the government would like to pursue!).

The predictable impact of such 'shock therapy' in Russia was hyper-inflation, combined with the collapse of the material productive sectors of the economy. The annual inflation rate has averaged 523 per cent during 1990-96, wiping out the life savings of the elderly and reducing them to destitution, while real wages of workers have fallen drastically to less than half over the same period. Industrial output went into a downward spiral and by 1996 was only 45 per cent of the 1990 level (World Bank estimates). Wrong economic policies can devastate economies faster than war: the rate of destruction of output through 'shock therapy' in Russia has been faster than the destruction achieved by the Nazi onslaught over a comparable duration in the Second World War. (All figures cited in the Tables are from World Bank and UNDP publications, and various editions of *Plan Economy, Review and Outlook for the Former Soviet Republics*).

There has been a burgeoning of 'tertiary sector' activities ranging from private trade , restaurants, wheeling-dealing and organized crime to gun running and prostitution, but all these new activities have not pre-vented the national income from declining to 51 per cent of the 1990 level over the following six years. *Russia is back to the level of income it had at the end of the Second World War.* Since the population has become static and is indeed slightly declining, this is the same order by which the per capita income has also declined. The official Russian estimates of poverty are the most laughable in the world since they actually manage to show a decline at the same time that real per capita income has been halved.

The estimates of independent scholars using expenditure and income data considered to be reliable, shows that the percentage of the poor in the population has gone up vertiginously from almost nil in 1990, to 36.5 per cent in 1992, and to 46.5 per cent in 1995. While Table 1 shows that real consumption has not fallen as much as real wages, this reflects the sale of assets and durable consumption goods by households desperately trying to prevent a decline of consumption to starvation levels. In a nation where poverty had been virtually eliminated, nearly half the population is in poverty today; and the depth of poverty (the fraction of the poor who are well below the poverty line) is also high. This may well be an underestimate since not only has real income declined, but a range of social facilities— free health care and highly subsidized housing—are no longer available. If a nation as opposed to an individual can be said to be committing *harakiri*, it is the Russian nation in the nineties.

The economic collapse and the 'market pricing of health' have combined to raise mortality rates rapidly (Table 2). Over a mere four years of the reforms the Infant Mortality Rate per thousand live births has risen to 18.6; Russia is worse off than is Kerala today with an IMR of 16. The expectation of life (EOL) at birth for the average Russian has declined by six years in as many years of the reforms, from 64 years to 58 years. *Russia is now worse off with regard to male EOL than is India.* The nearly ten per cent fall in life expectation is in turn not owing to a rise in the IMR alone but is mainly owing to the sharp rise in mortality amongst the able bodied (i.e., excluding the children and the old), especially among males. Indeed this mortality rate has almost doubled, and the main reasons put forward are the fall in real income, the inability to afford treatment for illnesses after the dismantling of the free socialist health care system, despair-induced alcohol abuse by men in particular, and the unchecked proliferation of spurious liquor containing poisonous substances, produced by private enterprise.

At the same time that the death rate has risen, the birth rate in Russia has fallen drastically to below the death rate and the overall population has started declining. Fertility is sensitive to falling nutrition, and decisions to have children are always postponed when times are bad.

The demographic collapse is the most pitiful index of the economic and social disaster initiated by the restoration of capitalism. The unregulated market has proved itself once again to be an efficient dispenser of death. Those responsible for the economic policies which have unleashed such misery for millions of people are guilty of crimes against humanity no less than were those who gassed victims in concentration camps during WWII.

Table 1
Annual Growth Rates of GDP, Wages and Consumption

Year	Real GDP	Real Wages	Real Consumption
1991	-9.0	-5.2	-8.0
1992	-19.0	-31.7	-41.0
1993	-12.0	-2.8	11.0
1994	-15.0	-9.0	10.0
1995	-2.7	-26.0	-7.0
Index (1990 = 100)			
1991	91.0	94.8	92.0
1992	73.7	64.8	54.3
1993	65.0	63.0	60.2
1994	55.3	57.3	66.2
1995	53.7	42.4	61.6
1996	50.6	44.6	61.0

Source: *UNDP Poverty Report* for 1998 and 2000 (New York).

Table 2
Mortality Rates and Life Expectation in Russia

Year	Infant Mortality Rate*	Mortality of Able-bodied**	Male Life Expectation in years
1990	17.4	488	64
1992	18.0	581	62
1994	18.6	841	58
1996	na	na	58

*Per 1,000 live births   **per 10,000 in group

Table 3
Headcount Measures of Poverty

Year	Official Measures	Expenditure Measures	Income Measures
1992	32	25.2	36.5
1993	31	31.9	...
1994	23	26.8	...
1995	26	35.8	46.5

Note: Tables 2 and 3 from data in *Plan Economy, Review and Outlook for the Former Soviet Union*.

People's Democracy, October 19, 1997

THE LOSS OF FOOD SECURITY IN SUB-SAHARAN AFRICA

Colonial structural patterns of specialization are being replicated in the contemporary developing world to a remarkable degree, albeit in new forms given the absence of overt political control by the metropolitan powers. The main control mechanism initially in the 1970s and 1980s, was debt. Problems of trade deficit and external balance obliged developing countries to implement specific economic policies as a condition for receiving loans from the international financial institutions – the International Monetary Fund and the World Bank, or the Bretton Woods Institutions (BWI). However, even after the BWI loans have been fully repaid and the foreign exchange situation is comfortable, as in India, these policies continue to be mindlessly implemented by the ruling elites who have internalized the hegemonic neo-liberal dogmas on free trade and fiscal contraction.

These neo-liberal policies are remarkably reminiscent of colonial conditions: complete openness of the developing economy to trade and investment flows, restriction on the freedom to impose protective tariffs, removal of domestic subsidies protecting producers and consumers, domestic demand-restricting budgetary policies, and encouragement of exports with special emphasis on primary sector exports. Verily, *plus ça change, plus c'est la même chose.* The inclusion of agriculture in the WTO discipline has meant a renewed pressure on developing countries to specialize according to the needs of the advanced world, and to change their cropping pattern in order to keep the supermarket shelves filled in Northern countries, regardless of what happens to their own food security.

All indicators show that food security has been already severely undermined in the poorest countries in the world, many located in Sub-Saharan Africa, owing to their export thrust to serve Northern consumers. The next section gives some results derived from calculation of the per capita food crops output for the 46 countries of Sub-Saharan Africa, using the data provided by UNDP in its *Africa Development Report, 1992.*

Structural Adjustment, Trade Liberalization and Loss of Food Security
Since the import dependence of the North on tropical agricultural production was already high at the time of post-War de-colonization, it might be thought that little scope existed for a further increase in the demands made on scarce tropical lands by temperate region populations. In the course of the last two decades however, a substantial shift in the consumption patterns of rich Northern populations has been gathering momentum, one which involves new demands on tropical bio-diversity. This shift is taking place largely owing to a growing awareness of what constitutes a healthy diet and life-style which, from being the preserve of a few practitioners earlier considered to be eccentric, is now spreading rapidly to the general population of North America and Europe.

Prone to obesity, heart diseases and digestive tract disorders, under medical advice the well-to-do consumers in Northern countries are cutting down on the high-fat dairy and meat products their own agriculture produces, introducing more fish and white meat as well as more fibrous green vegetables and fruit into their diets, and replacing fat as a cooking medium with vegetable oils low in polysaturates. Only a small fraction of the new products demanded can be supplied by Northern agriculture, and this consists mainly of reducing the refining of grain in order to retain more germ and fibre. The emergence of the giant supermarket chains in retailing from the late 1960s has been associated with direct sourcing by the increasingly vertically-integrated transnational food business companies, of fresh fruits and vegetables from dozens of developing tropical countries under the system of contract farming, which is spreading rapidly. This represents in a new form, the old colonial phenomenon of control by metropolitan capital over the cropping pattern of tropical lands, which is altered to suit the composition of advanced country demand. Seasonality of supply of fresh produce, which was a feature of Northern consumption even up to the 1960s, has disappeared since fresh and frozen fruits and vegetables are sourced all the year round by the TNCs from a large number of developing countries to keep the supermarket shelves well stocked.

Further, as the cumulative adverse effects of using synthetic chemical pesticides, fertilisers, preservatives, flavours and food dyes become better known, there is now a premium on biological pest control, use of organic fertilizer, natural vegetable sources of preservatives, flavours and dyes. All this involves a new phase of increased demands by the North on tropical agriculture, and a determined, sustained attempt to acquire control over research with the basic genetic material underlying tropical bio-diversity, through revised patent laws and other means. Thus there is today a veritable new assault on the limited productive capacity of Third World agriculture, combined with the transfer of genetic materials to Northern laboratories.

On the other hand, agriculture in the advanced countries is characterized by large overproduction of cereals, fatty meat and dairy products relative to domestic absorption. Faced with an unprofitable product line, a capitalist in manufacturing would simply switch to another product. Owing to the climate-soil specificity of crops, however, this is not possible in agriculture except to a very limited degree. If wheat and potato growing in Idaho under free market conditions do not pay, then farmers in that region cease to exist as farmers, unless they are helped by the state to survive. Indeed they are helped by the state not only to survive but to produce far in excess of domestic demand and by exporting, dominate the global market in these products although their cost of production per unit in every product is much higher than in the developing countries.

This is only possible because massive annual subsidies are doled out by the state to farmers and agro-business in North America and Europe, paying farmers often to restrict acreage, and to reach a target price which is higher than the market price. Under the April 1994 GATT Agreement, subsidies in the North will not be reduced, as is mistakenly believed by many; it is merely the *form* of subsidy which is changing already, from product-specific price maintaining subsidies to direct budgetary cash transfers, since advanced countries have been careful to write into the Agreement on Agriculture that such transfers are permissible.

Clearly it is in the interest of advanced countries to export their artificially maintained surpluses of cereals and dairy products to the rest of the world. The main players in the world wheat export market are the U.S., Canada and the European Union. The former Soviet Union used to purchase feed grains on a large scale in the late 1980s but imports of the different states of the new CIS have now fallen sharply with their economic collapse (see the essay 'The Economic and Demographic Collapse in Russia' in this volume). This has meant that advanced countries are seeking alternative markets, and are now exerting strong pressure on the developing countries to do away with import restrictions. The largest potential buyers of food grains are the populous Asian, Latin American, and some of the African economies, whose per capita income may be low, but whose populations precisely for that reason spend a high fraction of their income on basic food grains and constitute a large potential market in absolute terms.

However, for potential buyers to become actual buyers, the developing countries concerned must lose their self-sufficiency in food grains production and become net food importers. An important part of 'structural adjustment policies' implemented under the guidance of the BWI, is precisely to ensure this. The policies made mandatory for every developing country under SAP - opening up the country to unrestricted trade, removal of subsidies to producers and promotion of agro-exports – lead to a decline in the basic food staples output per head of population. This happens because, with the diversion of food growing land and resources to export crops, the food grains growth rate falls below the population growth rate.

Further more, as large numbers of developing countries are made to compete with each other to export under the same set of policies, the unit value, namely the international dollar price of their crops, falls and the earnings from fast growing volumes of exports hardly register any rise. There is therefore little or no increase in the capacity to import the food grains which are needed, as domestic output grows slowly or becomes stagnant with the displacement of land and resources away from basic food staples towards exportables. If the process goes far enough it increases the vulnerability of already poor populations to famine, which can then be precipitated by any moderately severe economic shock.

The basic reason for the loss of food staples self-sufficiency by the developing country which opens up its economy fully to global trade by reducing or removing existing protective measures (like quantitative restrictions and tariffs), is quite simple. Implementing such 'trade liberalization' subjects its agricultural cropping and output pattern to the pull of international purchasing power and hence, international demand. Over four-fifths of the world's purchasing power is concentrated in the pockets of one-sixth of the world's population residing in a handful of Northern countries. These countries have based their rising consumption standards historically on their privileged, monopoly access to tropical goods exercised through colonial systems, and their demand as we have seen has now entered a new phase.

The average consumer's per capita income in the North is $18,000 compared to about $360 in Asian countries including India, and somewhat less in most Sub-Saharan African countries. Even purchasing power adjusted average income in India is only 5 per cent of average Northern incomes. The income of less than one percent of India's population would approximate the average level in the US. The richest elites of the Third World countries do tend to model their consumption patterns on those of the metropolitan centres, so we may think of the 'metropolitan demand' as comprising two parts – the domestic high-income mainly urban segment in the concerned developing country, and the part representing demand emanating from advanced metropolitan countries. The latter far outweighs the former in its impact once full trade liberalization is put in place.

Estimated Decline in Food Output in Sub-Saharan Africa during the 1980s

We observe clearly in the case of Sub-Saharan Africa, precisely a decline in per head food output and availability to an extent severe enough to produce pre-famine conjunctures. This has been the direct corollary of increased agricultural exports under BWI guided policies against a background of declining terms of trade. The crop-wise data I have analysed (Patnaik 1992) relate to 46 countries in Sub-Saharan Africa and have been taken from the UNDP, 1992 publication titled *African Development Indicators*. I have taken the reported gross physical output in tonnes of all food grains (comprising all cereals), and added to it all tubers and plantains output, at the conversion rate of 5 kg. tubers and plantains = 1 kg. grain, to arrive at the total food staples production by country. Note that in India only cereals and pulses comprise food grains but since in SSA tubers and plantains are important basic staples in many regions, we would get an underestimate of food staples output and availability if they were not included.[1] My measure however somewhat overestimates the food available for local consumption since a part of cassava is converted to starch and a part of bananas and plantains are exported.

The initial per capita output of the food staples so defined for the whole of SSA was only 138.5 kg. in 1980, a reasonably normal harvest year. This was already low by developing country standards: for comparison the per capita gross output of foodgrains alone excluding tubers was 190 kg. in India and 285 kg. in China at that date. But the SSA countries have been experiencing actual decline in average per head GDP during the decade of the 1980s, a decline which has persisted at a slower rate in the decade of the 1990s, on which more below. A substantial decline in per head food output during the 1980s is also observed from the data we have analyzed. Absolute per capita food output reached only 122 kg. for the three year average ending in 1989 and represented a nearly 12 percent decline over a little less than a decade (Table 1). Northern scholars immediately say that "output is underestimated" though they are unable give evidence to support their presumption or to hazard by how much there is underestimation. Even if we add a generous 15 percent to output at both dates to take account of alleged underestimation, we get a decline from 159 kg. to 141 kg. where the terminal figure remains one of the lowest in the world.

The SSA region as a whole is not densely populated, but there are individual countries which are populous. These are identified in the literature as the following six countries: Nigeria, Kenya, Tanzania, Sudan, Ethiopia and Zaire. These six most populous countries account for 60 percent of the total population of 46 countries in SSA. The situation with regard to these countries is worse than in the Sahelian countries as Table 1 shows: cereal output per head fell by as much as one-third while total food per head declined by 20 per cent in less than a decade – which is a faster rate of decline than during the inter-War colonial period in India, and faster even than in Bengal during 1911 to 1947, where per head food output had fallen by 38 percent over 35 years. It is not surprising that most countries in SSA other than South Africa and oil-rich Nigeria, are teetering on the verge of famine every time there is a slight shock by way of bad rainfall, and require food aid to avoid large mortality.

Each of the six most populous countries have been implementing SAP under the guidance of the BWI, have liberalized trade and followed an export thrust from agriculture which has been very 'successful' in terms of the volumes of commodities pumped out, but predictably much less so in terms of exchange earnings which have stagnated or risen little owing to declining prices. Three of the six countries have taken more than one structural adjustment loan (SAL), and therefore have been obliged to undergo 'intensive adjustment', which simply means that they have had to cut public expenditures to a greater degree, remove barriers to trade faster, and devalue their currencies to a larger extent than other countries.

Table 1
Index of Food Output Per Annum Per Head of Population
in Sub-Saharan Africa, 1980-89 (Base 1980 = 100)

Country/Group	1980	1987-89	Per cent Change
1.*Six Most Populous Countries*			
Cereals	100	66.7	- 33.3
Tubers and Plantains	100	106.8	+ 6.8
All food	100	80.0	- 20
2. *Sahelian Countries*			
Cereals	100	125.8	+ 25.8
All food	100	125.8	+ 25.8
3. *All 46 Countries*			
Cereals	100	83.4	- 16.4
Tubers and Plantains	100	105.8	+ 5.8
All Food	100	88.4	- 11.6
All 46 countries, absolute			
All- Food in Kg. per annum	138.5	122.4	- 11.6
Adding 15 percent*	159.3	140.8	- 11.6

Source: Calculated by author from country and crop-wise data on gross output, available in UNDP 1992, African Development Indicators and first presented in Patnaik,1992.
'Six most populous countries' are Nigeria, Kenya, Tanzania, Sudan, Ethiopia, and Zaire.
Food output from which indices are calculated are in thousand tonnes and per capita output is in kilograms per annum. Cereals include wheat, maize, barley and millets; tubers include cassava, yams and potatoes; plantains include bananas and plantains.
Grain is added to tubers & plantains to obtain All Food, by following the convention 5 kg. tubers & plantain = 1 kg. cereal. There was no tubers and plantains output recorded for the Sahelian countries.
*15 percent is arbitrarily added to take account of alleged under-estimation in the statistics.

While the decline of food output per head is a widely recognized fact, the analysis of the reasons leave much to be desired. Neither Northern scholars of the region nor African intellectuals have pin pointed the real reason, which lies in the diversion of the best irrigated land and investment resources towards non-food export crops for stocking Northern supermarket shelves, while the growth rate of the staples consumed by local populations declines and becomes negative in the case of the intensively adjusting countries; namely stagnation or absolute decline in staple food output is observed. As Table 3 shows from the UNDP 1992 data, the growth rate of non-food crops (excluding sugarcane and palm oil [1]) has been high to very high in the case of Sudan, Nigeria, Kenya and Ethiopia, ranging from nearly 4 % in Ethiopia to nearly 14 % in Sudan, and these high growth rates are associated with *absolute decline in food output* for the first three countries (negative growth rate) and stagnation for the last country. 'Successful' volume exports to advanced country supermarkets is the underlying real cause of declining per capita food output and it represents a severe undermining of food security.

However it could be argued that decline in per head food production might be compensated by increased net food imports using the exchange earnings from non-food exports, thus leaving availability for local populations unchanged. But this is not the case. As Table 3 shows, the annual net imports (net of food aid) was absolutely lower in terms of tonnage during 1990 for all the six populous countries compared to a decade earlier in 1980, even though population was larger, domestic food output was lower, and imports should have been much higher.[2] The reasons were that first, exchange earnings did not increase much though export volumes did, because prices fell; and second, food imports using scarce foreign exchange, are not a priority for the elites running governments. Food aid from abroad was not enough to maintain nutrition standards: four out of the six countries registered a decline in per capita calorie intake per diem over the same period, while intake was virtually stagnant in Zaire and rose substantially only in Nigeria (where oil revenues probably helped to increase non-cereal food imports).

It is important to note that the supply-side factors of diversion of resources to export crops cannot be sustained if there is rapid increase in the local population's income level, because such rise in mass purchasing

Table 2
Annual Growth Rates of Food and Non-food Crops,
Selected SAP Implementing Countries in SSA

Country	Period	Non-food crop growth, %	Cereal crop growth, %
SUDAN	1980-85	13.9	- 2.3
NIGERIA	1986-89	11.3	- 6.1
KENYA	1975-80	6.5	- 9.5
ETHIOPIA	1986- *	3.7	0.9

*The period for Ethiopia is shown as open-ended in the data source although a closed interval must have been assumed to calculate the growth rate. Non-food crops here exclude sugarcane and palm oil.
Source: Growth rates taken directly from UNDP 1992, *African Development Indicators*.

power would automatically express itself as market demand for the basic food staples and maintain the profitability of producing them. So an important part of the SAP and associated policies is to reduce the growth of mass incomes and thereby reduce the growth of aggregate demand by making it mandatory for the concerned developing country governments to slash public investment and development spending. Since every Rs.100 cut in such spending generates employment loss and income loss by a multiple, there is a reduction of Rs.400 to Rs.500 in incomes, depending on the multiplier value which is likely to lie between 4 and 5 in a developing country.

It is not mere coincidence that SSA per capita GDP has been steadily declining at the same time that volume exports from agriculture are booming. Per capita GDP has been made to decline under the expenditure-reducing policies advised by the BWI, and faithfully and foolishly implemented again and again by 'intensively adjusting' countries. Keynes himself was a humanist who developed his brilliant theory of income determination and advocated increase in public expenditure to reduce unemployment and loss of incomes during the Great Depression. But his theory can as readily be used by the anti-humanists who, exploiting their status as global moneylenders, are forcing dozens of developing countries

Table 3
Declining Net Imports and Declining Calorie Intake in
Selected SAP Implementing Countries in SSA

Country	Cereal Imports (000 T.)		Food Aid, Cereals (000 T.)		Change in Imports net of food aid	Change in Calorie Intake, %
	1.	2.	3.	4.	5.	6.
	1980	1990	1979 - 80	1989 - 90	1980 to 1990	1979-81 to 1989-91
ETHIOPIA	397	687	111	538	- 137	- 9.92
TANZANIA	399	73	89	22	- 259	- 2.17
UGANDA	52	7	17	35	- 63	- 6.0
KENYA	387	188	86	62	- 175	- 9.86
ZAIRE	538	336	77	107	- 232	1.54
NIGERIA	1828	502	-	-	- 1326	15.45

Source: P.Patnaik 1999. For columns 1 to 4, various issues of the World Development Report, annually published by the World Bank; for column 6, FAO, Food Balance Sheets, 1992-94, Rome.
Note: Column 5 is cols. (2- 4) – (1 –3).

to do the opposite, to cut public expenditures, raise unemployment and slash mass real incomes. SSA is the worst case where there is absolute reduction in even current income per head, while elsewhere as in India, current income per head continues to rise but real income per head for the major part of population, declines. This serves the purpose of restricting aggregate demand growth, reduces the use of energy, and diverts land and resources for production to fill Northern supermarket shelves at the expense of falling nutrition for local populations.

A World Bank study of SSA countries showed that during the period 1980 to 1989, out of 33 countries studied, 12 countries, with 41 percent of the total population of the entire set of countries, saw decline in real per capita GDP at the rate of up to 2 percent per annum, while another 9 countries accounting for 40 percent of total population, registered decline at more than 2 percent per annum. Thus over four-fifths of the population showed actual decline in per capita real income. Taking all countries of SSA, per capita GDP fell at 1.1 percent annually over the decade, and the fall has continued in the next decade 1990 to 2000, at a slightly slower rate (a reported total of 9 percent over the decade). As part of Fund-guided wage restraint policy, real average and minimum wages were cut by a quarter in just five years, 1980 to 1985, in two-thirds of the countries for which wage data are available (World Bank and IMF reports, summarized in van der Hoeven, 1994).

Such sustained reduction in income per head, given no reduction and probably increase in inequality, has meant greater hunger reflected in steady fall in average calorie intake for the SSA population. All countries except the oil exporters and South Africa, are affected by income decline and rising hunger, and there is little doubt that this lowered nutritional status has been a contributory factor in the virulence of pandemics including the devastation wrought by AIDS. Reduction in income means fall in mass aggregate demand. This is of direct benefit to the advanced countries, which sustain their voracious appetite for tropical goods and for variety in diet by using up more and more of scarce tropical land through the TNC's extension of contract farming, for the purpose of supplying the metropolitan centre with products ranging from coffee to green beans and cut flowers. These are lands which should have been feeding local populations if only they were permitted to maintain their purchasing power.

The vicious route of expenditure deflation and reduction in aggregate demand of local populations has meant a steady intensification of hunger, reflected in the fall in the daily energy intake. The countries with the largest fall in daily calorie intake (Kenya, Ethiopia) however, are not necessarily those which have the highest rate of growth of the non-food exports, since the rate of investment in agriculture also matters in sustaining output. Given our knowledge of the steep decline in food staples output and availability discussed earlier and depicted in Tables 1 and 2, we would expect the largest decline to be in calorie intake from the food staples. This is indeed what the FAO's *Food Balance Sheets* giving country wise data show (Table 4 gives two case studies). Obviously the large fall in energy intake from vegetal foods is

Table 4
Examples of 'Dietary Diversification' and Worsening Welfare:
Kenya and Tanzania, 1974-76 to 1992-94 :
Calorie Intake Per Head Per Day

Country	Vegetal Origin	Animal Origin	Total	Percentage shares Vegetal%	Animal%
KENYA					
1974-76	2003	217	2220	90.2	9.8
1982-84	1810	230	2040	88.7	11.3
1992-94	1672	245	1917	87.2	12.8
Change 1992-94					
Over 1974-76	- 331	+28	- 303		
TANZANIA					
1974-75	2009	150	2159	93.1	6.9
1982-84	2148	138	2286	94.0	6.0
1992-94	1906	147	2053	92.8	7.2
Change 1992-94					
Over 1974-76	- 103	- 3	- 106		

Source: Food and Agriculture Organization (FAO), Rome. Food Balance Sheets 1992-94, pp.236, 435.

far from compensated by the slight rise in Kenya in energy intake from animal origin foods giving a substantial net decline.

The non-staple foods intake may be unchanged, may rise (Kenya) or may even decline (Tanzania), but in all cases including the last one, Tanzania, where it is falling, these non-staple foods of animal origin show up as a higher *share* of the declining calorie intake; in short diets are more 'diversified' as hunger increases. Thus in Tanzania even though there is a slight absolute decline in calories of animal origin, their share of it in total calorie intake has gone up from 6.9 to 7.2. This is owing to the much steeper fall in calorie intake from staples of vegetal origin.

The same data as for Kenya and Tanzania are available for every other reporting country in SSA from the FAO's *Food Balance Sheets*, with much the same pattern of decline in overall calorie intake combined with fall in the share of basic food staples. In India too the share of the staple food grains in food expenditure has been falling, along with falling calorie intake from all foods per head per day in rural India. The share in this falling total calorie intake contributed by the non-staples and by foods of animal origin have been rising. All this has been rationalized by the government and by establishment economists in India, as an 'Engel's Law' indicating that every segment of the population is getting better off and voluntarily reducing staple grain intake. The statistician Ernst Engel, on the basis of budget studies of 153 Belgian households in the mid-19th century, had found that *as per capita income and expenditure rises*, the consumer devotes a lower share of total spending to food. This was confirmed by later studies of consumer behaviour and additionally it was found that as income rises, the consumer devotes a lower share of food expenditure to starchy staple foods like bread and a higher share to high-protein products of animal origin.

What a travesty of logic it is to argue, in a situation where *per capita income and expenditure is falling, and total calorie intake from all foods is falling,* that a higher share of spending on non-staples and a higher share of calorie intake from non-staples, indicates betterment! Ernst Engel would turn in his grave to hear the foolish arguments being put forward in his name by our luminaries, arguments which confuse necessary and sufficient conditions. A falling share of food staples in expenditure is a necessary indicator of betterment but it is not a sufficient indicator, because such a falling share is also an indicator of worsening. The sufficient condition for betterment is given by rise in expenditure and therefore rise in calorie intake. Does the fact that the average Kenyan, Tanzanian or citizen of other SSA countries, is getting a higher *share* of falling calorie intake from foods of animal origin, indicate that she is better off, when the higher share is solely owing to the huge fall in intake of foods of vegetal origin, and results in an overall large decline in daily energy intake? Ideology, not reason, explains the desire to justify increasing hunger as betterment.

Extracted and revised from a paper first presented at an international conference in July, 1992 at the School of Oriental and African Studies, University of London whose expanded version was published under the title "Peasant Subsistence and Food Security in the Context of the International Commoditization of Production – the Present and History" in Peter Robb, ed., *Meanings of Agriculture* (Delhi: Oxford University Press, 1996).

Notes

[1] The precise conversion rate adopted here is followed in China where the practice is to add tubers (mainly potato) output to cereal output at the rate of 5 kg. tubers = 1 kg. grain.

[2] Oddly, sugarcane and palm oil were counted along with the food staples and designated as 'food crops' in the UNDP source. I have separated out these two crops and calculated All-food as cereal plus tubers and plantains, as indicated in the text. The 'non-food crop' growth rates, excluding sugarcane and palm oil, are given in the UNDP data source and are quoted in Table 2. I am not able to recalculate the growth rates including sugarcane and palm oil as their weight in total non-food crops, is not available.

[3] In view of my argument that decline in per head food output meant decline in food security in the six most populous countries, P.Patnaik calculated the food imports net of aid and found that food availability had indeed declined. P.Patnaik, 'The Pitfalls of Bourgeois Internationalism' in R.M.Chilcote ,ed., *The Political Economy of Imperialism* (Boston: Kluwer Academic Publishers, 1999).

ASIA MUST STARVE TO FEED THE WEST
THE RICE DEBACLE IN THE PHILIPPINES

One of the most destructive effects of economic liberalization in agriculture with its attendant policies of export promotion is the ongoing undermining of food security for the masses in Asian countries.

We have been analyzing this process for Sub-Saharan Africa (SSA) and for India in earlier essays, and have shown how there has already occurred a one-third drop in cereals output per head for 60 percent of the population of SSA during the decade of the 1980s. This has brought them to the brink of starvation and actual famine in some areas, despite their increasing food aid dependence, for their ability to pay for food imports has fallen at the same time. This is owing to the sharp fall, in the price per unit of their agro-exports to about half of the 1980 level, while conversely wheat which is exported by the rich countries, has been rising in price. In short the terms of trade have worsened for these countries.

India has opened up the agricultural sector to virtually unprotected trade and launched agro-export promotion less than five years ago, and already the area under food grains has fallen by 5.4 million hectares while per capita food output has been on a declining trend with crop and resource diversion to exportables like cotton, prawns, fruits and vegetables and flowers. The large food stocks of over 30 million tonnes with the government at present is the result of the poor being unable to buy to the same extent as before, being impoverished further through a deliberate near doubling of issue prices in order to satisfy the Fund-Bank theology of cutting subsidies and deflating mass incomes.

The government has already quite blatantly manipulated the method of calculating poverty, by ignoring the current consumption figures from the National Sample Survey (NSS), to claim that poverty has fallen while the reality is the opposite. The people are, as a matter of deliberate policy, being disenfranchised economically, thus clearing the way for the consumers in advanced countries – as well as the Indian rich – to restructure land and resource use towards their own high-protein and diversified consumption requirements.

Prawns for the Rich

Can such a basic necessity as food grains, whose availability at an affordable price affects the very life of millions of our people, be left to the operation of 'market forces', that is, set on a declining trend because the rich abroad and at home, demand products out of our limited tropical lands? It is monstrous that in order that Europeans and North-Americans can eat prawns, cheap low fat meat cooked in healthy vegetable oils, fruits and vegetables their own lands cannot produce in winter, and give flowers to each other, that Asians must see their food security destroyed and that our poor cannot get enough food to keep body and soul together. Yet it is precisely this scenario – a replication of the Sub-Saharan Africa experience – which awaits us in Asia under the present policies.

The undermining of our food producing capacity, in order to divert land and resources to export crops which satisfy the demand of the rich consumers abroad, and thus become dependent ourselves on the Northern countries for wheat imports, is the aim of GATT provisions on market access in grains and which will be enforced by the WTO, a body not subject to any controls by developing countries.

A recent conference in Manila on Food Security and Free Trade attended by academics and activists, in which this author also participated, discussed the situation in South-East Asia, where also we see emerging this familiar basic foods problem common to all developing countries with trade liberalization and export promotion in agriculture. Among South-east Asian countries, Vietnam and Thailand alone are rice exporters while Indonesia, Malaysia, Cambodia, Laos and Philippines are rice importers. Every single country is also by now a substantial wheat importer with the Philippines forming a virtual captive market for US wheat (Table 1). The world wheat trade is dominated by the USA, Canada and the European Union who together account for 75 per cent of all trade, another 15 per cent being on account of Argentina and Australia. Some five million tons of additional wheat exports to SE Asia region has taken place since 1989-90 with the largest market gain being in Indonesia though wheat imports into Malaysia and Philippines are also growing fast.

Philippines Going the African Way

Since the early 1980s the Philippines has been following policies of opening further to trade along with adjustment policies. Subsidies on fertilizer and farm credit were scrapped between 1981 and 1985, rediscounting facilities to rural banks withdrawn, and funds allocated for infrastructure projects saw a sharp decline, adversely affecting irrigation, electrification and flood control programmes. Earlier price support to farmers for the production and distribution of rice and corn were suspended.

The Philippines as a highly diversified tropical country produces a large variety of fruits and vegetables; the Corazon Aquino administration however allowed import of fruits and vegetables resulting in a flood of apples and grapes into the Filipino market, while wheat and flour imports were opened up from 1987. Having reduced the competing capacity of its own farmers, the government faced farmers' agitations which resulted in the pushing through of the *Magna Carta of Small Farmers* which seeks to control the import of rice and corn. Section 23 of this *Magna Carta of Small Farmers* specifically prohibits the import of commodities which are produced locally in sufficient quantity.

The Act includes the procedures for regulating such imports as necessary, and mandates strict compliance by the concerned Ministries. This Act still has the force of law because it has not been amended as yet by Congress even though the Philippines Senate has ratified the 1994 GATT agreement. However, given the political complexion of the government it seems to be only a matter of time before the full liberalization of food crops imports that the Northern countries are so eager to see, becomes a reality. For the moment the Filipino progressive movement has secured a breathing space and is pressing for prioritizing of food production owing to the recent eruption of the rice crisis, the background to which is as follows.

The Rice Crisis

Despite all the farmers' struggles, the government had proceeded to sabotage food security by simply running down its procurement operations in line with the Fund-Bank theology of scrapping state intervention in the food economy. Between 1990 and 1994 the National Food Authority (NFA) reduced its purchases of rice from 600 thousand tons to less than 50 thousand tons even though absolute output rose. When a combination of drought and floods hit the country last monsoon season in 1995, the price of common rice shot up, doubling from 12 to 24 pesos per kilogram in less than two months (or about 0.45 to nearly 1.00 US dollars per kilo). Rice is thus now over four times more expensive than in India, though the average Filipino income is only twice as high.

When the price started to go up the NFA was found to have less than two days supply, hence no ability to intervene in the market where speculators had a merry time. The sacking of the head of the NFA and the resignation of the Secretary of Agriculture has not altered the fact that prices have ratcheted up to stay at an unprecedented high, and that one-third of the population, the poorer Filipinos who spend 60 per cent of their income on grains, have seen their real income fall substantially.

The rice crisis is the manifestation of a deeper trend involving large scale decline of rice and corn growing area, only partly replaced by other uses and associated with the export thrust (in just two regions, Central Luzon and Southern Tagalog, food grains area declined by 170 thousand hectares during 1989 to 1993). Combined with the axing of all support to its farmers, the Philippines is all set to go in for even larger imports most likely of cheaper wheat replacing rice as it is already doing. These outcomes will delight the world grain sellers.

Subsidies Rising in Developed World

The outcomes described above are not spontaneous but are manipulated by advanced countries through the high and rising subsidies they give to their farmers and agro-business. One of the most successful myths assiduously propagated by the advanced countries is that it is cutting subsidies to its own farmers under GATT 1994. Exactly the opposite is true: the level of producer subsidy for wheat and coarse grains in USA and EU has actually risen according to the latest OECD Report to over $26 billion annually; the producer subsidy on all crops receiving the subsidy, is a whopping $ 107 billion. How are such enormous subsidies compatible with the Agreement on Agriculture enforced by WTO, which says subsidies are supposed to be reduced?

The advanced countries have played a trick: they have already taken good care to put direct payments – which are made out of the budget - into special categories (green box and blue box) which are not subject to any reduction commitments, in the Agreement on Agriculture. These types of payments are defined- by these same countries - as allegedly, 'not distorting trade'. So they are going on raising subsidies to support their agriculture and penetrate developing country markets, simply by altering the form of the subsidy so that it is now direct cash payments, and not linked to crop area as earlier. Some data from the OECD 1995 Report are given in Table 2 below. The producer subsidy alone (which has to be added to normal income of a similar order) per farmer in the US in 1994 was 16,000 dollars and in the EU about 18,000 dollars, whereas the per capita total annual income of the Filipino farmer is less than 800 dollars (and of the Indian farmer below 400 dollars).

The 'unit PSE' shows the subsidy per ton for the concerned crop, which is very high in both US and EU, given that world wheat price was about $144 per ton and coarse grains price $100 per ton in 1994. We can easily calculate that the subsidy on wheat was 46% of price for the US and 80% of price for the EU while that on coarse grains was 19% in the US and 114 % for the EU. (Europeans produce at higher unit cost and so give higher subsidy rates).

It is these huge subsidy rates which enable the advanced countries to dump wheat on the third world and get them hooked to wheat. Without the subsidy the world wheat price would be nearly doubled and this wheat would be unable to penetrate developing countries, whose farmers produce at much lower cost than advanced countries do and moreover have very meagre state support. This is the reality of the 'level playing field' of which we hear so much!

Some of our economists are misguided enough to say that subsidized wheat should be allowed because it benefits 'the consumer'. They forget that the majority of consumers in developing countries like Philippines and India, are themselves peasants and labourers dependent on agricultural employment, whose livelihoods get destroyed and thereby consumption levels get reduced owing to unfair competition from heavily subsidized foreign grain. In fact, these economists think of 'consumers' as simply being urban people like themselves, and think of farmers and labourers as simply 'producers' born to work for the benefit of the urban consumers. They forget that farmers and labourers are not just producers but are also consumers, in fact the majority of our consumers, who have a right to prevent further erosion of their already low income and consumption levels.

Table 1
Net Trade in Food and Feed grains in SE Asia
(Exports minus Imports, million tons)

	Rice	Wheat	Coarse Grains
Indonesia	-0.27	-2.52	-0.32
Malaysia	-0.39	-1.00	-1.80
Philippines	-0.07	-1.85	-0.03
Thailand	4.77	-0.57	-0.37
Vietnam	1.68	-0.35	-0.05
Region	**5.53**	**-6.30**	**-1.73**

Source: *Grain: World Markets and Trade.* Note that negative sign means imports are greater than exports. Note that 'Region' also includes other smaller countries so the individual figures in the table will not always sum to the Region figure.

Table 2
Producer Subsidy Equivalent (PSE) for Cereals in the USA and EU, 1994

Wheat	US	EU
Total PSE (mn. Dollar)	4,179	9,223
Unit PSE (dollar/ton)	66	114
Coarse Grains		
Total PSE (mn. Dollar)	5,016	7,888
Unit PSE (dollar/ton)	19	111
ALL CROPS with PSE		
Total PSE, mn. Dollar	26,227	80,480
PSE per farmer	16,000	18,000

Source: OECD Reports 1995

People's Democracy, March 10, 1996

PEASANT RESISTANCE TO GLOBALISATION
CHIAPAS A SYMBOL

The economic dynamics of globalization entail the sacrifice of the interests of the ordinary mass of peasants in third world countries, for, once there is complete trade liberalization, withdrawal of price support and subsidy cuts, it means that the protection of mass livelihoods and guarantee of subsistence have ceased to be the aim of state policy. It is replaced by the promotion of agro-exports and the reversal of land reforms, in the interests of advanced countries and their transnational corporations, through the medium of a small minority of domestic capitalist farmers and companies. This process is not an uncontested one: it is sooner or later resisted by those who are losing out.

Unfortunately peasant resistance usually builds up only when the process of marginalization and distress is already quite far advanced, so that this resistance becomes a species of desperate rearguard action, delaying but not stopping the victorious march of global capital.

We in India, after six years of trade liberalization, have now come to the end of what might be termed the first or initial phase of the dismantling of the earlier national agenda for protecting our farmers' livelihoods. So far whereas agro-exports were being strongly promoted, restrictions on imports from advanced countries had been retained. Under unremitting pressure exercised through the WTO by the US and other interested countries to give up quantitative restrictions on trade, the government which was incumbent until recently, had reportedly already taken a decision to do so some weeks ago. In June this year representatives are expected from the WTO, to begin the process of removal of quantitative restrictions on trade including agriculture, and negotiate tariffs at low levels acceptable to Northern countries. The present political uncertainty is unlikely to affect the timetable which will be insisted on by the WTO regardless of the complexion of the government.

Secondly, the demand for reversing land reforms by way of removal of restrictions on companies acquiring land for export production has also become more strident, and some states have either amended their laws already to accommodate this demand, while others are quietly allowing land-grabbing of communal or tribal land by companies to proceed without formal amendment of laws.

At this juncture it is necessary for the Kisan movement to be aware of what the experience has been in other countries which have earlier trodden the same path. The Chiapas rebellion in Mexico has emerged as a potent symbol of resistance to the devastating effects of globalization. It provides a lesson, namely, the economic agenda of globalization must not be allowed to go to that point where the livelihood of the majority of the rural population is sacrificed for the sake of profits for a domestic minority and to guarantee markets for food grains dumped by the Northern countries.

Mexican Story

What lies behind the Chiapas rebellion? The story goes back to over twenty years of trade liberalization and structural adjustment under debt-conditionalities in Mexico. During the 1980s, more than four-fifths of the 1,555 companies run in the public sector by the Mexican government were sold or dissolved, in what the IMF and the World Bank hold up as a model of privatization. Their sale reduced employment for lakhs of workers and enriched further the top 13 fabulously rich Mexican families.

Between 1981 and 1989, state infrastructural investment in rural areas was cut by 65 per cent as part of the containing of the fiscal deficit by reducing public expenditures; agricultural subsidies were reduced and regulations were relaxed to permit foreign holding of Mexican land. Average Mexican tariffs on imports declined from the already low levels of 27 per cent in 1982, to only 8 per cent in 1992. To keep exports competitive and make devaluation effective, real wages were slashed—on top of the earlier decline, there was a further decline of wages in the 1980s, the total decline by 1992 amounting to 60 per cent compared to the 1974 level.

Large masses of poor farmers were displaced from subsistence agriculture based on the food staples maize and beans, owing to the preference given by state policies to export agriculture, heavily dominated by the US transnational food companies. These displaced peasants swelled the ranks of the unemployed seeking work in the cities. Mexico became a large net wheat importer for well-to-do consumers, but the demand for the local staples declined as mass incomes were cut, pushing more people into under-nutrition.

The Mexican government promised that membership of NAFTA (North American Free Trade Association) would usher in an era of prosperity, and in order to show its good behaviour vis-à-vis the US in 1992, it pushed through a notorious amendment to Article 27 of the constitution. Under this amendment, Indian community land held in common (*ejido* land) which traditionally was available for use to the poor peasants and farm workers and was not allowed to be alienated, now was thrown open to foreign investors, who were privileged over local peasants in accessing this land. The communitarian traditions and revolutionary heritage underlying the Mexican constitution were given up at one stroke.

All this in political economy terms amounted to a total reversal of the earlier national economic agenda of stabilizing livelihoods for the mass of the population: in effect the mass has been sacrificed by the Mexican elite to globalization. Mexico after this long period of 'good behaviour' and preparation in 1994 became a member state of NAFTA, comprising Canada,

USA, and Mexico. Regional free trade associations of this type can be seen as an intermediate step to the eventual complete subordination of national interests to global financial management benefiting the advanced countries through trade under the terms embodied in the WTO.

Within the terms of the NAFTA, existing price support, in Mexico, to the basic food staples, viz., beans and maize, were to be phased out completely. Lakhs of *campesinos*, who are the subsistence farmers, were to face the competition from heavily subsidised North American maize and wheat (in 1994 the US paid out 28, 000 dollars per full-time farmer and 90 billion dollars in total transfers, but recognized only four billion dollars of this as qualifying under GATT 1994, to be cut by year 2000).

The Uprising[1]

On New Year's Day, 1994, impoverished peasants in Chiapas province rose in revolt against NAFTA in particular, and the social and economic effects on them of globalization, in general. This was the day from which implementation of NAFTA became effective. The movement emerged as a coalition of *campesino* and women's organizations, and called itself the *Ejercite Zapatista de Liberacion National*, harking back to Mexico's famed revolutionary peasant leader Emiliano Zapata.

Why Chiapas province in particular? While the issues involved all Mexican small farmers, in Chiapas the contradictions unleashed by the globalization project had reached acute proportions. This was a region where huge coffee plantations and cattle ranches surround small peasant farms struggling to survive. Near landless and totally landless *campesino* represent the incomplete nature of land reforms; they had been permitted to colonise the Lacandon jungle, produce coffee and cattle, and use the timber. In the 1980s all the product prices fell and government prohibited logging by peasants, whereas the large timber companies continued felling trees. The opening up of so far inalienable communal lands for sale and for foreign investment, and the deregulation of commodity markets especially in maize was the last straw. Zapatista communiqué put it in the following words:

Oil, energy, cattle, money, coffee, bananas, honey, corn, cocoa, tobacco, sugar, soya, melons, mamey, mangoes, tamarind, avacados, and Chiapan blood flow out through a thousand and one fangs sunk into the neck of Southeastern Mexico, millions of tonnes of natural resources go through Mexican ports, railway stations, airports, and road systems to various destinations: the USA, Canada, Holland, Germany, Italy, Japan—but all with the same object, to feed the empire... The jungle is opened with machetes, wielded by the same campesinos whose land has been taken away by the insatiable beast... Poor people cannot cut down trees, but the oil company, more and more in the hands of foreigners, can... Why does the Mexican government take the question of national politics off the proposed agenda of the dialogue for peace? Are the indigenous Chiapan people only Mexican enough to be exploited, but not Mexican enough to be allowed an opinion on national politics?

The Mexican government reacted to the Chiapas rebellion by setting up a 'National Commission for Integral Development and Social Justice for Indigenous People' and promised more funds. The Zapatistas have however rejected this as merely another step in their economic assimilation within a continued programme of adjustment and globalization, which they reject *in toto*. They have instead drawn up their own plans for the restoration of land to *campesino*, abolition of debts, reparations to Indians whose human and natural resources have been seized without recompense, and have set up new organizational forms of cooperation among the diverse groups in the area. They demand the inclusion of *campesino* organizations at the national level in all decision-making affecting the rural economy. Their demand for local self-government to ensure the relevance to the peasant masses of local development projects, is strongly reminiscent of the revival of effective *panchayat* functioning in our own country in states led by the Left Front governments.

Note

1   The factual information and quotation is taken from the useful study by Philip McMichael, *Development and Social Change–A Global Perspective* (1997), pp. 134–137.

People's Democracy, April 20, 1997

MASS INCOME DEFLATION, BURGEONING FOOD STOCKS

A common misconception held by many people is that the distress caused by the new economic policies in force since mid-1991 is a temporary 'price' to be paid for 'restructuring' the economy and the economy will, if it has not already, 'turn the corner'. That this misconception is so widespread is an indication of both the success of official propaganda efforts as well as the general ignorance about the experiences of other third world countries under structural adjustment programmes (SAP). The truth is, however, that the very basis of these Fund-Bank guided programmes is an implacable and continuing attack on the real incomes of the mass of the third world populations, at the same time that their ruling classes are offered freer access to international living standards, thus sapping their commitment to any national cause.

Latin American, African Experiences

All over Latin America and Africa, for fifteen years now, working class real incomes have been falling owing to the specific requirements of contractionary policies and wage-cuts imposed by the Fund and the Bank. According to a recent survey of the impact of SAP, carried out by IMF officials (R. van der Hoeven & G. Rodgers, *The Poverty Agenda – Trends and Policy*

Options), in Latin America between 1980 and 1990, taking all countries implementing SAP, the agricultural wage declined by 26.5 per cent, the minimum wage by 31.7 per cent, and per capita GDP by 9 per cent. The proportion of the poor rose to 44 per cent with a larger impact on the urban poor, and the absolute numbers rose to 132.7 millions over the decade compared to 91.4 millions earlier.

There is of course a great deal of variation underlying the dismal average, with some countries containing the damage, while others are disaster scenarios for the masses with up to 25 per cent fall in per head income (Bolivia, Argentina, Haiti, Nicaragua). Needless to say the Latin American rich flourish as never before.

All these countries are highly export-oriented. Similarly, highly export-oriented economies of sub-Saharan Africa, according to World Bank data summarized in the source earlier quoted, show that in 21 countries implementing SAP, *per capita GDP declined over 1980 to 1989, at the rate of up to 2 per cent annually in 12 countries, and at more than 2 per cent annually in 9 countries.* For the whole of SSA, per head income has fallen at 1.1 per cent annually, and continues to fall in the nineties. Substantial fall in the share of industry in the workforce and in GDP (de-industrialization) has also taken place.

The extent to which incomes have fallen and home industries displaced by imports, is a measure of the success of the real, as opposed to the declared Fund-Bank agenda. Such mass income deflation imposed on developing countries is quite unprecedented in the post-war era, and marks nothing less than an economic re-colonization. It marks the success of the *real agenda* of the Fund-Bank as opposed to its declared agenda.

Now mass real income deflation is being imposed 'successfully' from the liberalisers' point of view, on India as well from mid-1991. Our rate of industrial growth has shifted down dramatically from 8.5 per cent annual average for the seven years up to 1990, to barely 4 per cent in the following four years up to 1994-95. Poverty has risen from 36.6 per cent to 48 per cent in rural areas during 1990 to 1992 according to the Tendulkar-Jain estimate; and during 1990 to 1994, from 35 to 37 per cent in rural areas, according to the Abhijit Sen estimate.[1]

From the era of import substituting industrialization, we are being pushed by loan-conditionalities, into the era of import augmenting de-industrialization. The pressure by the IMF and the World Bank to continue the policy-package pushing down our mass incomes, and to continue the process of our own de-industrialization, will mount further, not decline – just as in SSA and in Latin America.

The Dynamics of Imperialism

What is the basic reason for this implacable pressure? What have the ruling classes in the advanced world to gain from mass incomes declining in the third world? They stand to gain a great deal, given the premises of capitalist dynamics. The gain is no less than maintaining the economic and social stability of capitalism at the core.

One aspect of this is that the tropical third world has been richly endowed by nature and can produce a range of primary sector goods the temperate North is physically incapable of producing, but on which its living standards and segments of industry crucially depend. But, given the regime of falling investment, the third world can continue to meet the rising demands of the North *only by curtailing the demand of its own population for basic foodgrains.*

This is 'achieved' by cutting mass incomes. Both under direct colonialism and at present, the North reduces the third world populations' own market demand and absorption of their own products, in order to divert their land and resources to exportables. This maintains a cheap and elastic supply to the metropoles, of those goods which are only producible in tropical lands and which by now form an essential basis for high Northern living standards. Hence the continuous tirades to the third world to reduce their populations and reduce their growth through 'fiscal discipline'. Hence the relentless new pressure on the indebted third world countries to promote agro-exports, and 'open up to the international market'.

At the same time non-agricultural market access to these countries is sought by the North, under GATT and through debt-conditional trade and investment liberalization, to ensure that despite falling mass incomes a larger market share for manufactured goods can go to metropolitan capital through de-industrializing the third world country concerned.

It is in this context that the 'function' of the sharp rise in prices of essential foodgrains since 1991 in India is to be understood. While fiscal contraction increases unemployment and cuts incomes, inflation in food prices is another most potent way of slashing real incomes by reducing mass purchasing power. This in turn, by economically disenfranchising the poor, paves the way to a restructuring of cropping, away from meeting the domestic population's basic needs to meeting the metropolitan population's demands.

Comparing 1990 and 1994 we find that the government has raised the minimum support price for rice (common variety) by around half, while the central issue price for rice has gone up by as much as 86 per cent. The Issue price for wheat has been raised by 82 per cent. The gap between the open market and ration price has been narrowed by now to near vanishing point and a gap exists only for sugar. The consumer food subsidy in real terms has been cut drastically as required by the SAP package.

The effect of this near doubling of food prices has been to price out substantial numbers of the poor from the ration shops altogether. They simply cannot afford these prices: the offtake from the fair price shops has declined drastically to 14.3 million tonnes from 19.7 million tonnes four years ago. With steady harvests and the rising support price, procurement has picked up precisely with the savage attack on mass purchasing power through a combination of cutting growth and raising food prices. The customary rise in the central issue prices in the spring of the following year was postponed given falling offtake, but the rise in December 1994 made the respite brief and ineffective. Huge stocks exceeding 30 million tonnes, involving steeply rising costs of storage, have piled up while people go hungry. The paradox is that the total subsidy burden is rising, not in order to help to feed more needy people, but in order to carry the larger stocks arising from the sharp reduction in the numbers able to buy owing to the engineered inflation.

Thus Table 2 shows that the consumer subsidy has fallen absolutely, and as per cent of total subsidy it has dropped from nearly 87 per cent to only 61 per cent. It is the subsidy to the FCI on the costs of holding vertiginously rising stocks alone which accounts for the Rs.1,100 crore rise, amounting to one-third rise in total subsidy in the last four years.

Any attempt to cut subsidy by raising the issue price in a poor country, is bound to have the apparently perverse effect of actually raising the subsidy further. This is the same as the famous 'paradox of thrift' that Keynes had explained: if all individuals try to save more, it actually reduces savings in the economy because there is decline of aggregate demand and incomes. Here in India the government wrong-headedly tries to reduce subsidy through issue price rise but it merely thereby reduces effective demand, so excess stocks build up which cost more to hold and raise the subsidy bill sharply. The correct measure for reducing subsidy now is to raise aggregate demand through a combination of reduced issue price and food-for-work, which will increase offtake, benefit the hungry poor, and automatically do away with the irrational subsidy for holding excess stocks.

There is at present a struggle over the future form and role of the public distribution system (PDS), both within the government and outside. The extension of the PDS to rural areas and further subsidizing food for the poor by the Left Front and some non-Congress governments such as the Telegu Desam, has been a major factor in the popular support these parties enjoy. Alarmed at the erosion of Congress support following the disastrous reform policies, many in government in May 1995, urged the prime minister to adopt a food-for-work programme and reduce ration prices. However, this proposal was rejected by the finance minister on the grounds of an unsustainable rise in the food subsidy, which no doubt could not be defended before his Fund-Bank mentors.

The irrationality of a situation where people go hungry, food stocks rot in the godowns, and the government is too paralysed by its fear of the Fund-Bank to do anything, is becoming clear to increasing sections of the

Table 1
Revised Support Minimum Price, Central Issue Price

Season		SMP (Rs)	CIP (Rs)	Date increase
RICE				
Pre-Reform				
Kharif 1989-90	C	185	289	25.6.1990
	F	195	349	
	S	205	370	
Kharif 1990-91	C	205		
	F	215		
	S	225		
Post-Reform				
Kharif 1991-92	C	230	377	28.12.1991
	F	240	437	
	S	250	458	
Kharif 1992-93	C	270	437	11.1.1993
	F	280	497	
	S	290	518	
Kharif 1993-94	C	310	537	1.12.1994
	F	330	617	
	S	350	648	
Kharif 1994-95	C	340		
	F	355		
	S	375		
Kharif 1995-96	C	360		
	F	375		
	S	395		
WHEAT				
Rabi 1990-91		215	238	1.5.1990
Rabi 1991-92		225	280	28.12.1991
Rabi 1992-93		250 + 25 bonus	330	11.1.1993
Rabi 1993-94		305 + 25 bonus	402	1.2.1994
Rabi 1994-95		350	427	
Rabi 1995-96		360		
Rabi 1996-97		380		

C: Common variety   F: Fine variety   S: Superfine variety
Source: *Fifth Report of (Parliamentary) Standing Committee on Food Supplies and Public Distribution 1994-95*

Table 2
Break-up of Total Food Subsidy between Consumer Subsidy and the
Carrying Cost of Stock-Holding 1991-92 to 1994-95

Year	Sale Qty. (mn. t.)	Consumer Subsidy on Sales (Rs. crores)	Average Buffer (mn. t.)	Carrying Cost (Rs. crores)
1991-92	21.363	2890.9	5.580	432.7
1992-93	17.950	3223.8	4.348	450.7
1993-94	18.646	3175.0	10.629	1245.3
1994-95	18.815	2736.0	16.590	1719.0

Year	Total Subsidy (Rs crores.)	Percent of Consumer to Total Subsidy, %	Provided for in GOI Budget, Rs. crores
1991-92	3323.7	86.98	2850.0
1992-93	3674.5	87.73	2785.3
1993-94	4420.3	71.83	5537.1
1994-95	4455.0	61.41	5100.0

Source: *12th Report of the (Parliamentary) Standing Committee on Civil Supplies and Public Distribution 1995-96, presented to Lok Sabha on May 9, 1995, p. 5.*

Table 3
Sales of Wheat and Rice Through PDS Relative to Procurement During
Reform Period

Year	Procurement (in mn. tonnes)			Sales (mn. t.)	Stocks Held (mn. t.)
	Wheat	Rice	Total		
1991-92	7.753	9.240	16.993	19.70	19.798
1992-93	6.380	11.790	18.170	17.20	13.862
1993-94	12.835	18.652	26.487	17.70	24.163
1994-95	11.868	18.884	30.752	14.30	30.749

Source: *12th Report of the (Parliamentary) Standing Committee on Civil Supplies and Public Distribution 1995-96, presented to Lok Sabha on May 9, 1995, p. 10.*

public. Once within the trap of structural adjustment conditionalities, the loss of sovereignty is palpable. The paralysis will cost the Congress its mandate to rule the country after the next general elections. To what extent the attack on working people can be reversed will depend on the building up of popular pressure.

Note

[1] These estimates are based on the official method of price-adjustment to a 1973-74 poverty line, and the serious problem with using this method, namely that it de-links poverty from any nutrition norm, was not known to me when this piece was written. Actual poverty as it turns out was much higher – by 1993-4, 50th Round, 75 percent of the rural population was in poverty – unable to access 2400 calories daily intake – compared to 70 percent in 1983. See 'Theorizing Food Security and Poverty' in this volume.

People's Democracy, February 11, 1996

FOOD STOCKS AND HUNGER
CAUSES OF AGRARIAN DISTRESS

Fallacious Theories Underlie Intellectual Apathy

In the year 2000-01, long before the drought, the availability of cereals in the country dropped to an all-time low of 141.4 kg. per head and that of pulses per head similarly dropped to below 10 kg. Adding the two, foodgrains availability was 151 kg. in 2001, nearly 26 kg. lower than at the beginning of the nineties. The last time such abysmally low levels of availability were seen, was during the hungry thirties and World War 11 in colonial times, and again briefly for two years only during the food crisis of the mid-sixties. *An average family of four members thus absorbed 104 kg. less of foodgrains in 2001 compared to the early nineties – a truly massive decline.* A given average fall implies a far larger order of fall for the poorer majority of the population, since for the top income groups the absorption of foodgrains has been rising – for let us remember, this refers not only to directly absorbed grains but also indirectly absorbed grains via conversion to animal products.

The following has been excerpted from the above paper published in *Social Scientist*, July-August 2003.

Yet the majority of academics and many activists seem to be complacently unaware of the depth of the hunger stalking India's tribal areas, villages and urban slums. Their complacence arises from the fact that while the crisis over forty years ago was caused by a *deficiency of supply* which everyone could understand, the problem today is caused primarily by a massive *deficiency of demand*: and most people, it appears, simply cannot comprehend how the existence of 40 million tonnes of surplus food stocks can be compatible with increasing hunger. Their understanding is not helped by the fact that the explanations put forward by official, government publications as well as by many professional economists, are materially and logically fallacious, and seek to rationalise the present abnormal situation solely in terms of 'voluntary choice' by consumers and by attacking allegedly 'high administered prices'. These explanations are not correct: in some cases there is open apologetic intent, in others material facts are ignored, or there is simply an incorrect process of inference from the premises.

There are a number of fallacious arguments which have been advanced to explain this unprecedented build-up of public foodgrains stocks in the country, which by July 2002 were 40 million tonnes in excess of the revised buffer norm for this time of year. One fallacious argument in official documents like the *Economic Survey 2001-02* is that the excess stocks are to be explained by the fact that minimum support prices (MSP) to farmers have been "too high" resulting in excessive procurement during 2001 despite a dip in grain output. This is complemented by the related argument that the excess stocks are a surplus over what people *voluntarily wish to consume*. The excess stocks represent a "problem of plenty", as the *Economic Survey 2001-2002* puts it: it says that the growth rate of superior cereals have been higher than population growth owing to allegedly too high administered prices of rice and wheat, and stocks have built up because *all consumers voluntarily* wish to reduce their intake of cereals and rather consume fruits, vegetables and animal products (milk, eggs, chicken etc.) as their income rises. NSS consumption data are quoted to show that over time there is a declining *percentage share* of food expenditure on cereals and a rising share on non-cereals, in almost all expenditure groups (in fact for the lowest groups it is static). Hence, it is argued, there is a mismatch between what consumers want, and the actual output structure resulting in excess stocks (See *Economic Survey 2001-02*, pp.118-130).

The RBI's *Annual Report 2001-02* (pp.20-25) repeats this argument, explaining the alleged mismatch between supply and demand as arising from rising administered acquisition price for rice and wheat against the global trend of falling market prices, leading to wrong price signals to the farmers and hence to excessive output and procurement of these crops. A third argument put forward by some rather well-meaning but misguided people is that the excess stocks are at the expense of lowering of consumption for the majority of people, hence the surplus is notional; while up to this point the argument is correct, they then go on to say that two successive years of drought would make the stocks disappear. It almost seems that they are asking for droughts to solve the problem, and indeed have got their wish since 2002-03 is a severe drought year. The last argument is as mistaken as the first two are.

All these arguments are not only incorrect but are highly misleading for policy. The argument on MSP being "too high" in 2001-02, ignores the fact that stocks started building up from four years before the quoted rise in the MSP. The argument is not situated within other well-known trends affecting grain sales, namely the falling prices or arrears of payment for cash crops like sugarcane and cotton grown in North India. In fact the logical fallacy involved is of the type *'post hoc ergo propter hoc'* namely a temporal sequence is mistaken for causal sequence. Declared MSP was raised and a bonus given in 2001, followed by high procurement in the *rabi* 2002, and it is wrongly inferred that high MSP *caused* high procurement, without reference to any other facts. Our own hypothesis is that record procurement, higher by 5.3 million tonnes in the year 2000-01 compared to the preceding year, was rendered abnormal by the fact that it came out of a cereals output which was *lower* by nearly 11 million tonnes. This indicates the presence of *distress sales of cereals* by farmers already affected for the preceding five years, by crashing prices for their other commercial crops. The typical farmer in Punjab, Haryana and Uttar Pradesh does not produce food grains alone but operates a mixed cropping pattern including non-food grain crops. The prices of cotton and sugarcane, by 2001 were at two-fifths to half the levels prevailing in 1996: while MSPs for these crops were declared, they were both lower than before and not fully implemented; further, sugar mills are notorious for their large arrears of payment to growers. Only the public procurement of cereals gave farmers some relief and led them to sell even at the expense of their own consumption, in trying to cover losses on other crops. We believe that without the bonus paid in that year on wheat, farmers would have sold an even higher tonnage, because they were already on the backward bending segment of their supply curve.

The suggestion that MSP should be lowered is irresponsible, given the crisis of falling prices of commercial crops that farmers currently face. There has been a phenomenal increase in farm subsidies over the last five years in the advanced countries, whose governments are supporting their farmers in the face of globally falling farm prices, and our farmers are forced to compete, after removal of quantitative restrictions, against these increasingly heavily subsidised foreign products. They can certainly do without being attacked by their own economists via recommended lowering of MSP. What is required on the part of government is to follow the example set by advanced countries, especially USA, and increase its budgetary support to farmers in their hour of distress as well as maintain MSP.

The second argument on voluntary dietary diversification *by all population segments* away from cereals towards fruits, vegetables, milk, eggs and chicken can be likened to Queen Marie Antoinette's alleged, notorious comment on the hungry poor of Paris agitating for bread in the bitterly cold winter of 1789: "If they have not bread, let them eat cake." This was rational enough advice when confined to the nobility who indeed had no difficulty in substituting cake for non-available bread, but it showed a callous ignorance of the condition of the poor. In retrospect we may perhaps forgive Marie Antoinette her ignorance, for she was raised in feudal opulence with no contact with the people, and surely she paid a heavy price when the guillotine separated her head from her body. But what shall we say of our own economists with their doctorates who operate with the same assumption, that voluntary dietary diversification is possible for all segments of the population? Both Marie Antoinette's remark and the arguments of those writing the *Economic Survey* and the Reserve Bank of India's *Annual Reports*, contain the same fallacy – the *fallacy of composition*. This common fallacy in applied logic, is of the following type – a proposition is true for a *part* of the whole (example: the paper A in a collection of essays is very good), but from this the incorrect inference is drawn that the proposition is true for the whole (the entire collection of essays is very good).

The argument on voluntary dietary diversification ignores the fact that the distribution of food in our society is highly skewed owing to the highly skewed distribution of incomes; that this skewness is likely to have been increasing over time as reform policies have favoured the rapid growth of incomes for particular top segments of the population and immiserized other, poorer segments who have a much higher income elasticity of demand for foodgrains. At the highest income levels, say taking the top decile of the population ranked by income, which has seen rising per capita disposable incomes over the last decade, there is indeed a voluntary diversification of diets towards higher value foods accompanied by rising nutritional levels. For those with below average incomes (roughly, the lowest six deciles) 'diversification' is the result of a cut in access to basic foodgrains owing to a combination of falling purchasing power and denial of BPL ration cards, and hence this diversification is accompanied by falling per head calorie levels and deepening hunger. The average picture of overall decline is the outcome of diametrically opposite trends for these different segments of the consuming population – a rise for the minority and a large fall for the majority. What we see as the outcome, is the weighted average of opposite trends.

Further, *"diversification"* (measured by falling average share of food grains in total expenditure, or alternatively, by falling average share of calories from food grains in total calories), is a necessary, but is not a sufficient condition for inferring an improvement in welfare. This is because diversification can be as much an outcome of declining income, declining average nutrition and hence declining welfare, as it can be of improving income, improving average nutrition and improving welfare. It is a grave logical mistake to think that dietary diversification is identical with betterment: one may as well think that one is standing at the top of a mountain while actually standing at the bottom of a valley, because both are flat. The simple arithmetic behind the proposition that diversification is a necessary feature of lowered welfare as much as it is a necessary feature of improved welfare, is discussed towards the end of this paper.

While presenting their rosy view of a voluntary diversification of diets by all segments of the population, most economists consistently suppress the fact that the NSS, the source of the share of spending figures showing 'diversification', also shows that per head daily total calorie intake ('total' in the sense of 'from all foods'), has been falling in both rural and in urban areas from already inadequate initial levels, and falling much more rapidly in the 1990s than before. Even the controversial 55th Round data show that rural average calorie intake has fallen below the urban level for the first time. Those economists who do reluctantly mention the falling calorie intake figures, tend to put forward the argument that there is a voluntary trade-off, of lower calories for a more diversified diet. This is hardly credible, since these lowered grain intake and lowered calorie intake levels prevalent in India by 2001-02, even before the drought, were even lower than the sub-Saharan African countries had a decade ago, and since all other developing countries not subject to deflationary reform policies have improved their average calorie intake, some like China quite dramatically, as their average diet has diversified (see the country data in the 'Food Balance Sheets' calculated periodically by the Food and Agriculture Organisations, Rome).

'Diversification' has a radically opposite significance when it is associated with falling average nutrition, compared to when it is accompanied by rising average nutrition, but this elementary fact is ignored in the literature. Table 2 details the data on increasing diversification for two SSA countries, Kenya and Tanzania, as their per capita income declined. Perhaps it is the unwise and dogmatic commitment of many pro-reform economists to the untenable proposition that economic reforms have been of benefit to all, that leads to their present conceptual blindness and to the bad theory that we see today, which produces grotesquely apologetic interpretations of deepening hunger and starvation, as 'voluntary choice'.

The third argument on droughts drawing down food stocks, ignores the fall in farmers and labourers' income, further loss of purchasing power and increasing distress, that droughts entail: it fails to see that mere supply does not create its own demand, i.e. Say's law does not operate, and that no amount of droughts alone will lead to more sales from the PDS and drawing down of stocks, unless there is intervention to lower the issue price on the one hand and to increase mass purchasing power through large -scale food-for-work on the other.

While there has been about 5.6 million tonnes actually disbursed in drought-affected Rajasthan through food-for-work, which while inadequate has staved off higher mortality, the story is different in Andhra Pradesh, where several districts were drought-stricken in 2002. During that year, the following were the police records of farmer suicides in the three worst affected districts: 1,220 in Karimnagar, 903 in Warangal and 457 in Nizamabad; the total for these three districts comes to 2,580 which is over three times the total number of suicides for all districts summed over the preceding five years. Suicides also continued in the remaining districts during 2002, and in the worst-affected districts during the summer of 2003. Over a thousand poor additionally died in Andhra Pradesh in May-June 2003 reportedly owing to heat-wave, but obviously because their already weakened bodies could not stand the stress. A drought which follows five years of falling prices and employment, has a very different impact from a drought in normal times.

Despite the severe drought of 2002-03, no *general all-India programme* to raise rural purchasing power by the required extent and get back the 27 kg. per head loss of grain consumption suffered over the last decade, is remotely in sight, and the fundamental reason is the incorrect diagnosis of the problem presently being offered by all those economists and policy makers in a position to influence the government.

All the arguments detailed so far miss the basic point about these stocks, that they are the result of a very large increase in the inequality of access to food in Indian society, over the last five years in particular. The increased inequality of access in turn is the outcome of two sets of processes – absolute decline in real incomes and hence loss of purchasing power through unemployment and income deflation for a substantial section of the population, and targeting in the PDS. The first, the cut in purchasing power of the poorer majority of the population, especially in villages, itself has two components – contractionary, public-expenditure reducing economic reform policies in the nineties resulting in a collapse of rural employment growth and hence income growth, and sharply falling farm prices for commercial crops both globally and locally from 1996-7, also reducing incomes, for the extent of price fall has rivalled the extent of price crash in the years of agricultural depression preceding the Great Depression. Both processes have been discussed in three of my recent papers (Patnaik 2002, 2003a, 2003b) and the interested reader is referred to these for a more detailed analysis.

The collapse of employment in rural areas is indicated by a deceleration of employment growth rate which was 2% annually during 1993 to 1998, to less than a third of this rate at 0.58% annually during 1987 to 1993. Further, the employment data for 1999-2000 gives the startling finding that there has been absolute decline of number employed in agriculture by 5 million compared to 1993 – over this period employment growth has been negative, and the situation is bound to have worsened further after 1999. This total collapse of employment has been mainly the outcome of the reverse multiplier effects of the sharp fall in development expenditures in rural areas implemented under reform policies: from nearly 4 percent of NNP in the 7th Plan period before reforms began, rural development expenditures have halved to less than 2 percent of NNP by 2000-01. The apologists of 'economic reforms' are quick to point out that the share of agriculture in GDP has also gone down so it does not matter – which is a nice example of fallacious argument, of putting the cart before the horse: for, of course, the share of agriculture going down is precisely because of collapse in output growth in that sector, directly owing to the sharp fall in public development expenditures which includes the spending on vital infrastructure like irrigation and power, apart from employment generation programmes. The well-known trends of falling crop output growth rates are detailed in Table 3 (p.155).

The second process leading to worse access to food on the part of the poor is implementation of targeting the food subsidy, which has been an utterly disastrous policy. The maximum cut in mass purchasing power, from 1997-8 onwards (as price falls came on top of job losses) were already taking place when, under pressure to "target" the food subsidy, government gave up the earlier system of unconditional and universal access by households to the Public Distribution System, and thereby initiated the institutional denial to the poor of access to cheap food, owing to the sadly misconceived system of above-poverty-line and below-poverty-line (APL-BPL) introduced from 1997-98. This means that while the permit-licence system in every other sphere has gone, it is only the poor who have to have a new permit now – recognized BPL status – to draw cheap food and further, their entitlement has also fallen. The result has been a drastic drop in off-take (sales) from the PDS (for a useful discussion see Swaminathan 2002). The combination of all these processes have led to the present situation of increasing hunger.

We have seen that foodgrains availability per head in the country hit a low of only 151 kg. in the year 2001, 26 kg. lower than in the early nineties. Only the AIDS-ravaged Sub-Saharan African countries and some least developed countries have a lower level than this at present. The last time such a low level was seen was in colonized India on the eve of the Second World War. The level of India's gross foodgrains output in 2002-03, following the drought in Monsoon 2002 , is now estimated to be no higher 181.3 million tonnes, a seven-year low while population is higher by 265 million. Hence per capita net output works out to 149.5 kg. for 2003, the second worst level reached in the 20th century in British India during war time. No doubt in 2003-04 output will improve, but once the perception of drought ends, what will happen to food-for-work and to domestic absorption remains to be seen.

Even progressive academics and intellectuals in a position to influence policy, are, with a few honourable exceptions, in the main oblivious to the seriousness of the long-term situation owing to the wrong theories in which their thinking is locked. They are rendered conceptually blind to increasing hunger, and are putting forward all kinds of untenable arguments to rationalise the present crisis (vide the official explanations of the RBI Report and Economic Survey cited earlier, which say nothing at all about the drastic fall in food availability even while positing positive Engel effects). It is a mistake to think that the victims of these disastrous economic policies will revolt and make their distress obvious to our obtuse intellectuals and policy makers by agitating or rioting: they are scattered over thousands of atomistic villages, tribal areas and urban slums, and as they face increasing unemployment, income loss and deepening undernutrition, they are struggling merely to survive. Rising graphs of suicides and organ sales are indicators of deepening agrarian distress. Starvation is already a reality in many tribal communities. The ongoing rise of fascist forces in India is a classic process in which the victims of rising economic distress (tribals, *dalits*, retrenched textile mill workers) are easily mobilised by the communal-fascist forces and their blind anger turned against the minorities who are made scapegoats for their distress, in areas where the progressive movement is weak.

Why rising per head income but falling per head foodgrain absorption?
We know that in the 1990s the foodgrains growth rate has slowed down drastically to 1.7 % annually and fell below the population growth rate of 1.9%, so that per head annual net foodgrains output has fallen by about 4 kg. from a peak of 181.6 kg. in the three years ending in 1994-95, to 177.7 kg. by the three-year period ending in 2000-01.

Since the per head income in the country has been growing at least at 3% annually during this period, normally in such a situation of supply shortfall there should have been a need for *food imports* to satisfy demand.

Annual net imports of about 3-4 million tonnes without any change in stock levels, would have just maintained the early- nineties grain absorption level, and in fact, even higher imports than this should have been required since per head income growth has been good and average absorption should have risen, everything else remaining the same.

It is a grave mistake to think that the absorption of grain per head falls with rising income: on the contrary, all empirical evidence shows that the absorption of foodgrains for all purposes, always goes up with rising per head income under normal conditions (this includes both the direct use plus the indirect consumption through conversion of grain as feed into animal products). In short, the elasticity of demand for foodgrains for all purposes, is positive with respect to income. This rise of per head foodgrains absorption is true in a cross-sectional sense looking at countries at different levels of income – compared to below 200 kg. in India, the Chinese, with over double the per capita income of India, absorbed 325 kg. of cereals per head in the mid-nineties, Mexico absorbed 375 kg., while high-income Japan, Europe and North America absorbed over four times as much as India, with the USA registering 850 kg. per head annually of which about 200 kg. was direct consumption and the remainder was converted to animal products.

With rising grain absorption, a rising percentage of the grain is devoted to feed for producing animal products. Needless to say, the higher the grain absorption, the higher is the total calorie intake per head from all foods. (We adopt the same definition of 'foodgrains' for the purpose of international comparison, namely the cereals, excluding potatoes. We also take the same definition of availability, namely gross output plus net imports and minus net addition to stocks. Gross rather than net output is adopted as the deduction on account of seed, feed and wastage might vary across countries and we do not have information on how it varies).

The rise in per head grain absorption is also found to be true when we study any individual developing country over time provided its per capita income is rising – Brazil and a host of other growing countries have higher per head absorption of grains today than they did a decade ago and they also have higher per capita total calorie intake. Conversely, the sub-Saharan African countries, with falling GDP per head, show falling per head grain absorption and falling per head calorie intake from all foods. In short, development always sees rising total grain intake per head and this is associated with improving nutrition, namely rising total calorie intake per head, while the opposite is true with fall in income.

Yet, in India despite the shortfall in supply with per head output falling, and despite positive overall income growth per head, far from any need for imports, as already discussed we see precisely the opposite situation, namely both the build-up of public food stocks as well as net exports – equivalent to the drastic fall in absorption of foodgrains per head of population. The question is, why should average grain absorption be falling in India despite rise in average income? Nowhere in the world has such a phenomenon been observed under normal conditions.

Further, the daily per capita calorie intake from all foods – not just foodgrains – has been falling slowly in urban areas and at a faster rate in villages, according to the NSS data, and the period 1983 to 1993-94 has seen a drop in rural areas by 156 calories, from 2309 calories to 2153 calories. The only exceptions have been the states of Kerala and West Bengal, which according to the same NSS consumption data, have seen rising per head cereals intake and hence, have also posted rising per head total calorie intake *in both rural and urban areas*, in sharp contrast to all other states. The pro-poor policies in these two states have helped to enhance nutritional security. In the states other than Kerala and West Bengal, taken together, the fall in both variables, obviously, has been greater than the all-India average fall.

The only answer lies in a very large increase in the *inequality of income distribution* during the nineties of a specific type, namely income deflating policies reducing the absolute real income of a majority of the population, and also in the poor being institutionally denied access to grain since 1997-98 owing to the misconceived targeting system under which large numbers of the actually poor are not being identified as such and are not being issued BPL ration cards for accessing cheap food.

The proportion of rural development expenditures to NNP halved to 1.9 percent over the 1990s. The growth rate of total employment in rural areas has crashed from over 2 percent annually during 1987 to 1993, to only 0.6 percent during 1993 to 1998 and employment in agriculture has declined in absolute terms. A large segment of the textile industry, particularly the small scale and unorganized segment of handlooms and powerlooms, has experienced closure and job losses. The crisis of the textile industry in turn is directly the result of trade liberalisation entailing raw cotton and yarn exports, driving up raw material costs, hikes in power tariff and a credit squeeze.

Economic reform policies of expenditure cuts and trade liberalisation, along with targeting, by inducing demand deflation on the one hand and administratively excluding the poor from the PDS on the other, have reduced a functioning PDS to a shambles before our very eyes and gravely undermined the little food security that the people had. While the top one-eighth of our population ranked by income levels, which accounts for at least fifty percent of national income, is undoubtedly approaching advanced country levels of food consumption with rising nutrition levels accompanied by dietary diversification, the bottom six deciles, with less than a fifth of national income, are being pushed further into the ghetto of undernutrition. They have already become the sub-Saharan Africa within India.

Diets can show diversification when average nutrition falls: as earlier argued it is a grave logical mistake to associate diversification solely with improvement. For example, in Kenya where per capita income has been falling for the last two decades at nearly 1 % annually, average calorie intake has been falling as well mainly owing to a drastically lower availability of the food staples which includes cereals and tubers – just as in India of late – while calories from animal products have risen but only very marginally, leading to a large net loss of calories per day. The average Kenyan by the mid-nineties was pushed way below the poverty line calorie intake owing to a large net loss of 303 calories compared to the late 1970s. But in percentage terms the share of calories from foodgrains has fallen and the share from animal products has risen – viz. the diet is more "diversified", and someone who looks only at the trend in percentage shares without looking at the trend in the absolute totals, might be misled (Table 2).

Similarly in Tanzania by the mid-nineties a more diversified diet was consistent with fall in the average nutrition level.

We have given Table 2 as an example of dietary diversification accompanying worsening nutrition. Since it is always a large loss in grain intake – the biggest component of vegetal sources of calories – which produces the nutrition decline, the percentage share of grains and vegetal sources generally will also show a decline – viz. diets will be more "diversified". This is a simple logical matter, that given a ratio x/y where x < y, and a constant deduction of A from both numerator and denominator, the ratio x-A/ y-A will always be lower than x/y. (The opposite is true if x>y, namely then x-A / y-A > x/y).

If C(F) / C(T) is the initial share of calories from foodgrains to total calories, then a fall in foodgrains calories by the amount A, by lowering the denominator by the same amount, will produce the new share {C(F) - A / C(T) - A} which will always be lower than the initial share C (F) / C(T). (Always, because C(F) is necessarily always less than C(T). The share of calories from the non-vegetal sources, on the other hand, will rise, viz. C(T)-C(F) / C(T) will rise. It is obvious that the only very special situation in which the shares will be unchanged when C (F) is declining, is when non - foodgrains calories also decline in exactly the same proportion.

Diversification is a necessary condition, but not a sufficient condition for inferring improvement in welfare at the average level. We need to look at a crucial additional fact – is the per head total calorie intake going up, in which case nutrition is improving – or, is it going down, in which case nutrition is worsening and so is welfare. Both the bottom of a valley and the very top of a mountain are flat, viz. flatness is a necessary condition for a maximum as well as a minimum. We need to know an additional, crucial fact to know where we are, and that is whether we have been climbing, or sliding down. The second-order condition must also be known before we can correctly answer the question of whether we are at the top of the mountain or the bottom of the valley. It is perhaps not accidental that those

Table 1
Change in Average Calorie Intake per Diem from
All Foods, in Rural and Urban India, 1983 to 1998

Year	RURAL	Index	URBAN	Index
1983	2,309	100	2,010	100
1987-88	2,285	99.0	2,084	103.7
1993-94	2,157	93.4	1,998	99.4
1998	2,011	87.1	1,980	98.5
Change				
1993-4 over 1983	- 152		- 12	
1998 over 1993-94	- 146		- 18	

Source: NSS Surveys on Consumer Expenditure up to 1998. The 55th Round data for 1999-2000 are not apparently comparable with earlier Rounds owing to change in recall period. Note that average rural calorie intake has always been higher than urban owing to the physically more demanding work performed in rural areas .

who are so eager to argue that Engel's Law has been operating favourably for the *entire* population, suffer amnesia when it comes to this crucial additional fact of declining per capita calorie intake from all foods, and do not even bother to mention it.

There is no need for our economists to be so confused by the fact that average grain absorption and calorie intake from all foods are going down despite rise in per head income: *sharply worsening income distribution plus institutional denial of food access to the poor owing to targeting, is the answer.* This proposition is supported by the estimates made by Radhakrishna and Ravi (2002) in their study which indicates that the lowest three deciles of the consuming population in both rural and urban areas can be expected to have experienced a drastic fall in per capita total calorie intake to around 1300 calories by 1998.

The nadir of food availability had been reached in British India with 136 kg. per head during 1945-46. The present Government, through its inaction, is doing its level best to ensure that this nadir is reached once again. Simply lowering the APL issue price a little as has been done is not

Table 2

Examples of Dietary Diversification and Worsening Welfare: KENYA and TANZANIA, 1974-76 to 1992-94 : calorie intake per head per day

KENYA	Vegetal Origin	Animal Origin	Total calories	% shares in Total Vegetal	Animal
1974-76	2003	217	2220	90.2	9.8
1982-84	1810	230	2040	88.7	11.3
1992-94	1672	245	1917	87.2	12.8
Change, 1992-94 Over 1974-76	- 331	+28	- 303		
TANZANIA					
1974-75	2009	150	2159	93.1	6.9
1982-84	2148	138	2286	94.0	6.0
1992-94	1906	147	2053	92.8	7.2
Change 1992-94 Over 1974-76	- 103	- 3	- 106		

Source: Food and Agriculture Organisation (FAO) *Food Balance Sheets 1992-94*, p.236, 435.

enough, for the implicit assumption behind the measure is that the population is on the same demand curve as earlier. The fact that the demand curve itself has shifted down sharply for a large segment of the population, including for the farmers who were well-to-do earlier, owing to severe income deflation, is still not theoretically recognized: hence, the prognosis as regards corrective macroeconomic action remains very bleak. Without determined measures to raise purchasing power through an expansionary fiscal stance, by raising development expenditures in rural areas, the danger of continuing income deflation and even more widespread starvation will become a reality. But, no such expansionary policy is remotely in sight.

The statement regarding starvation is not idly made. Food security systems can collapse very fast with wrong policies, the system has been already severely undermined, and in a still poor country, mass starvation is a hair's breadth away. There is nothing wrong in principle with the PDS or with its distribution mechanism, and despite all its problems it worked reasonably well for three decades from 1967 to 1997. The reason it started packing up from 1998, and has reached a crisis point today, is because purchasing power especially in villages, has collapsed under a combination of government's contractionary fiscal policies and the effects of globally falling farm prices as protection was removed, and the poor have been excluded from the PDS by the misconceived targeting of the food subsidy.

The immediate and urgent measure is to abandon the disastrous attempt to target the food subsidy and to go back to the earlier universal system, issue ration cards to all who want it, and make foodgrains available at the present BPL rates. The Report on Long-term Grain Policy by the A. Sen Committee (August 2002) had put forward two excellent recommendations – scrapping targeting and restoring universal access in the PDS, and food-for work pogrammes on a large scale, not only in drought hit areas but elsewhere as well. Continuing food-for work beyond the perceived end of the drought would raise the off-take from the PDS by at least about 8-10 million tonnes a year, but excess stocks would still remain.

Longer term policies of restoring purchasing power need to be started on an urgent basis, and the stepping up of food-for-work programmes to cover every state whether drought affected or not, as well as increased development expenditures on vital infrastructure – irrigation and power – constitute the obvious answer. It has been pointed out by Shetty (2001) that with the banking system awash with liquidity and industry in recession, Rs.16,000 crores annually can be mobilised safely for infrastructural development. To this we may add that with unutilised excess foodgrains stocks, it is only the callous neo-liberals who would hesitate to launch a massive food for work programme for restoring mass purchasing power and at the same time ensuring infrastructural and social sector development in rural areas. There is no objective basis like a well-grounded fear of inflation, which can possibly explain the mindless deflationism still being followed by the government despite recession, unutilised resources and mass hunger. India has never experienced a period of hyper-inflation as Germany had seen after WW1, which is cited as the reason for deflationist sentiment even with rising unemployment in the Weimar Republic period, nor has it ever experienced the kind of high inflation rates that many Latin American countries have had in the more recent past. The only reason for the Indian government's continuing refusal to adopt an expansionary fiscal stance is subservience to the current deflationist dogmas of the Bretton Woods institutions – the same 'humbug of finance' which today is succeeding in pushing the material sectors of the global economy into recession, in the same manner the capitalist world had been ultimately pushed into depression seventy years ago (see P. Patnaik 1998, U. Patnaik 2003a).

Farm and agro-business interests in the advanced countries, faced with declining global prices for their grain and dairy exports, have secured massive increases in subsidies from their governments. Between 1998 and 2002, the USA added 30.8 billion dollars in transfers to farmers to its 1998 level of $84 billion. That is not all: on November 2002 the USA enacted a law which will give additional subsidies totalling over $56 billion, annually phased over the next six years. By 2007, an *increase* of over $100 billion in farm transfers in the USA will be a reality compared to a decade earlier. Already, the share of subsidy in the US wheat price per tonne is over 70 %. The European Union has also added rapidly to its farm subsidies. In such an unfolding scenario of increasingly unfair competition, the Indian economists' and government's disregard of the interests of its own farmers and the interests of the poorer majority of consumers through the refusal to adopt an expansionary fiscal stance, will have far-reaching implications in generalizing the spread of the strong income-deflationary tendencies already visible in the economy. The associated process of political destabilization via the rise of the communal-fascist forces, is visible already.

References

Food and Agriculture Organization. 1996. *Food Balance Sheets, 1992-94* (Rome: Food and Agriculture Organization).

Ministry of Finance, Government of India. *Economic Survey* for the years 2000-01, 2001-02, and 2002-03.

Patnaik, P. 1998. 'The Humbug of Finance', *Chintan Memorial Lecture,* reprinted in P.Patnaik, *The Retreat to Unfreedom* (Delhi: Tulika).

Patnaik, U. 2002 .'Deflation and Deja-Vu' in V.K.Ramchandran and M.Swaminathan (Eds.), *Agrarian Studies – Essays on Agrarian Relations in Less Developed Countries* (Delhi: Tulika).

—— 2003 a. 'Global Capitalism, Deflation and Agrarian Crisis in Developing Countries', *Journal of Agrarian Change,* Vol.3 Nos.1-2, January and April.

—— 2003 b. 'Food and Land Use: Sustainable Development in India in the Context of Global Consumption Demands' in R. Sengupta and A. Sinha (Eds.), *Challenge of Sustainable Development – the Indian Dynamics* (Kolkata: Indian Institute of Management, Kolkata in association with Manak Publications).

Reserve Bank of India, 2002. *Annual Report, 2001–02* (Mumbai: Reserve Bank of India).

Swaminathan, M., 2002. 'Excluding the Needy: the Public Provisioning of Food in India', *Social Scientist,* Vol.30, Nos.3-4, March-April 2002.

THE REPUBLIC OF HUNGER

Introduction

In the course of the last five years (1998 to 2003), the population of the Republic of India has been sliding down towards sharply lowered levels of per capita foodgrains absorption, levels so low in particular years that they have not been seen for the last half century. Between the early 1990s when economic reforms began, and at present, taking three-year averages, the annual absorption of foodgrains per head has come down from 177 kg. to 155 kg. Such low absorption levels were last seen in the initial years of World War II – from where they had fallen further still. Again, after some recovery, the very first few years after Independence half a century ago and the food crisis of the mid-1960s, are comparable to present average absorption levels.

Over four-fifths of the total fall has taken place in the last five years alone, from 174 kg. in the three years ending in 1998 to 155 kg. taking the average of the two pre-drought years. This steep and unprecedented fall in foodgrains absorption in the last five years has entailed a sharp increase in the numbers of people in hunger, particularly in rural areas, and for very many it has meant starvation. The average downward movement in turn is the outcome of divergent trends – foodgrains absorption is rising fast for

Public Lecture on the occasion of the 50th Birthday of Safdar Hashmi, organized by SAHMAT (Safdar Hashmi Memorial Trust) on April 10, 2004, New Delhi.

the (mainly urban) well-to-do, and is either the same or falling faster than the average for the bulk of the (mainly rural) population.

This phenomenon of increasing numbers in hunger, can be established both on the basis of the hardest and most reliable data (on output, trade and stocks) that we have from official data sources, as well as from the ground-level experience of individual researchers and of organizations working in rural areas. The phenomenon is completely independent of the recent drought, and indeed the lowest levels of foodgrains absorption to date, has been registered two years *before* the severe drought of 2002-03.

The perception of the government and of the majority of academics, is however very different from that expressed above: they interpret the development as nothing out of the ordinary and many indeed even see it as a positive development, indicating a voluntarily chosen, more diversified basket of consumption by all segments of the population including the poor. When as a ground reality, the incidence of hunger rises, a 'denial mode' amongst those who govern and also amongst those who are associated with making or influencing policy during the period concerned, is common and is to be expected. But in the present case the divergence between the reality of increasing hunger, and the prevalent bland justifications of the phenomenon as a positive one, is so stark and so striking, that this divergence itself perhaps requires a theoretical explanation. Never before in the independent history of our country have we seen the kind of wholesale denial of a negative trend, and of its packaging and presentation as a positive development, as we are seeing at present. Moreover, the packaging and the justifications are not being put forward only by the right-wing political class which through its policy measures, is responsible for the present debacle. That the present government and ruling class in this country should seek to sanitize and justify the deeply anti-humanist and negative trend of increasing hunger, is to be expected. What is disturbing is that a large number of hitherto liberal academics are also advancing these justifications on the basis of various theories which are, needless to say, quite fallacious.

The International Context of the Discussion

Before going on to the details of the story in India, let us situate this story within the broader context of the past international approaches to hunger and famine. For this I will take up two cases – the alleged massive famine in China during the Great Leap, 1958-61, and the internationally unrecognized famine in Russia in the first half of the 1990s. When we look at these cases it becomes clear enough that the entire field of the discussion of hunger and famine is a highly ideological one, and has been routinely characterized by the abandoning of the minimum academic criteria with respect to evidence and estimation.

First, let us consider the allegation that 27 to 30 million people died in China during the 'Great Leap' period. This allegation is contained in the books of two US demographers Ansley J. Coale (1984), and Judith Banister (1987). Few in the developing world however would have bothered to read the discussion of these demographers, couched in technical language. The main popularizer and ardently uncritical supporter of the conclusions of these US demographers has been Amartya K. Sen, and it is through Sen's writings first in the *New York Review of Books* and subsequently in his many lectures and books including *Development as Freedom* (1999) that the world, and the reading public in this country has been informed that "China has had what is almost certainly the largest recorded famine in history (when thirty million people died in the famine that followed the Great Leap Forward) in 1958-61 whereas India has not had a famine since independence in 1947" (Sen, 1999, 43). The figure of 30 million has passed into popular folklore. However, a study of how it has been arrived at, shows that this estimate has no scholarly basis whatsoever.

The facts are that there was a run of three bad harvests and a steep 30% drop in foodgrains output took place in China in 1960, while the government's procurement from the villages did not decline, lowering availability per head. The official death rate, which had been falling up to 1958 owing to public health and sanitation measures, registered a rise to 25.4 per thousand in 1960. (This peak 'famine' death rate in China was however little different from India's actual, 'normal' death rate, 24.6, in the same year). The birth rate also fell steeply in 1958, mainly owing to labour mobilisation for collective work.

Two alternative routes have been used to estimate 'famine deaths', both of very dubious validity. In the first, the 'missing millions' totalling 27 millions in the population pyramid during 1958 to 1961, have been identified with 'famine deaths'. The problem with this is that not only the people who were actually living and who died in excess of normal numbers are included in the missing millions, but so are all those hypothetical persons included, who were never born at all and who 'should' have been born if the birth rate had not fallen. This is not a common-sense definition nor is it a logical definition of famine deaths: for, to 'die' in a famine, a minimum necessary condition is to be born in the first place. The Chinese are a highly talented people but even they cannot achieve the feat of dying without being born! If a person is told that 30 million people died, then quite correctly she would infer that those 30 million were alive and then died. The fact that 19 million of them never existed because they were never born in the first place, is not conveyed by the formulation. Hence, there is disingenuousness involved in saying that 30 million people 'died': it is an untrue proposition.

The second route, followed by the demographers Coale and Banister, is perhaps even more dubious. They take the population totals yielded by the official 1953 and 1964 Censuses in China to be correct, but dispute the official fertility rate even though it was based on a very large sample of 30 million persons or 5% of the then population, especially canvassed along with the 1953 Census as Nai-Ruenn Chen (1966) had informed us. Instead, they use the much later Census 1982 study to project back very high fertility rates to the past, thus constructing an entirely hypothetical larger total of births between 1953 and 1964.

If more people were born over the inter-censal period 1953 to 1964, correspondingly these extra people must also have died over the same period: for both authors despite rejecting every official vital rate, display a most touching faith in the absolute Census population totals at these two dates. Hence the official increase in population is kept unchanged, enabling them to assume exactly as many extra deaths as they assume extra births.

With this procedure the official figure of total deaths over the inter-censal period was raised by a heroic 60 percent. Both authors then arbitrarily allocated the assumed higher numbers of deaths over the individual inter-censal years by assuming varying rates by which deaths were allegedly 'under-reported' during each of these years. In short it was entirely up to the demographer how many extra deaths he or she assigned to the Great Leap years, and the totally arbitrary nature of the procedure can be gauged by the fact that Coale raised the 1960 death rate to nearly 39 while Banister raised it to 44.6 (compared to the official death rate of 25.4). There is no reasonable basis for either figure.

Nor is this all: a linear time trend was then fitted by both to deaths derived from a variable – the death rate – which always behaves non-linearly, and the extent to which the (arbitrarily constructed) death rate was above this declining trend was then used to derive total 'excess deaths', the figure being 27 million for Coale and 30 million for Banister. We know that deaths in a population can never reach zero, so fitting linear trends makes no sense. The linear trend procedure implies that the Chinese population would have reached zero deaths and attained immortality in a few years – a remarkable achievement indeed, an impossible achievement outside the nonsensical statistical procedures followed by the US demographers.

It is a travesty of the norms of academic integrity that grossly exaggerated estimates of 'famine' deaths derived in this arbitrary manner have been uncritically quoted and promoted and that they enjoy so much currency. In my detailed critique (Patnaik 2002) I have also shown the inconsistency of the peak death rates constructed by Coale and Banister, with the foodgrains output and availability figures in China. My calculations also show that the lowest possible availability figures we can get for China after taking into account government procurement, is still higher than in India, and it is a puzzle why, given a much more egalitarian distribution, the death rate should have risen even to the officially declared level. Because the internal political developments in China after 1978 were in the direction of attacking Maoist egalitarianism and the commune system, no repudiation from Chinese sources of the US estimates are to be seen.

In sharp contrast to the retrospective, patently ideological construction of hypothetical large famine deaths in China's Great Leap period and the publicizing of these figures, we find that the demographic collapse in Russia in the first half of the 1990s has been met with a deafening silence from the same academics. The estimation methods which they applied to China, are not applied by them to Russia. The facts are that the so-called 'shock therapy' to usher in capitalism, under the advice of Western experts, led to a catastrophic collapse of GDP in the former socialist states between 1990 and 1996. As Table 1 summarizing the United Nations data shows, the GDP level was half or less in Russia and Ukraine by 1996 compared to a decade earlier, and collapsed to only one-fifth of the mid-eighties level in Georgia, which was the worst affected. Never in peacetime have we ever seen such a comprehensive destruction of productive capacities and outputs, entirely owing to the wrong macro-economic policies advised by foreign experts and followed by the local policy makers. The human effects have been devastating, with a sharp reversal of the decades of improvement in all economic and human development indicators. The infant mortality rate rose, and the death rate among the able-bodied rose to 58 from nearly 49 (per thousand in the group) comparing 1992 with 1990, and rose further to 84 by 1994.[1] The male expectation of life declined by nearly 6 years in Russia. With the steep rise in the death rate, the total population of Russia showed absolute decline – again, an unprecedented situation in peacetime.

Where were those academics who profess to be concerned with hunger and famine, when it came to analyzing the economic and demographic collapse in Russia? It can hardly be argued that journalists and the media had no access to the country after 1990. I have said earlier that it is not reasonable to count the effects of the decline in the birth rate if any, to estimate 'famine deaths'. If we apply a reasonable method of simply taking the 1990 death rate in Russia as the bench mark and calculate the cumulated extra deaths by 1996 owing to the observed rise in the death rate, we get a figure of 4 million excess deaths in Russia alone. Expressed in relation to Russia's population, this famine was three times larger than the great Bengal famine in India in 1943-44 and twice as large as the Chinese excess mortality –accepting the official figures – during the Great Leap years. The Russian famine is neither internationally recognized nor publicized, for the very good reason that Russia was making a transition to *capitalism* and it is this process which gave rise to the famine. Those who are eager to discredit socialism even at the cost of indefensible statistical procedures, appear to be less than willing to recognize the existence of famine or estimate famine deaths in a 'transitional' society like Russia, even though the case is a contemporary one and is well documented.

The Significance of the Decline in India's Food Absorption in the Light of Historical Trends

We have not yet reached in India, the nadir of average foodgrains absorption seen in Sub-Saharan Africa under economic reforms and trade liberalization, where from 139 kg. per head in 1980 there has been a decline to below 125 kg. by the mid-1990s, and the masses are perpetually on the verge

Table 1
Drop in real GDP and male life expectancy in the countries of the former Soviet Union, 1985–1995

Country	Real GDP in 1995, percentage below real GDP level in 1985	Change in male life expectancy, no. of years
Armenia	–62	–1.1
Belarus	–39	–2.9
Georgia	–82	—
Kazakhstan	–55	—
Kyrgyzstan	–50	–3.2
Russian Federation	–45	–5.9
Tajikistan	–60	–1.0
Turkmenistan	–40	–0.2
Ukraine	–54	–2.4
Uzbekistan	–17	0.0

Source: UNDP Poverty Report 1998, New York; and UNDP Poverty Report 2000, New York.

of being pushed over into famine whenever there is drought (see p.64). The six most populous countries of Sub-Saharan Africa, accounting for 60% of the entire region's population, have seen declining calorie intake per diem, because declining food aid is not compensating for lowered domestic food production.

A large segment of the rural masses in India with a much lower foodgrains absorption than the average, have been already reduced to the nutritional status of Sub-Saharan Africa. On the basis of the NSS data on calorie intake for 1999-2000, I estimate that about 40% of the rural population was at the low absorption level of the SSA average. It is not for any lack of effort by the Indian Government that the situation is not worse. If the present incorrect policies of official denial of the widening ambit of hunger, failure to undertake expansionary development policies, and the official promotion of export oriented corporate agriculture continue to be followed, it may well be only a matter of another five years or so before we see the descent of the whole of rural India to the present average SSA nutritional status.

It is hardly possible to imagine a more drastic reversal of the goal of food security than has been seen in the last five years. The fifty years of a dying colonial rule before Independence had seen a decline of annual foodgrains availability per head by a quarter, from 199 kg. to 148.5 kg., considering five-year averages and leaving aside the individual post-war year which was even lower (see Table 2). The War years included the terrible Bengal famine with a mortality of at least 3 million. I have elsewhere argued (Patnaik 1999) that although the proximate cause of the famine was the inflationary burden of financing the war which was unjustly placed on India, the actual toll in the Bengal famine would not have been so large, without the preceding three decades of declining nutrition in Bengal which had seen a much larger than average drop in per capita foodgrains availability, by nearly 40% between 1911 and 1947.

Many who had seen the Bengal famine before their eyes, and in particular P.C. Mahalanobis, had an important role in formulating post-Independence policy: the goal of attaining food security at least in the limited sense of foodgrains self-sufficiency was given priority, and we saw a rise, albeit a painfully slow one, in the foodgrains availability per head from 152 kg. during 1950-55 to 177 kg by 1989-91 (see Tables 3 and 4). While the new agricultural strategy and green revolution no doubt had many drawbacks as regards equity of distribution, the average rise in per head output and availability was a major achievement which should not be underrated.

Forty years of effort have been lost in the last decade of neo-liberal economic reforms, with over four-fifths of the loss taking place in the last five years alone. The most remarkable and disastrous feature of the last five years of NDA rule in India has been the slide-back to the low level of 151 kg. per head food absorption in rural areas by 2001, a level not seen for fifty years. Reports of starvation, farmer suicides and deepening hunger should cause little surprise when we consider the recent trends in the official data on foodgrains output and availability. If we exclude the abnormal drought year 2002-03 and consider the average output of the preceding two years, we find that net foodgrains output per capita has fallen by about 5.5 kg. compared to the early nineties, owing to a slowing of output growth. This fall in per head output had been anticipated by this author (Patnaik 1996): as agriculture was opened up to the pull of global demand, 8 million hectares of foodgrains growing land has been diverted to exportable crops between 1991 and 2001, and yield has not risen enough to compensate, leading to a sharp decline of annual output growth which has fallen below population growth (even though the latter itself has been falling): hence we see fall in per head output.

Even more striking than output decline, however, has been the decline in foodgrains availability, or absorption per capita over the same period. Availability (which is defined as net output plus net imports and minus net additions to public stocks) has fallen by four times as much as output, or by 22 kg., as Table 4 shows. A large gap between per capita output and availability was last seen during the food crisis of the mid-1960s, but in the opposite direction: at that time, since output fell, 19 million tonnes of foodgrains were imported over two years to ensure enough domestic availability, apart from existing stocks being drawn down for the same purpose. By contrast in recent years even though output per head has fallen, both very large additions to stocks as well as massive food exports have taken place, resulting in large availability decline.

Availability is the same as the actual *absorption* of foodgrains, and the two terms will be used interchangeably. There was a slow decline in the absorption of food grains per head of the country's population between 1991-2 and 1997-8, after which it has fallen very sharply, from an average annual level of 174.3 kg. in the three year period ending in 1997-98, to only 151 kg. by the individual pre-drought year 2000-01, an abysmally low level last seen during the early years of the Second World War, which included the years of the terrible Bengal famine. Thus, in 2000-01 *the average Indian family of four members was absorbing 93 kg. less of foodgrains compared to a mere four years earlier – a massive and unprecedented drop, entailing a fall in average daily intake by 64 gms. per head, or a fall in calorie intake by at least 225 calories from foodgrains* which accounts for 65 to 70 percent of the food budget of the poor. Adequate energy intake from cereals normally ensures adequate protein intake and the converse is also true, as NNMB Reports point out.[2] Since the richest one-sixth to one-fifth of the population, mainly urban, has been improving and diversifying diets, the nutritional decline for the poorer three-fifths of the population, mainly rural, has been much greater than the average fall indicates.

Last year's severe drought, despite very low output, galvanized efforts to implement food-for-work in the drought-hit areas, and therefore resulted in somewhat improved availability per head compared to 2000-01, though it remained lower than the 158 kg. level of the previous year, 2001-02, which had registered the highest foodgrains output ever seen, of 212 million tonnes. Nevertheless the average annual cereals absorption taking all three years ending in 2002-03 is only 146 kg., and the cereals plus pulses or foodgrains absorption is only 155 kg. per head, an absolutely inadequate level given the large inequality in its distribution.

Often the argument is heard that since per capita income is rising it is to be expected that people should consume less cereals and pulses which become inferior goods, and consume more high-value foods: in short, people would diversify their diets. A falling share of grains in the consumer budget as income rises, is known as Engel's Law. So, it is argued, there is nothing wrong if we see falling availability/absorption of foodgrains per head. This is a total misconception regarding Engel's Law and it seems to have contributed to the incorrect official explanations of large stocks as arising from 'overproduction', discussed a little later. It is a misconception because Engel was referring to the fall in the share of food expenditure for the *direct* consumption of grains as income rises, and not to the total absorption of grains which includes both direct use as well as indirect use as feed for livestock (to produce milk, eggs, meat and so on), and as industrial raw material. The absorption of foodgrains per capita is always found to rise, not fall, as the consumer's average income rises. The figures of availability we have given, as indeed the official figures of availability, refer to absorption of grain *for all purposes*. (Note that availability figures do not require any consumption data but are calculated directly from output data, which is the hardest data we have, and this is adjusted only for trade and for stocks, so by definition it has to meet all possible final uses).

Availability of foodgrains thus includes not only direct consumption (as *roti*, boiled rice and so on) but also the part converted to animal products by being used as commercial feedgrains, and at present a part of these animal products are exported. (The conversion coefficients are quite high, for example a kilo of mutton can require 3-4 kilos of feedgrain to produce). Availability also includes the part of grain converted to industrial products like starch and alcohol, and into processed foods like cornflakes and noodles with an urban market. The availability, or absorption of foodgrains per head, *because it is for all uses, always rises as a nation's per capita income rises*. This is a very well known fact and is supported by an extensive literature on the responsiveness of demand for cereals to rising incomes, and by the FAO food balance sheets which give data over time for output, trade and stocks by individual crops, and cover virtually every country.

China, with about double India's per capita income, absorbed 325 kg. per capita of foodgrains (excluding tubers) in the mid-1990s compared to

India's less than 200 kg. at that time. Mexico absorbed 375 kg.per capita, high income Europe absorbed over 650 kg. per capita and USA absorbed the maximum, 850 kg. per capita of which less than a quarter was directly consumed and the rest converted to animal products, processed or put to industrial use (Calculated by the author from FAO, Food Balance Sheets for 1992-94).

The recent trend in this country of sharply declining foodgrains absorption per head while average per capita income has been rising, is thus highly abnormal, not only in the light of international experience but also in comparison with our own past experience – we have always seen rising grain absorption per capita as average incomes rose in the past in India. Between 1950 and 1991 per capita absorption rose slowly from 152 kg. to 177 kg. as per capita incomes rose.

As earlier observed these gains of four decades have been wiped out in a single decade of economic reform, and while availability fell by 3 kg per head in the seven years up to 1998, over eight-tenths of the total fall, namely a fall of 19 kg., has taken place in the mere five years of NDA rule (from 174 kg. average for the three years ending in 1998 to 155 kg. average for the three years ending in 2002-03).

What lies behind the decline in absorption of foodgrains? The massive decline at present compared to 1998, is the result of an unprecedented decline in purchasing power in rural areas following directly from a number of deflationary policies at the macroeconomic level, combined with international price declines for the larger volumes of export crops produced in India following trade liberalization. Both deflationary policies and opening up to trade are integral to neo-liberal economic reforms. This has resulted in a deflation of effective demand as far as the mass of the rural population is concerned.

The continuous decline in purchasing power, hence decline in foodgrains absorption for direct consumption purposes, resulted in a continuous decline in foodgrains sales from the PDS, which therefore got reflected in the continuous and increasing additions to public food stocks year after year starting from 1998, with the total stocks standing at 63.1

Table 2
British India, 1897 to 1946: Net Output, Imports and Availability of Foodgrains (Five-year average except last year)

Period	Net FG Output m. ton	Net FG Imports m.ton	Net FG Avail. m.ton	Popu-lation m	Per Capita Output Kg.	Per Capita Availa-bility Kg.
1897-1902	44196.84	-475.00	43721.84	219.74	201.1	199.0
1903-1908	41135.94	-1105.83	40030.11	225.79	182.2	177.3
1909-1914	47292.59	-1662.83	45629.76	231.30	204.5	197.3
1915-1920	45298.31	-336.00	44962.31	232.81	194.6	193.1
1921-1926	44607.21	-203.67	44403.54	239.18	186.5	185.6
1927-1932	43338.46	858.83	44197.29	253.26	171.1	174.5
1933-1938	41786.79	1374.67	43161.46	270.98	154.2	159.3
1939-1944	42702.91	521.83	43224.74	291.03	146.7	148.5
Individual year						
1945-46	41397.13	596.00	41993.13	307.00	134.8	136.8

Source: Net Output is obtained from gross output data in G. Blyn (1966) *Agricultural Trends in India 1891-1949*, by following the present day practice, of deducting one-eighth from Gross output on account of seed, feed and wastage. Net import figures also from the same source. Last two columns are roughly comparable with present day concepts of per head output and availability detailed in Table 3 and 4 below.

million tonnes by the end of July 2002. This was nearly 40 million tonnes in excess of buffer norms – and this in spite of declining per capita foodgrains output, and 2 to 4 million tonnes of grain exports every year up to June 2002, after which exports undertaken by the government have surged to unprecedented levels.

Last year, the worst drought year for two decades, between June 2002 and June 2003, the NDA government exported a record 12 million tonnes of foodgrains out of stocks and continued to export a million tonnes a month, bringing the declared total exports to over 17 million tonnes by November 2003. Independent India has never before seen such huge grain exports, only made possible by more and more empty human stomachs over the preceding years. Most of the exports was used as feedgrains for European

Table 3
Annual per capita output, imports and availability of foodgrains 1950-1 to 1989-90 in Kilograms (Five-year average)

Period	Net Cereals Output	Net Import	Change in Stocks	Net Annual Availability of Food Grains per Capita			Pulses/ Total, %
				Cereals	Pulses	Total	
1951-55	122.74	6.06	- 0.33	129.13	23.59	152.72	*15.4*
1956-60	121.81	8.30	- 5.82	135.93	24.84	160.77	*15.5*
1961-65	135.02	10.99	- 0.31	146.32	22.12	168.44	*13.1*
1966-70	129.83	12.45	1.34	140.94	17.78	158.72	*11.2*
1971-75	135.48	6.17	1.11	140.54	15.47	156.01	*9.9*
1976-80	147.13	- 0.77	0.57	145.79	15.63	161.42	*9.7*
1981-85	153.19	2.30	3.54	151.95	14.34	166.29	*8.6*
1986-90	155.95	0.65	- 1.56	158.16	14.61	172.77	*8.5*

Change in per Capita Availability, percent	
1951-55 to 1971-75	2.15
1971-75 to 1986-90	10.74
Total Change, 1951-55 to 1986-90	13.12

Source: Calculated from net output and availability data in Ministry of Finance, *Economic Survey* for various years, supplemented by Reserve Bank of India, *Report on Currency and Finance* for various years.

cattle and Japanese pigs. It is an utter scandal and a disgrace, that at the same time that more millions of the rural poor were going hungry and those already hungry were being pushed into starvation, rather than undertake widespread food-for-work programmes the government preferred to feed foreigners and their cattle by exporting foodgrains, applying a heavy subsidy of over Rs.4,000 crores to beat low world price. The f.o.b. export price was lower than the domestic price for the Below Poverty Line consumers. The concerned Ministry has had the gall to put full-page advertisements in newspapers in March as part of the government's pre-election 'shining India' campaign, celebrating among other things its export earnings.

Table 4
Summary of Annual *per capita* Foodgrains Output and Availability in India in the Nineties (Three Year Average)

Three-yr. Period Ending in	Average Population million	Net Output per Head Cereals Kg.	Foodgrains Kg.	Net Availability per Head Cereals Kg.	Pulses Kg.	Foodgrains Kg./ Year	Gms / day
1991-92	850.70	163.43	178.77	162.8	14.2	177.0	485
1994-95	901.02	166.74	181.59	160.8	13.5	174.3	478
1997-98	953.07	162.98	176.81	161.6	12.6	174.2	477
2000-01	1008.14	164.84	177.71	151.7	11.5	163.2	447
Individual Year							
2000-01	1027.03	157.79	167.43	141.42	9.64	151.06	414
2001-02	1046.44	165.40	177.01	146.76	11.61	158.37	434
2002-03*	1066.22	140.54	150.09	148.14	9.55	157.69	427
Average of the Years 2000-01 & 2001-02	1036.74	161.63	173.30	144.51	10.64	155.15	425

Change in Per Capita Availability of Foodgrains, %	
Triennium ending 1991-92 to Triennium ending 1997-98	- 1.6
Triennium ending 1997-98 to biennium ending 2001-02	- 10.9
Total Change, 1991-92 to 2001-02.	-12.3

Source: As Table 3. Population growth rate calculated as 1.89% using Census population totals of 1991 and 2001. The population figure for 2001 used above, is the March 2001 Census total of 1027 million which is 6 million less than the mid-2001 figure of 1033.3 million used in the *Economic Survey, 2002-03* in its Table S-21. Population for 2002 and 2003 in the table above, is obtained by applying the growth rate of 1.89% to this March 2001Census figure. The under-estimation of population by us is deliberate. The reader can check that actual availability per head would be lower by about 1 kg. in each year from 2001 using the official population figures.

* Note that 2002-03 estimate of availability is provisional, based on assuming the correctness of the data on individual items like procurement, off-take, and export over the months of 2002-03 as reported in RBI, *Report on Currency and Finance 2002-03*, Table 2.13 on p.12. It may be noted that the opening and closing stocks figures given in the same table are not consistent with the reported change in individual items – about 13 million tonnes of foodgrains are not accounted for.

Now that the perception of drought has ended, food-for-work projects have been wound up, and the media are full of a good monsoon and record projected grain output in 2003-04, the prognosis for a recovery of absorption levels to anywhere near that of 1998 remain very bleak. Let us remember that millions more than before were going hungry at only 158 kg. average absorption level in the year of the largest harvest seen to date – 212 million tonnes in 2001-02, or 177 kg. average output. The difference of nearly 20 kg. per head, between output and absorption, was going into addition to stocks, held at increasing cost, and into exports.

While a look at Table 3 shows that the difficult late 1960s and early 1970s also had fairly low availability, only somewhat higher than at present, it has to be recognized that the situation for the rural poor is worse today compared to then, because a larger part of the lowered absorption of today is going into animal products (the consumption of which is highly concentrated with the well-to-do) and into open market sales to processing units. Thus while in the last drought year 2002-03, a total of 33 million tonnes of grain were procured, the sales through the PDS plus allocations to special schemes for weaker sections amounted to almost the same, 35 million tonnes, implying that the mountainous stocks of 63 million tonnes were drawn down by a negligible 2 million tonne only, on this account.

Thus no policies were followed of an expansionary nature to reduce stocks by implementing large-scale food-for-work schemes in all rural areas in order to generate employment and restore purchasing power to earlier levels, as had been widely suggested by the progressive movements. All that was done was to allocate larger amounts of foodgrains to relief works in drought-hit areas alone. It is the massive 12 million tonnes of exports plus 6 million tonnes of open market sales which mainly reduced stocks by July 2003, and these obviously did not benefit the poor. The very fact of as high as 33 million tonnes procurement in a severe drought year also indicates distress sales by farmers (see RBI, *Report on Currency and Finance 2002-03* for these figures).[3]

Neither government nor its policy makers are prepared to recognize the fact that falling availability reflects a contraction of effective demand.

On the contrary, the explanation put forward in official publications of the Finance Ministry and the RBI and propagated by most academic economists, is precisely the opposite, namely that there is 'overproduction'. The *Economic Survey 2001-02* (pp.118-130) argued that excess stocks were a surplus over what people voluntarily wish to consume, and represented a "problem of plenty". NSS data on falling share of cereals in the spending on food were quoted to argue that not only the well-to-do, but all segments of the population were voluntarily diversifying their diets to high value foods away from cereals. It said that minimum support prices (MSP) to farmers have been "too high" resulting in excessive output and procurement. The RBI's *Annual Report 2001-02* (pp.20-25) repeated this argument, explaining the alleged mismatch between supply and demand as arising from rising administered acquisition price for rice and wheat against the global trend of falling market prices, leading to 'wrong' price signals to the farmers and hence to 'excessive' output and procurement of these crops.

Evidently the authors of these arguments have never heard of the difference between direct consumption of grain and the absorption of grain for all purposes – both direct and indirect – which has been already explained: if they had, they could not have given the above arguments or talked of overproduction, especially given the fact that the very same Reports show massive fall in availability per head. Further, their arguments might have had some little persuasive power if rural growth rates, employment and incomes had been rising. But all the NSS and official data show that precisely the opposite is the case. For a country which has been seeing sharp deceleration of agricultural growth in the nineties, falling per capita foodgrains output and sharply rising rural unemployment, these arguments on voluntary dietary diversification for all rural population segments, are illogical to the point of being foolish. We now know why the central government undertook massive food exports last year in a situation of steeply falling food availability and despite a severe drought: it has all been justified and rationalized already, simply by interpreting deepening hunger and starvation as 'voluntary choice,' and way below-normal consumption as over-production, in a grotesque travesty of reality.

J. Maynard Keynes had once remarked that the world moves on little else but ideas: and the socially irrational outcome we see before our eyes, of increasing hunger amidst relative plenty, illustrates starkly the effects that fallacious theories and wrong policies following from them, can have in lowering mass welfare. The fallacy involved in the official view is the *fallacy of composition,* where a statement which is correct for a *part* of the whole, is wrongly inferred to be correct for the whole. With income distribution shifting sharply in their favour, the top one-sixth of the population has certainly been voluntarily diversifying diets, but the poorer majority of the population cannot afford to do so, any more than the hungry poor of Paris crying for bread, could heed Queen Marie Antoinette's advice to eat cake.

It seems that the question of effective demand, and of *demand deflation* is simply not understood by most people. While everyone understands food shortage as in a drought, namely a physical output shortfall which curtails *supply*, it appears to baffle many that even more severe consequences can arise when the *effective demand,* the purchasing power of the masses falls, so that even though the physical supplies of foodgrains are there, people starve or move into hunger, owing to their inability to purchase food or to access food.

The reasons for declining rural mass effective demand in the nineties to date are many, and are all connected with deflationary neo-liberal reforms combined with trade liberalization. They will be summarized only briefly here as they have been discussed at length elsewhere (Patnaik 2003). First, public rural development expenditures, including infrastructure, which averaged 11 % of NNP during the period 1985-90, before reforms, were reduced to 8% of GDP by the early nineties as part of the deflationary policies advised by the BWI. Since 1998 they have been reduced further, averaging less than 6% of GDP and in some years falling to less than 5%. In real terms there has been a reduction of about Rs.30,000 crores annually in development expenditures on average during the last five years, compared to the pre-reform period. If we assume a plausible value of between 4 and 5 for the Keynesian multiplier, this means a drop in incomes in agriculture annually to the tune of between Rs.120,000 crores to 150,000 crores – a massive contraction indeed. This order of income fall, combined with real income declines owing to other causes detailed below, is broadly consistent with the observed fall in the contribution of agriculture to GDP during the nineties, from around one third to just over a fifth at present.

Let us remember that rural development expenditures include all employment generation programmes, special areas programmes, village industry, irrigation and flood control, energy and transport, apart from agriculture and rural development. Further, public fixed capital formation in agriculture has also continued its decline even more sharply in the nineties. It is hardly surprising that the rate of agricultural growth has slowed drastically in the nineties and has fallen below population growth for the first time in thirty years, and that the NSS employment surveys show an alarming collapse of rural employment growth to below 0.6% annually during 1993-4 to 1999-2000 compared to 2% annually during 1987-8 to 1993-4. Rural job losses are reflected in a lower participation rate, higher open unemployment, and an absolute decline in the numbers employed in agriculture.

Despite all its recent strident talk of development and the costly media publicity to every project, the reality is that no government has followed more systematically anti-development policies than has the NDA during the last five years. (It must be remembered that a rise in the size of the budget deficit as such, is no indicator of an expansionary impact on material production, if the rise is owing to reduction in the tax-GDP ratio and increasing interest payments to the well-to-do, as has been the case with reform policies). The decline in rural purchasing power has also contributed substantially to industrial recession, through demand linkages for simple consumer goods and manufactured inputs. The economy has undergone de-industrialization with the contribution of industry to GDP, which had been rising in the eighties, falling from 28% to just over 25% in the course of the nineties, and large net job losses have taken place in the organized sector. The only sector which has grown fast is the services sector which has ballooned, at the expense of the material productive sectors. As income distribution has shifted to the urban elites, a modern version of the medieval

Mughal economy is emerging with dozens of service providers to each individual rich household. Only a small segment of the services sector is highly-paid IT related services: the major expansion comes from lower-paid service activities.

Second, at the very same time that unemployment was growing and real earnings of the rural masses falling owing to deflationary policies, the government, years before it was required to do so under WTO, bending to the pressure of advanced countries, removed all quantitative restrictions on trade by April 2001 and exposed our farmers to unfair trade, global price volatility and recession-hit external markets. While global primary prices were rising up to 1996, they went into a prolonged decline thereafter, with between 40-50% (cereals, cotton, sugar, jute) to 85 % (some edible oils) fall in unit dollar price between 1995 and 2001. Some goods like tea and coffee continue to fall for growers, and others have seen only 10 to 15 percent rise from the trough, in the last two years. It is one thing to open the economy to trade when markets are expanding and quite another to do so when the world capitalist economy is in recession.

Anyone with a rudimentary knowledge of the past behaviour of global commodity markets should have been able to predict the crashing prices after the sharp rise of the early nineties, and also predict the fact that advanced countries would immediately raise their subsidies as they have always done (this author had warned of both in a 1997 paper), but India's policy makers have been unequal to the task and have in effect sacrificed our farmers on the altar of the BWI and WTO dogmas. These free trade dogmas ensure reduction of protection to their own producers by gullible developing country governments, at the same time that advanced countries increase their non-tariff barriers and massively raise their subsidies – the greater part of which they have, for their own convenience, already defined as non-trade distorting and placed outside reduction commitments in the Agreement on Agriculture. The bound tariff rates on agricultural products which the Commerce Minister had repeatedly assured as being adequate (bound rates averaged 115%) have not been actually implemented to provide protection to our farmers. On the contrary even under the regime of sharply falling global prices, duties continued to be reduced by the Finance Minister in every budget, far below the bound rates and averaged only 35% by 2000, allowing imports of rice, fruit and dairy products, undermining local incomes.

Producers of all export crops in India including raw cotton have also been badly hit by falling global prices, especially as input prices also rose with reform policies, inducing a severe squeeze on their already low incomes. With the implementation of the Narasimhan Committee Report after 1994, bank credit became more expensive and reliance on private high-cost credit perforce rose. Reduction of input subsidies and higher power tariffs, all part of the reforms pushed by the BWI, were mindlessly implemented even as farmers were already in difficulty, plunging virtually all farmers including the normally viable ones, into a downward spiral of indebtedness and causing many to lose land as the latest data indicate. Sale of kidneys and suicides are stark indices of deepening agrarian distress.

While the main prize for servile implementation of deflationary BWI dictates against mass interests goes to the central government and its policy advisers, the consolation prize for the most adverse state-level policies should go to the TDP government of Andhra Pradesh which, entering into a direct structural adjustment programme with the World Bank, has hiked power tariff on five occasions. This state has seen more than three thousand recorded farmer suicides in the last five years as well as suicides of entire families of weavers. In 2002 alone, according to police records (reported in *The Hindu,* Hyderabad edition of Jan.6, 2003) as many as 2,580 deeply indebted farmers killed themselves mainly by ingesting pesticides in three districts alone – Warangal, Karimnagar and Nizamabad. We have no record of suicides on this scale in colonial India: our present day politicians in their servile implementation of imperialist dictates routed through the BWI, have out-done even the colonial masters of the past in their disregard for the welfare of the mass of the people. At least agrarian distress at that time led to some official commissions of inquiry and amendments to laws to restrict land transfer for debt: at present all we see is bad theory and open apologetics.

Advanced countries, as they have always done in the past, have been increasing support to their farmers as global prices fell (the US has legislated subsidies into the future, which will give transfers to its farm sector of $180 billion by 2008 compared to $84 billion in 1998). The majority of our economists by contrast, are busy attacking the Indian farmer when he is already down, by saying that 'MSP is too high' and should be cut for these *kulaks*, and by shedding crocodile tears for the poorer farmers and labourers, on the ground that they are net food purchasers and would benefit from lower prices. They are obsessed with the question of support price alone, not the issue price which is the relevant one, and which can be lowered in principle without affecting support price. Further, by focussing on price alone, they implicitly assume that the population is on the same demand curve as before, whereas in fact the demand curve itself has shifted down so drastically for the mass of the rural population that tinkering with the support price is now likely to deepen the crisis.

They seem not to realize that unemployment and income deflation has swamped this sector, that every price is also an income, and cutting MSP today when there is already agrarian crisis, would further widen and deepen income deflation and lead to more indebtedness and more suicides. They forget that for years and decades India's surplus farmers, the much reviled 'kulaks', sold grain without complaining to the FCI at half the global price when global price was high, thus ensuring cheap food for urban areas. Now, when the global price has fallen below the local price, these farmers have a moral right not to be abandoned to unfair competition from heavily subsidized foreign grain and other products, and a right to be given enough price support to prevent their total ruin. If those misguided economists who put forward unethical arguments about lowering MSP, were seriously interested in the cause of the poorer farmers and labourers they should be demanding an expansionary fiscal stance, a large hike in public investment and in rural development expenditures to restore employment and purchasing power.

Thirdly, the introduction of PDS targeting in 1997 divided the population into 'above poverty line' (APL) and 'below poverty line' (BPL) with lower prices being payable by the latter but with a cut in quantity. The problem of wrong exclusion of large numbers of the actually poor from BPL status (which is determined by arbitrary criteria) has been a serious one and the denial of ration cards has further aided the fall in sales from the PDS already taking place owing to decline in purchasing power. Hardly 10 million tonnes were sold by 2000-01, compared to 21 million tonnes in 1991 despite the population needing ration grains, being much larger (Swaminathan 2002).

While real disposable incomes for the top segments of the urban population have been rising fast owing to reform policies of tax cuts and cheapening of primary goods and durable goods, on the contrary rural mass incomes in terms of command over goods have been falling faster than is evident from consumption data, since higher indebtedness and asset losses have taken place to maintain already low consumption. There is rising absorption of foodgrains for the elites with a higher proportion going to processed foods and animal products, while the majority in rural areas are plunged into deepening undernutrition, owing to their reduced purchasing power and reduced institutional access to food. Very recent analysis of NSS data by fractile groups has confirmed my earlier diagnosis of sharply widening inequalities in the last five years.

The five-year period of NDA rule has seen the most violent increase in rural-urban income inequalities ever seen since Independence. The urban elites have every reason to feel good as they play with their new toys in the form of the latest automobiles and consumer durables, enjoy a more diversified diet, eat out more and reduce their resulting adipose tissue in slimming clinics: but the same neo-liberal policies which have benefited them have immiserized millions of their fellow country men, women and children who are getting enmeshed in debt and land loss, and struggling harder merely to survive.

The Imbroglio of Indirect Poverty Estimates

The NSS Rounds on consumption expenditure collect data not only on the expenditure on food and non-food items but also the physical quantities of foods, and since the average calorie equivalent of different foods is known it also computes and presents the calorie equivalent of average diets by expenditure groups. When we directly inspect this available NSS data on the calorie intake corresponding to the quantities of foods consumed by persons in the various per capita expenditure groups, we see that by 1999-2000, seven-tenths of the rural population was below the norm of 2400 calories per day (the norm originally adopted in all poverty studies), about one-tenth had an intake around the norm and only one-fifth had an intake above the norm (See Table 5). *Thus at least seven-tenths of the rural population was in poverty in 1999-2000.* About two-fifths of the urban population was below the lower urban norm of 2100 calories. This method is direct, simple and transparent, and requires no estimation by the reader. Even if a much lower level of 2100 calories, equal to the urban norm, is considered for rural areas, we see by direct inspection that over half the rural population was below this level.

Even though the official and academic estimates of poverty started by using exactly the same poverty norm of 2400 calories for rural areas, they now arrive at an estimate of population in poverty which is 27 % or less for the same year, 1999-2000, and this, as we can see from Table 5, corresponds to a calorie intake of less than 1900 per diem. The very low estimate from the Planning Commission and the academics today, is because they all now use an *indirect* and non-transparent method of estimation, which moreover has proved to be increasingly incapable of capturing the ground reality of larger numbers of people moving into under-nutrition. This indirect method requires some explanation for the lay reader.

The direct inspection of calorie equivalent of quantities consumed by different expenditure classes was carried out by the Planning Commission using the 28th Round of the NSS for 1973-74, a date which is now thirty years in the past. From this, the per capita monthly expenditure whose food expenditure part gave 2400 calories per diem in rural areas and 2100 in urban areas at that time, was obtained and this was called the poverty level income (though more correctly it is the poverty level *expenditure.* It came to Rs.49.1 for rural and Rs. 56.6 for urban areas).

For later years no similar direct inspection of the calorie equivalent of changing expenditures was done, even though the relevant NSS data were there for many years, exactly in the same form as for the year 1999-2000 given in Table 5. *Instead, in order to estimate poverty for later years, it was assumed that the quantities people consumed, hence the pattern of consumer expenditure, remained unchanged from 1973-74,* and a price index was applied to the old poverty line to update it. The new rounds of consumer expenditure data, did not enter the picture for directly revising the poverty line at all. Only the distribution of persons by expenditure groups was used to read off what percentage of persons came below the new poverty level, estimated indirectly by applying a price index to the old poverty level. Thus the method used amounts to a Laspeyres index, with quantities in a base year which by now is three decades in the past, and with adjustment being done only for price change.

If the Planning Commission, when it first estimated the poverty line expenditure for 1973-74, had said that it would base its estimate on quantities of foods people consumed thirty years earlier in 1943-44, obviously no-one would have taken its estimate seriously. Present day Planning Commission and academic estimates are based precisely on a three decade old consumption pattern relating to 1973-4, and they no longer deserve to be taken seriously. In fact they are no longer worth the paper on which they are written.

There had been no dearth of earlier, detailed criticisms of the indirect method, starting from the valid argument that it makes no sense to assume an unchanged consumption pattern for it has changed considerably over time, and not necessarily owing to voluntary reasons: labourers are no longer paid wages in kind as grain and meals, not fully valued earlier or valued at low farm-gate prices, and now have to purchase food at retail prices with money wages (Suryanarayana 1996); common property resources giving free goods have disappeared so that fuel and fodder have to be purchased, all impacting on the quantities of food that can be purchased by the poor out of a given real income (Ibid., and Mehta and Venkatraman 2000). As a result, a considerably larger total real expenditure is actually required than

Table 5
The Population in Poverty in India from direct observation of Calorie Intake, against expenditure group and distribution of persons, 1999-2000, NSSO

RURAL			URBAN		
Monthly per capita Expenditure Rupees	*Calorie Intake per diem per capita*	*Per cent of Persons %*	*Monthly per capita Expenditure Rupees*	*Calorie Intake per diem per capita*	*Per cent of Persons %*
Below 225	1383	5.1	Below 300	1398	5.0
225- 255	1609	5.0	300- 350	1654	5.1
255- 300	1733	10.1	350- 425	1729	9.6
300- 340	1868	10.0	425- 500	1912	10.1
340- 380	1957	10.3	500- 575	1968	9.9
380- 420	2054	9.7	**575- 665**	**2091**	**10.0**
420- 470	2173	10.2	665- 775	2187	10.1
470- 525	2289	9.3	775- 915	2297	10.0
525- 615	**2403**	**10.3**	915- 1120	2467	10.0
615- 775	2581	9.9	1120-1500	2536	10.1
775- 950	2735	5.0	1500- 1925	2736	5.0
950 & more	3178	5.0	1925 & more	2938	5.0
ALL	2149	99.9	ALL	2156	99.9
SUMMARY					
470- 525 and less	2289 and less	69.7	500- 575 and less	1968 and less	39.7
525- 615	2403	10.3	575- 665	2091	10.0
615-775 & more	2581 & more	19.9	665- 775 & more	2187 & more	50.2 & more

Source: National Sample Survey Organization 55th Round, 1999-2000, Report No. 471, *Nutritional Intake in India* and Report No. 454, *Household Consumer Expenditure in India – Key Results.*

Note: The monthly per capita expenditure, refers to the expenditure on both food and non-food, with the food expenditure part giving the calories indicated against each group. For the three groups in the summary, the rural average per capita monthly expenditure was Rs.496.7 and less, Rs.566.62, and Rs.686.0 and more. (This average expenditure is very close to but not exactly the mid-point of the relevant expenditure group owing to inequality within each group). Two graphs are drawn from the data – first, the ogive of persons below specified per capita expenditure levels, and second the per capita expenditure against per capita calorie intake. The rural poverty-level expenditure, which commanded food quantities giving 2400 calories per day (almost equal to the 2403 average in the Rs.525 to 615 class) is found to be Rs.565 per month (Rs.19 per day) and 75 percent of all persons consumed below this level. In urban areas 44 percent of all persons consumed below the urban calorie norm of 2100, closely approximated by the actual calorie intake 2091 of the expenditure group Rs.575 to 665. For comparison, how unrealistically low the official 'poverty level' expenditure (estimated by inflating the 1973-74 poverty line by the Consumer Price Index for Agricultural Labourers) is can be seen from Table 6.

before, so that its food component can satisfy the calorie norm. The price-adjusted poverty line is therefore found to correspond to an actual calorie intake which over time is further and further below the original calorie norm (thus the 1999-2000 indirectly estimated official poverty line of Rs.328 per month corresponds to less than 1900 calories per diem as inspecting Table 5 shows. The direct estimate gives a poverty line of Rs.565, over 70% higher than the official one).

The increasing divergence between the direct and indirect estimates have been pointed out by many scholars, as have the anomalies and arbitrariness in the indirect estimation method. An early demonstration of the divergence of the results using both the direct and the indirect method for two different years in the 1970s compared to a base year in 1961-2, had been carried out in her doctoral thesis by Rohini Nayyar (1991) who had explicitly concluded that "there is no doubt that the poverty estimates based on actual consumption data and set out in Table 3.4 are superior to those derived from a price-adjusted poverty line, particularly as the use of a deflator [price–index] poses many problems…" (Nayyar 1991, 38). She also pointed out that the two methods gave results which while different (the difference was 19% of population in 1977-8) did move in the same direction over time: but this conclusion no longer holds in the late nineties, for reasons discussed later.

Mehta and Venkatraman (2000) gave the 1993-94 NSS consumption expenditure groups and calorie levels, which showed that 69.7% of persons were below the group with an average of 2410 calories. Since the lower part of the latter group also have to be added, the actual percentage below 2400 calories was 75 percent. Thus this direct estimate for rural areas included an additional 37 % of the rural population, who were being excluded by the official indirect estimate (which was 37.2%), a difference far too large to be ignored. They rightly questioned the logic of continuing with the indirect method.

All these criticisms have been completely ignored by the official and academic poverty estimators who use the indirect method, and who have continued full sail on their unregenerate course: they are rapidly discrediting the entire area of indirect-estimation poverty studies for their unreal estimates are foundering on the rocks of hard macroeconomic facts which contradict their estimates and which cannot be wished away. The fallacious official views on voluntary reduction in foodgrains absorption, and resulting official apathy and callousness towards the reality of increasing hunger, have been reinforced by the wrong official estimates using the indirect method, showing an actual *reduction* of the rural population in poverty to 27% by 1999-2000 in the face of the opposite ground reality of increasing hunger with 75 % of the rural population actually consuming below the calorie intake norm.[4]

A number of academics (A.Deaton, K.Sundaram and S.D.Tendulkar, S.Bhalla and others) have published the papers estimating poverty for 1999-2000 by the indirect method, which they had presented at a conference (see *Economic and Political Weekly* January 25-31, 2003). There is scope for variation in results among them as different price indices can be used. The estimate by A. Deaton using new price indices places the rural poverty percentage in India at 25% , even lower than the official 27% (Deaton 2003b). Other estimates are either of a similar order to the official one or are even lower.

Another way of characterizing all the estimates using the indirect method would be : *Statistical poverty reduction via clandestine reduction of the calorie norm.* The official Planning Commission (Rs. 328) and Deaton *b* (Rs.303) price-index updated poverty line for monthly per capita expenditure for 1999-2000 gives a daily calorie intake which is 1890 and 1860 respectively, as Table 6, derived from Table 5 shows – a far cry indeed from the original 2400 calorie intake norm in the base-year. But they do not inform the public about the nutrition implication of their estimate. *To meet the 2400 calorie norm, Table 5 data, when plotted, show that a person needed to spend at least Rs 565 per month or Rs.19 daily, equivalent to US 44 cents at the then exchange rate of Rs. 43.33 to a dollar. This is the realistic poverty line, not the official one of Rs.328 per month.*

The Planning Commission is asking us to believe that people could survive taking all their requirements on a mere Rs.11, or U.S. cents 25 daily, while Deaton's estimate means that Rs.10 daily or US cents 23 is considered quite enough! This is less than a quarter of the World Bank's own rough and ready dollar-a-day measure. When the level of consumption corresponding to the poverty line is quietly pushed down to such a sub-human level, it is hardly surprising that not many people are found to exist below it. At this rate poverty can be statistically eliminated completely from India by the indirect method with just a little more effort by the estimators to get a lower rise in the price index giving, say Rs.240 per month rather than the lowest poverty lines so far for 1999-2000, which are Rs.303 (Deaton b) and Rs.265 (Bhalla 2003). This, from Table 5, would reduce the poverty percentage dramatically to only 7, and as these people too would soon be dead, there would be a 'final solution' to all indirect estimation problems.

It is to be noted that none of the quoted papers making the low, indirect poverty estimates and published in *EPW* (Jan. 21-25, 2003), tells the reader that the implication of their method is that the calorie standard is thereby being drastically diluted and the original concept of poverty based on a nutritional norm, itself is being altered. To present estimates which imply a 500 calorie per diem or more cut in the calorie intake norm without explicitly informing the reader about it, is not acceptable by any academic standard. The NSS data for 1999-2000 relating *actual current calorie intake* to expenditure groups (which we have put together in Table 5) is not presented by any of those making indirect estimates, even though to do so they are using the percentage of persons by expenditure groups from the same source. Such selective use of the data is not an acceptable procedure either. None of these papers refer to even a single author among the several quoted earlier, who have criticized the indirect estimation method that they use. The student or newcomer to the area who reads the papers by the indirect method users, is not made aware that it is based on an invariant 30-year old consumption basket, does not know that any other, direct estimation method using the latest NSS consumption data, even exists and is instead given the impression that the indirect method is the only one by which poverty can be estimated, which is untrue.[5] Most economists in India not directly working with the data are not even aware that the nutrition norm has been abandoned in the official procedure.

The only type of non-comparability the indirect estimators discuss is that introduced by a change in the recall period in the 55th Round compared to earlier Rounds. According to them, the adjustment to make the 55th Round comparable with earlier ones raises the official and individual estimates of poverty by only 3 percent, with the official estimate going up at most to 30 percent from 27. Such adjustment would raise the percentage of people below the 2400 calories RDA, from 75 percent to more than 78 percent,[6] and increase further the distance between the direct and indirect estimates.

Quite apart from the problem of a far distant base year for quantities, the indirect method of updating an old poverty line using price indices now no longer captures even the trend of change correctly, leave alone actual numbers, *because the method can only reflect increase in poverty arising from rise in prices, and cannot capture increase in poverty arising from unemployment and income loss as development expenditures fall and as crop prices decline.* Further, when a population is already at very low calorie intake levels as in India, the processes of employment loss and income loss are likely not to be reflected fully in immediate fall in a flow variable like consumption alone but also involve stock changes, namely asset transfers through rising indebtedness by the distressed struggling to remain alive. In this sense even the nutrition data underestimate the adverse impact.

This fact is proving to be the final nemesis of the prevalent poverty studies, for in the second half of the nineties and especially from 1998, as we have seen, *worsening welfare in rural areas has been caused not by inflation, but owing to deflation and unemployment.* So pervasive has mass income deflation become that, significantly, a very bad drought year 2002-03, has seen a historically low inflation rate. Whereas the Consumer Price Index for Agricultural Labourers had risen by 60 percent comparing 1993-94 with 1999-00 (the period between the 50th and 55th Rounds) we find that between 1999-00 and 2003-04 the CPIAL has risen by a mere 8.2 percent.[7] This can bring no joy to even labourers, because it is part of the deflationary process of reduced development expenditures and falling growth, inducing rising numbers of days unemployed and fast rising open unemployment.

It is to be expected therefore, that the indirect poverty estimates should show, as they do, exactly the *opposite* trend compared to the actual ground reality of worsening welfare owing to a higher percentage of persons moving below the 2400 calorie norm (and a higher proportion moving below 1800 calories as well), hence both rise in poverty and increase in poverty depth. The situation now is even worse than direct inspection of Table 5 indicates because food grains absorption per head per diem has fallen further by 25 gms. by 2003, entailing a loss of another 95 calories on this account.

The bizarre element in all this arises from the loud celebrations of allegedly declining poverty by the government and by a number of academics engaged in indirect estimation, whereas the 'decline' is solely owing to the gross defects and the inappropriateness of their own indirect statistical methods. All the adverse macroeconomic trends the official data reveal regarding rising unemployment and falling food absorption, which are completely inconsistent with any story of declining rural poverty, are never alluded to by the practitioners of the indirect method nor, as already noted, are the available NSS direct consumption data with calorie equivalents, presented by them in their papers.

The poverty estimators using the indirect method are doing a grave disservice to the Indian people by continuing with an indefensible methodology which by now is giving the opposite result to the actual trends on the ground with respect to hunger. While in the late 1970s the difference between the direct and indirect methods was about 19% of the rural population and in 1993 the difference was 37%, for 1999-2000 the difference between the direct method (75% in poverty) and the indirect method is 48% of the rural population.

Whether they wish to or not, the officials and academics using the indirect method and claiming a reduction in poverty in the 1990s, are contributing to the formulation of incorrect policies further lowering mass welfare. If these poverty estimates remained in the ivory towers of academia and of Yojana Bhavan, it would not matter: but now targeted food distribution is being directly linked to poverty estimates. The present Government is currently slashing the numbers of people designated as being 'below poverty line', and grain allocations at a low price to the states are correspondingly sought to be lowered, on the ground that poverty has declined. The failure of the prevailing indirect estimates today thus does not lie in the failure to capture ground reality alone: they have become positively dangerous in spreading wrong information and inducing the opposite policy measures to those required. It is high time that the academics and administrators working in the area of poverty estimation used the direct indicators provided by the NSS consumption data and by per head foodgrains availability, if they are at all concerned about real trends as regards hunger.

In the middle of the Great Depression in 1931 with one-fifth of workers unemployed and factories closed, many economists in advanced countries continued to maintain that economics was about the allocation of 'scarce resources' among competing uses, and that sound finance meant that governments should cut expenditures. They are remembered today for their remarkable conceptual blindness, but considerable additional damage was done at that time since they dominated public policy. Today in India in the

Table 6
Calorie Intake Per Diem Corresponding To Planning Commission
and some Academic Poverty Estimates
RURAL INDIA, NSS 55th Round, 1999-2000

	Poverty Line MPCE Rs.	Daily Per Capita Expenditure Rs.	Percent of 'Poor' %	Highest Calorie 'norm'	Average Calorie Intake of 'Poor'
Planning Commission	328	10.9	27	1890	1687
Angus Deaton	303	10.1	23	1860	1676
Surjit Bhalla	265	8.8	12	1680	1520

Source: For poverty line and percentage in poverty, Deaton 2003b, for percentage in poverty, Bhalla 2003. Third column figures obtained by this author by plotting from NSS data, a) the ogive (percentage of persons below specified per capita expenditure levels) and b) the relation between average per capita expenditure and average per capita calorie intake, both by expenditure classes. The calorie 'norm' corresponding to the poverty lines of the first column, are read off from the graphs.

Figures in last column obtained by plotting the cumulative percentage of persons against the cumulative percentage of total calorie intake, reading the share of calorie intake by the specified percentage of the 'poor' and from this, calculating the average calorie intake.

Note: MPCE is Monthly per capita Expenditure at the poverty line, obtained by Planning Commission by applying a price index to update the original poverty line of Rs.49 in rural areas for 1973-74. Deaton has constructed his own price indices and poverty line while Bhalla's poverty line is implicit in his 12% estimate.

* The three estimates imply energy intake 'norms' of 78.75%, 77.5% and 70 % of RDA.

middle of rising rural unemployment, falling per head grain intake and a rise in the absolute and relative numbers in nutritional deficit, we find that those who make policy are talking of declining rural poverty on the basis of unreasonable estimation procedures and by ignoring all other trends. Posterity will remember them too for their remarkable conceptual blindness, but for the present the prognosis is bleak. Where the diagnosis of the problem of hunger itself is incorrect and a worsening situation is being interpreted as betterment, no remedial measures can be expected of the policy advisers and the rulers of this country which was once a developing economy, but which has been turned into the Republic of Hunger.

Notes

[1] These data were presented in a paper on poverty in Russia, by Prof. P. Gregory, at an international workshop on country studies on poverty held at UNDP, New York on September 11, 1997 and attended by the author. See also 'The Economic and Demographic Collapse in Russia' in this book.

[2] The National Nutrition Monitoring Bureau, in 25 Years of NNMB (Delhi, 1997) says on p.3: "The NNMB has consistently confirmed in successive surveys that the primary bottleneck in the dietaries of even the poorest segments of Indians is energy and not protein as was hitherto believed.....The data also indicate that measurement of consumption of cereals can be used as a proxy for total energy intake. This observation is of considerable significance as it helps to determine rapid, though approximate, estimates of energy intakes at the HH (household) level."

[3] We are assuming here that the individual items given month-by-month in Table2.13 on p.12 of the RBI Report on Currency and Finance 2002-03 up to November 2003, are correct. These individual items include procurement, off-take (given separately on account of PDS sales, allocations to schemes for weaker sections and open-market sales and exports). The doubt arises because the opening stocks and closing stocks figures given in the Table are not consistent with the total of the individual items, for closing stocks are found to be understated in many months. The final closing stock of October 2003 is given as 22.1 million tonnes, but it should be 35 million tonnes if we calculate from the individual items. Thus 13 million tonnes of foodgrains are unaccounted for! Did it rot, or was it destroyed: is the question.

[4] Since some of those falling below 2400 calories are in the lower part of the group with an average of 2403 calories, the exact proportion below the norm is found to be 75% when we plot the data on a graph. By using the ogive (cumulated frequencies of persons below expenditure levels) and the relation between per capita expenditure and per capita calorie intake, we can read off both the percentage of persons below the calorie norm, and the realistic poverty line, namely the expenditure required to access the calorie norm.

5   The only paper in the EPW Jan 21-25, 2003 collection which discusses calorie deprivation (Meenakshi and Vishwanathan) does not connect the current data on population below actual calorie intake levels to the intake implied by the indirect estimates presented in the same issue, nor does it discuss the crucial matter of the increasingly large difference over time, between the head count percentage of population in poverty obtained by the direct and indirect methods.

6   This is because more people would move down below Rs.328, which the indirect estimators take into account, but additionally more people would also move down into the expenditure interval Rs 328 to Rs 565, the second being the realistic directly estimated poverty line at which the RDA can be accessed.

7   Price indices are available in the Annual Economic Survey2003-04 Table S - 63.

References

Banister, J. 1987. *China's Changing Population* (Stanford University Press).

Bhalla, Surjit S. 2003.'Recounting the Poor 1983-99', *Economic and Political Weekly*, 38,4, January 25.

Coale, A. J. 1984. *Rapid Population Change in China, 1952-1982* (Washington, D.C: National Academy Press).

Deaton, A. 2003. a) 'Adjusted Poverty Estimates for 1999-2000"; b) 'Prices and Poverty 1987-2000'. Both papers in *Economic and Political Weekly*, Vol.38, January 25-31.

Mehta, J. and Venkataraman. 2000.'Poverty Statistics – Bermicide's Feast', *Economic and Political Weekly*, Vol.35, July 1.

Nai-Ruenn Chen. 1966. *Chinese Economic Statistics – A Handbook for Mainland China* (Edinburgh University Press).

Nayyar, R. 1991. *Rural Poverty in India* (Oxford University Press).

Patnaik, U. 1991.'Food Availability and Famine – A Longer View', *Journal of Peasant Studies*, Vol. 19, No. 1, October. Reprinted in U.Patnaik, *The Long Transition – Essays on Political Economy* (Tulika, 1999).

———. 1996. 'Export Oriented Agriculture and Food Security in Developing Countries and in India', *Economic and Political Weekly*, Nos. 35-37, September. Reprinted in *The Long Transition – Essays on Political Economy* (Tulika, 1999).

———. 1997. 'The Political Economy of State Intervention in the Food Economy', *Economic and Political Weekly* (Economy and Budget Issue), May 17-24.

———. 2002. 'On Famine and Measuring Famine Deaths', in S. Patel, J. Bagchi and Krishnaraj (Eds.), *Thinking Social Science in India – Essays in Honour of Alice Thorner* (Sage).

———. 2003. 'Food Stocks and Hunger – Causes of Agrarian Distress', *Social Scientist*, Vol.31, Nos.7-8, July-August .

Sen, A.K. 1999. *Development as Freedom* (New York: A Knopf).

Suryanarayana, M. H. 1996. 'Poverty Estimates and Indicators: Importance of Data Base', *Economic and Political Weekly*, Nos. 35-37, September.

Swaminathan, M. 2002. 'Excluding the Needy – the Public Provisioning of Food in India', *Social Scientist*, Vol.30, Nos. 3-4, March-April .

THEORIZING FOOD SECURITY AND POVERTY IN THE ERA OF ECONOMIC REFORMS

Introduction

The correct theorizing of the questions of food security and poverty has become particularly important at the present time, which is one of rapid changes in the economic environment in which small producers including farmers and workers are living. In a poor developing country, the incidence of poverty is very closely linked to the availability of food, in which the staple food grains still remain predominant, accounting for three-fifths of the daily energy intake of the population. The measurement of poverty in India has traditionally adopted a nutritional norm specified in terms of an average daily energy intake measured in calories. The National Nutrition Monitoring Bureau has informed us that "the NNMB has consistently confirmed in successive surveys that the main bottleneck in the dietaries of even the poorest Indians is energy and not protein as was hitherto believed... *the data also indicate that the measurement of consumption of cereals can be used as a proxy for total energy intake. This observation is of considerable significance as it helps to determine rapid, though approximate,*

Public Lecture in the series 'Freedom from Hunger', India International Centre, New Delhi, April 12, 2005. Revised November 2005.

estimates of energy intake at the household level."[1](emphasis added) It is this strong link between the staple food grains intake and poverty based on a nutritional norm, which enables us to put forward an analysis of the recent trends in food security and in poverty, in the light of the impact of changing economic policies during the last fifteen years.

The majority of academics and the Government of India today make two claims which I believe to be factually incorrect, claims which are underpinned by a wholly fallacious theoretical understanding of the current situation. They claim first, that there is 'over supply' of food grains relative to demand (which they assume to be growing normally), and so infer that food grains production should be cut back in favour of 'diversification'; second, that poverty has been declining in India in the era of reforms, specifically in the decade of the 1990s. My contention as regards both propositions is that they are incorrect, and that the correct position on theoretical and factual grounds is precisely the opposite. First, there is not over supply of food grains, but a decline in food grains supply and an even more drastic decline of effective demand for food grains especially in rural India, owing to an abnormally fast loss of purchasing power during the last six years: so, far from cutting back food grains output, the correct policy is to raise purchasing power and restore effective demand as well as restore access to affordable food grains through a combination of a universal, and not targeted, employment guarantee scheme and through reverting to a universal, not targeted public distribution system.

Second, far from the percentage of population in poverty declining as claimed, the factually correct position on the basis of current data is that poverty is very high, affecting at least three-quarters of rural and over two-fifths of the urban population. Moreover the data show that the depth of poverty has increased considerably during the fifteen years of reforms, with more people being pushed down into a poorer nutritional status than before in most of the Indian states and at the All-India level. The reason that many academics and the Planning Commission reach the conclusion that poverty is declining, is that they use an estimation procedure which has no basis in logic and is indefensible on academic grounds. What that estimation procedure is and how it differs from the correct procedure is one of the main questions I would try to explain, for I believe that it is part of the 'right to information' that the intelligent citizen should be able to independently reach a judgement about the validity of the official procedure and not simply take the truth of certain statements for granted. My lecture today will focus on the correct theorizing of these two main questions – of declining effective demand for food grains, and of the extent of poverty. This has become extremely important because the widely prevalent incorrect theorizing in academic and government circles is leading to policy formulations and measures which will only serve to worsen mass welfare and plunge even larger sections of the rural population in particular into higher unemployment and food deprivation.

The first and second sections will briefly discuss the deflationary macroeconomic policies combined with exposure to global price declines, which has led to massive loss of purchasing power in rural India in the last six years and is reflected in falling food grains absorption and falling energy intake. The third section discusses the interpretation of the decline in foodgrains absorption while the fourth and last section takes up the question of poverty estimation and how official and most academic estimates use a particular indirect method of estimation, which completely de-links poverty from nutrition norms by ignoring current data which show the ground reality of rising nutritional deprivation and increasing depth of poverty.

1. What Deflationary Policies and Trade Liberalization have meant for the Rural Economy in India

Deflationary macroeconomic policies are strongly favoured by international and domestic financial interest groups who are quite obsessive about controlling inflation and would prefer to see even an economy with a high rate of unemployment, growing slowly and raising unemployment further, rather than risk any possibility of prices rising owing to expansionary policies reducing unemployment. International creditors wish to maintain high real values of their financial assets and high real interest rates (inflation would erode both) - and are happy with bouts of asset deflation in

Table 1
Policies Followed by 78 Countries under Fund-guided Economic Reforms

	Percentage of Total Number of Countries Implementing Policy
1. Restraint on Central Government Expenditure	91
2. Limits on Credit Expansion	99
3. Reduction in Ratio of Budget Deficit to GDP	83
4. Wage Restraint	65
5. Exchange Rate Policy	54

Source: IMF study quoted in Cornia, Jolly and Stewart (eds.) *Adjustment with a Human Face,* Vol.1, p.11 (1987).

developing countries so that these assets can be snapped up at low prices by their corporations. Their insensate and obsessive fear of inflation can be seen in the policies advised uniformly by the International Monetary Fund to 78 developing countries in the 1980s and summarized in Table 1 from an IMF study. The first three policies – restraint on central government expenditure, limits on credit expansion, and reduction of budget deficit to GDP ratio, add up together to a strongly deflationary package and all three were actually implemented at the same time by four-fifths of the concerned countries, while two-thirds capped wages and over half devalued their currency.

The results of deflationary policies of the decade up to the mid-1980s have been documented as sharp decline in rates of investment in both capital formation and in the social sectors, leading to reduced or negative GDP growth and negative impact on the human development indicators (see in particular Cornia, Jolly and Stewart 1987). A number of studies since then have confirmed the adverse impact and have argued for expansionary policies. [2]

Table 2
Reduction in Rural Development Expenditures under Economic Reforms, Selected Years 1985-90 to 2000-01

	1985-90 average	1993-4	1995-6	1997-8	2000-01
1.Rural Development Expenditures as Percent of NNP	3.8	2.8	2.6	2.3	1.9
2. Above plus Infrastructure	11.1	8.4	6.9	6.4	5.8

Source: Government of India, Ministry of Finance, annual *Economic Survey*, for years 2001-02 to 2003-04, Appendix Table S-44. 'Rural development expenditures' here are the plan outlays of Centre and states under the five heads of agriculture, rural development, irrigation and flood control, special areas programmes, and village and small scale industry. Infrastructure includes all energy and transport including urban. Calculated from current values of expenditure and NNP at factor cost .

Table 3
Decelerating Growth rates of Agricultural Output

Period	Foodgrains	Non-Foodgrains	All Crops	Population
1980-81 to 1989-90	2.85	3.77	3.19	2.1
1990-91 to 2000-01	1.66	1.86	1.73	1.9
2001-01 to 2005-06	0.00	n.a.	n.a.	1.8

Source : Govt of India, Ministry of Finance, *Economic Survey, 2001-02*, p.189. Note that slowing down of output growth is much steeper than slowing down of population growth implying falling per head output.

Table 4
Employment Decline in Rural India

	Year 1983	Year 1993-1994	Year 1999-2000	Growth per Annum 1983 to 1993-4 %	1993-4 to 1999-00 %
RURAL					
1.Population,mn.	546.6	658.8	727.5	1.79	1.67
2.Labour force, mn.	204.2	255.4	270.4	2.15	0.96
3.Work force, mn.	187.9	241.0	250.9	2.40	0.67
4.Unemployed, mn. (2 –3)	16.3	14.4	19.5	- 1.19	5.26

Source: Govt. of India, Ministry of Finance, *Economic Survey 2002-03*, p.218.

India has been following exactly the same deflationary package of policies since 1991, whose impact has been especially severe in India's agricultural sector which saw sharp reduction in public planned development expenditures in rural areas, which has traditionally included agriculture, rural development, irrigation and flood control – all vital for maintaining output – to which we add also the outlays on special areas programmes, and village and small scale industry to define overall 'Rural Development Expenditures' or RDE. The employment-generating programmes had assumed a special importance from the drought year 1987 onwards.

Over the 7th Plan period marking the pre-reforms phase, from 1985 to 1990, Rs.51,000 crores was spent on rural development, amounting to almost 4 percent of Net National Product, and Rs. 91,000 crores or over 7 percent of NNP was spent on Infrastructure.[3] By the mid-1990s, annual spending on rural development was down to 2.6 percent of NNP, and after including infrastructure, less than 7 percent was being spent compared to 11 percent during the 7th Plan. Further declines took place so that by 2000-

01 the share of spending under these heads was down to 5.8 percent of NNP, the rural development part halving to only 1.9 percent (see Table 2). The per capita expenditures obviously declined even more sharply. I estimate that in constant 1993-4 prices about Rs.30,000 crores less was being spent by the end-decade year 1999-2000, compared to the beginning, 1990-91. A crude point-to-point comparison would suggest an annual income loss of between 120,000 to 150,000 crores of rupees assuming a multiplier value between 4 and 5. Actual income loss would have been greater taking the cumulative losses over successive years. This harsh contractionary policy had nothing to do with any objective resource constraint but simply reflected the deflationary policies of the BWI which were internalized and sought to be justified by the Indian government.

There is no economic rationale for believing that "public investment crowds out private investment" which is the common argument put forward for reducing the state's role in rural development. Precisely the contrary has been shown to hold for certain types of investment essential for an irrigation-dependent agriculture like India's such as irrigation projects of all types. Private tube-well investment is profitable only where the water table remains high owing to seepage from state-built canal irrigation systems, and where community integrated watershed management (planting trees and using check-dams) is encouraged with state help. Private over-exploitation of ground water has now reached a crisis point in many states in India, with the water table falling rapidly and with even the richest farmers unable to reach water after investing heavily in deep bore-wells and submersible pumps. Other infrastructure investment such as rural power projects, roads, bridges, school buildings, clinics and so on, are never undertaken by private investors but are vital for stimulating development and providing livelihoods both directly to those employed in building them and through the important multiplier effects on employment and incomes, of the increased wage incomes being spent on simple consumer goods and services within the villages. The market for machine made textiles and other goods also thereby expands.

The net result of the unwise cut-back of public investment and in RDE has been a slowing of the rate of output growth – both foodgrains and non-foodgrains growth rates have almost halved in the nineties compared to the pre-reform eighties, and both have fallen below the population growth rate even though this too is slowing down (Table 3). This has led to declining per capita output during the nineties, for the first time since the mid-sixties agricultural crisis, which however had been short- lived, whereas per head agricultural output continues to fall today even after a decade: even faster than earlier as the foodgrains output growth rate has become zero during 2000-01 to 2005-06. The Agricultural Universities had earlier played a major role in developing and helping to disseminate new crop varieties, and the cut in funding for research in these Universities by affecting the search for better rain-fed crop varieties, has also contributed to the deceleration in the growth of yields. With increasing use of land for commercial and residential purposes, the gross sown area in India has remained static since 1991, so it is only through yield rise that output growth can be maintained and it is here that the failure is evident.

The combination of decline in state RDE and the near-halving of agricultural growth has produced a major crisis of rising unemployment. There is both fast growing open unemployment and fall in number of days employed of the work force during the economic reforms period. Even with constant labour coefficients (labour days used per unit of crop output) a near halving of employment growth was to be expected given the decline in crop output growth, but the decline in jobs has been even more as mechanization especially of harvesting and use of chemical weed-killers as opposed to manual weeding, has led to falling labour coefficients. Further the rural non-farm employment growth, which was robust in the 1980s owing to reasonably high state RDE, had declined in the nineties. The ratio of labour force to population, or the participation rate, has declined (lower participation rate reflects difficulty of finding work), the ratio of work force to labour force has declined because open unemployment has been growing at over 5% annually (Table 4). The elasticity of employment with respect to output was 0.7 during 1983 to 1993-4 but has declined to 0.01 or virtually zero, taking the reforms period 1993-4 to 1999-00.

Let no-one imagine that unemployed rural workers are migrating and finding employment in industry: there have also been massive job losses in manufacturing during the reform period and the share of the secondary sector in GDP has fallen from 29 to around 22 percent during the nineties, in short India has seen de-industrialization. The agricultural depression has reduced the share of agriculture in GDP from about a third at the beginning of the nineties to just over a fifth a decade later, but the labour force and population dependent on agriculture has hardly fallen, reflecting the decline in per head incomes. Thus both the material productive sectors have declined and the only sector which has ballooned in an abnormal manner[4] is the tertiary or services sector which now accounts for over half of GDP.

Only a small proportion of the services sector comprises IT-enabled high income services, business process outsourcing, domestic tourism services and the like. The major part in employment terms, is still low-productivity activities in which the rural displaced workers stagnate at low income levels, servicing the requirements of the upper income elites who have been improving their real income position fast. Disposable incomes have risen even faster for this segment since a part of the neo-liberal reforms include reduction in direct tax rates. Advanced countries usually have this upper-income 10 to 15 percent minority of Indians in mind when they demand market access for their manufactures and agricultural products, and no doubt 100 to 150 million people is a large potential market. But the situation of the vast majority of the mainly rural population who not merely stagnate at low income levels but whose position is considerably worse today than a decade earlier, cannot be ignored: a potentially highly destabilising situation is in the making.

While income and employment reduction through deflationary policies is the first main reason for loss of purchasing power in rural India, the second main reason is the unwise opening to global markets through full trade liberalization at a time from the mid-1990s, when global markets went into recession and primary product prices started falling – a fall which continues to this day.

2. More Trade leads to More Hunger in Developing Countries under Global and Local Deflationary Conditions

The land resources of India, more so than in most developing countries, have the potential for producing a highly diversified range of products - not only the crops and fruits grown in the summer season in temperate lands but also the typically tropical crops, which cannot be grown at all in advanced countries located in temperate regions. The crops of our lands have been demanded abroad in advanced countries for over three centuries for meeting their direct consumption and raw material needs. *But, historically the growth of exports from tropical agriculture under free trade regimes, has always led to a fall in domestic food grains output and availability, plunging the mass of the population into deepening under-nutrition and in extreme cases into famine.* In the half-century before Indian independence, per capita foodgrains output fell by nearly 30 percent while export crops grew ten times faster than foodgrains. I have earlier discussed some historical and current cases in developing countries, of the inverse relation between primary sector exports and domestic foodgrains absorption.

This is bound to happen since land is not a reproducible resource, and heavy external demand made on our more botanically diverse lands by advanced countries to meet their ever-rising and diversifying needs, leads to diversion of our land and resources away from locally consumed food staples to meet export demands. The position is worsened by exports out of more slowly growing food output itself. The Ricardian theory of comparative advantage which says there is necessarily mutual gain from specialization and trade, contains a material and logical fallacy since the conclusion is based crucially on assuming that 'both countries produce both goods' which is factually untrue for agriculture. The advanced countries mainly located in cold temperate regions cannot produce tropical crops at all, so the cost of production of say coffee or rubber cannot even be defined in these countries, leave alone relative cost and transformation frontiers.[5]

In theory, more primary exports from developing countries can accompany more food production for domestic needs, but this can only happen when there is substantial rise in investment to raise productivity, for land is a non-producible resource whose 'supply' can only increase via investment permitting one hectare to produce what two hectares did earlier. It also requires that mass domestic demand grows, and is not held in check by income-deflating policies or excessive taxation as was the case under colonial systems.

The deeply disturbing feature of the current thrust for liberalizing trade is that it has been taking place within an investment-reducing, deflationary regime. I predicted in 1992 that given the deflationary climate, food security would be undermined with trade liberalization in India and that is precisely what has happened. As soon as trade was liberalized from 1991, within a few years, 8 million hectares of food-growing land were converted to exportable crops leading to fall in per head foodgrains output, but farmers did not benefit since their exposure to steeply falling global primary prices from mid-decade has plunged them into spiralling farm debt and insolvency. Nearly nine thousand recorded farmer suicides in India since 1998 are only the tip of the iceberg – there is a pervasive agrarian crisis and foodgrains absorption in India is back to the level prevailing fifty years ago.

Trade liberalization and an export thrust makes sense when local and global markets are expanding owing to expansionary developmental policies which promote growth in the material productive sectors, rising employment and incomes. But when the opposite is the case, when both globally and in local economies the dominant policy sentiment is strongly deflationary as at present, then trade liberalization spells lowered mass welfare in developing countries.[6] India's experience in the last fourteen years provides a good illustration of this.

India, as a signatory to GATT 1994, removed all quantitative restrictions on trade and converted to tariffs by April 2001, lowering the average tariff rate at the same time to 35%, or well below the bound rates which were 100% for crops and 150% for agricultural processed products.

India's thrust for trade liberalization could not have been worse timed, since advanced country markets were in recession and global primary product prices went into a steep tailspin with 40-50 per cent decline in unit dollar prices of all crops – cereals, cotton, jute, sugar, tea, coffee – and up to 80 percent decline in some oil crops between 1995 and 2001 as Table 5 shows. With a brief spike in 2002 prices have continued to fall and some prices are today lower than as far back as 1986. The price to growers is even lower than world price as the activities of the state marketing boards have been replaced by private transnational companies for many crops.

As prices fell for Indian producers of export crops, their access to low-cost credit was reduced under financial sector reforms. Since the nationalization of banks in 1969 agriculture and small scale industry had been treated as priority sectors offered bank credit at a lower than average interest rate but that ended with financial reforms, thrusting farmers into dependence on private moneylenders and high-cost credit (interest rates are usurious, ranging from 36 to 60 percent annually). Other crucial input prices including power tariff were raised as part of the neo-liberal dicta on reducing subsidies (which were already meagre compared to developed countries). Reduced tariff protection meant that producers of rice, fresh fruit and dairy products faced the undermining of their incomes from inflow of usually heavily subsidized foreign goods.

More than six thousand indebted farmers, mainly cotton farmers, have committed suicide in Andhra Pradesh alone since 1998 as its government which had entered into a state-level Structural Adjustment Programme with the World Bank, raised power tariff five times even as cotton price fell by half (Table 6). Over a thousand farmer suicides have also taken place in Punjab, mainly in the cotton belt, new rounds of suicides are recorded in Karanataka and Vidarbha, and in the four years from 2001, over 1,250 suicides are recorded in Wyanad in Kerala as prices to the local growers of coffee, tea and spices have nose-dived even more steeply than global prices once large companies have taken over purchase and marketing. Thus by 2003 the price of coffee to the grower was only one-quarter and that of tea and pepper only one-third of the prices prevailing in 1999.

The agrarian crisis was the main reason for the decisive mass rejection of neo-liberal policies and the May 2004 electoral defeat of the NDA coalition at the Centre as well as the TDP government in Andhra Pradesh. In recognition of the employment crisis the new United Progressive Alliance or UPA had promised to implement a National Rural Employment Guarantee Act which has been recently formulated and passed by Parliament, but which has been diluted by taking the household as the unit, where only one member is entitled to work, and by providing the option of setting the wage below the statutory minimum wage.

India has exported record volumes of wheat and rice during the last six years, and its share in global exports of rice and wheat has risen quite noticeably. Despite the drastic slowing down of output growth noted in Table 3, India exported 22 million tonnes of foodgrains during the two years 2002 and 2003 (Bhalla 2005), and the share of grain exports in total exports has risen from under one-fifth to almost a quarter. There is higher global trade integration reflected in rising trade-GDP ratio. During the severe drought year starting from monsoon 2002, despite grain output being 30 million tonnes lower than in the previous year, from June 2002 to November 2003, a total of 17 million tonnes of foodgrains were exported by the former NDA government. Superficially it looks as though policies of trade liberalization have 'worked'.

However the crucial fact which is suppressed in official publications and in the writings of pro-reform economists, and this is true even after the elections and the change in government, is that the vastly increased grain exports have been coming out of more and more empty stomachs as millions of rural labourers and farmers have suffered job loss and income decline. Food grains absorption in India today has reached a historic low as a result of the massive decline in purchasing power especially in villages owing to the combination of rising unemployment, rising input and credit costs for farmers and exposure to global price declines. Loss of purchasing power is pervasive affecting both the 158 million wage-dependent workers as well as the 120 million cultivating workers and their families. Targeting the food subsidy from 1997-8 by restricting supply of cheaper grain to only

Table 5
Prices of Some Important Traded Primary Products, in US Dollars

	1988	1995	1997	2000	2001 (Jan.)	% Change 2001 over 1995
Wheat (US HW)	167	216	142	130	133	- 38.2
Wheat (US RSW)	160	198	129	102	106	- 46.5
Wheat (Argentine)	145	218	129	112	118	- 45.9
Maize (Argentine)	116	160	133	88	80	- 50.0
Maize (US)	118	159	112	97	92	- 22.0
Rice (US)	265.7	-	439.0	271	291	- 33.7
Rice (Thai)	284	336	316	207	179	- 46.7
Cotton	63.5	98.2	77.5	66	49.1	- 50.0
Groundnut Oil	590	991	1010	788*		- 20.5*
Palm Oil	437	626	93.5	74.7*		- 88.1*
Soyabean Oil	464	479	625	71.4*		- 85.1*
Soyabean Seed	297	273	262	199	178	- 34.8
Sorghum Seed	110	156	111	102	99	- 36.5
Sugar	10.2	13.3	11.4	10.2	9.2	- 30.8
Jute	370	366	302	276*		- 24.6*

Source: *Food Outlook,* Various issues from 1986 to 2001; available from Global Information and Early Warning System on Agriculture, U N Food and Agriculture Organization; and *Monthly Commodity Price Bulletin,* UNCTAD 2001. For the cereals, edible oils and seeds the unit is USD per ton, for cotton and sugar, US cents per lb. and for Jute, USD per metric ton. * Relates to 1999, and percent change is 1999 compared to 1995. The 2004 price data show that sugar, cotton and jute prices continue to remain flat around 2001 levels while the cereals show some rise.

those officially identified as 'below the poverty line' has also added to the institutional denial of affordable food grains to the poor, not merely owing to mistakes of wrong exclusion from the set of the officially poor, but also owing to the gross official underestimation of the numbers in poverty, discussed at the end of the paper.

Table 6
Suicides of Farmers in Andhra Pradesh by District

No.	District	1998	1999	2000	2001	2002	Total
1.	Warangal	77	7	7	28	903	1022
2.	Ananthapoor	1	1	50	50	10	112
3.	Mahaboobnagar	14	2	25	10	—	51
4.	Karimnagar	31	10	6	30	1220	1297
5.	Guntur	32	10	1	6	—	49
6.	Khammam	20	5	3	6	2	36
7.	Medak	15	3	2	8	—	28
8.	Adilabad	9	8	5	13	—	35
9.	Nalgonda	5	1	10	11	8	35
10.	Nizamabad	9	1	—	11	457	478
11.	Rangareddy	5	—	3	6	—	14
12.	Kurnool	4	4	2	4	—	14
13.	Chittoor	3	—	—	2	—	5
14.	Krishna	4	1	1	3	1	10
15.	Prakasham	1	3	—	2	—	6
16.	West Godavari	1	—	—	5	—	6
17.	East Godavari	—	—	1	2	—	3
18.	Sreekakulam	—	1	—	-	—	1
19.	Cuddapah	—	—	—	4	—	4
20.	Visakapatnam	—	—	—	1	—	1
	Unknown	2	1	—	—	—	3
	Total	233	58	116	202	2601	3210

Note: The total number of suicides up to 2004 is over five thousand. Data from police records up to Jan. 27, 2002, presented by Kisan Sabha at a symposium on farmer suicides held at Hyderabad (Andhra Pradesh), 3 February 2002 and attended by the author. The Table has been partially updated by incorporating information for the entire year 2002, so far available for the three districts only (Warangal. Karimnagar and Nizamabad) as reported in *The Hindu,* Hyderabad edition, Jan.6 2003. For the other districts the figures given in the last column continue to refer to a single month, January 2002. Additional suicides numbering 1700 have taken place since then, for which the district break-up is not yet available.

3. Large Decline in Food grains Absorption per Head is Owing to Falling Purchasing Power, not 'Voluntary Choice'

The per capita availability or absorption of food grains in India has declined alarmingly during the decade of deflationary neo-liberal economic reforms, to only 155 kg. annually taking the three year average ending in 2002-03. This current level is the same as fifty years ago during the First Plan period, and it is also the level seen during 1937-41 under colonialism. This means that the food security gains of the four decades of protectionism up to 1991 have been totally reversed.

After Independence, from the early 1950s to four decades later, taking the 3 years ending 1991, the per capita food grains availability had climbed slowly from 153 kg. to 177 kg. – the achievement not only of 'Green Revolution' but of expansionary policies slowly raising mass incomes and demand, without too much rise in already high inequality. While the Green Revolution had many problems, its positive achievement in raising grain availability and absorption, should not be underestimated. All this was reversed from the early 1990s. As the new regime, of deflationary economic reform policies from 1991 eroded mass employment and incomes, we find a decline of per capita absorption to 174 kg by the triennium ending in 1998 and a very steep fall after that to the current abysmally low 155 kg level. Forty years of successful effort to raise availability has been wiped out in a single decade, with over four-fifths of the decline coming in the last six years. [7]

Availability or absorption, is calculated from the hardest data we have, on annual net output[8] adjusted only for change in public stocks and in trade, so by definition it has to cover all final uses – direct use for consumption as grain and its products, use as feed for converting to animal products (a part of this is exported), and industrial use. Per head availability/ absorption (the two are used as synonyms) is now one of the lowest in the world, with only Sub-Saharan Africa and some least developed countries registering lower absorption than India. Since urban India has been increasing average absorption and average calorie intake, it is rural India where the fall has been very steep. For comparison, China absorbed 325 kg. grains per capita (excluding tubers) in the mid-1990s compared to India's less than 200 kg. at that time, Mexico absorbed 375 kg., European countries absorbed 700 kg. or more and USA absorbed 850 kg. Except under abnormal conditions of war or famine, grain absorption is always observed to rise as a country's average income rises. This is why the fall in India is so unusual, and it is not being correctly theorized.

Although grain output per head fell by about 12 kg. over the five years ending in 2002-03, as may be checked from Table 7 the per head absorption has fallen much more, by 21 kg. over the same period. The average Indian family of five members is absorbing 100 kg. less of food grains annually than a mere five years ago and since in urban India absorption has risen (calorie intake has also risen), it is the rural family which is absorbing even less than the average fall indicates. This abnormal fall is because of the loss of purchasing power for reasons already discussed, and it got reflected in a massive build-up of unsold public food stocks, reaching 63 million tonnes by July 2002, some 40 million tonnes in excess of the normal stocks for that time of year. Rather than starting large-scale food-for work schemes to restore lost work and incomes, between June 2002 and October 2003, over 17 million tonnes of food grains were got rid of by the NDA government by exporting out of stocks with subsidy, and it went mainly to feed European cattle and Japanese pigs.

There can be two very different ways that such huge food stocks can build up: demand growth is normal but output increases much faster, or alternatively output increase is normal, but demand reduces very fast owing to loss of incomes, and the demand curve shifts downwards. In both cases supply exceeds demand, but for very different reasons. As already shown output growth has not been normal but has actually gone down, so the first reason does not hold. It is mass effective demand, hence absorption which has declined to a much greater extent, so it is the second reason and not the first which accounts for the present paradox of increasing rural hunger and record grain exports. If rural demand had been maintained even at the 1991 level, the absorption of foodgrains today would be 26 million tonnes higher than it is, and there would be no crisis in the agriculture of Punjab and Haryana, which have lost an internal market to that extent in the last six years alone. Instead of rural per capita calorie intake declining to below the urban average, as has been the case in the nineties, energy intake would have been maintained.

Since all-India per capita income has been rising during the reform period, such a drastic fall in food grains absorption is clearly, only compatible with a drastic rise in the inequality of income distribution as we had earlier pointed out (Patnaik 2003b). But rising inequality can also occur when all incomes are rising. Rising inequality per se is neither necessary nor sufficient for the observed drastic *absolute* decline in grain absorption.[9] The only scenario which is compatible with it, is a particular type of rise in inequality, namely absolute decline in real incomes and rise in absolute poverty, concentrated mainly in the rural areas, combined with a large rise in real incomes for the top fractiles of the population, concentrated mainly in urban areas. The data are partly reflecting this: one indicator is the decline in the per capita real expenditure on consumption by the lowest four-fifths of rural population during the end-1990s and very sharp rise by the top one-fifth of urban population, which has been noted by Sen and Himanshu (2004, 2005). But even these findings with *expenditure* are likely to understate the true extent of *income* decline for the mass of the rural population (we have no direct data on incomes). This is because this mass has been obliged to lose assets to maintain consumption and stay alive, while the well-to do have been saving much more over and above their greatly enhanced real expenditure and have entered real estate and financial markets. In short, there are in addition to the changes in observed flow variables like expenditure, also stock adjustments going on, namely changes in the distribution of assets which are adverse for the poor and which the data we have do not capture adequately as yet.

The official position is one of wholesale denial of these obvious facts and the creation of what can only be called a fairy tale, fit only for intellectual infants. It is argued that there is voluntary reduction in food grains intake and thus there is 'over-production' requiring a cut-back in cereals output – a position not supported by the facts. The full fairy tale set out in official publications goes like this: every segment of the population is reducing demand for cereals because average income is rising; (here, the increased income is assumed to be distributed in the same way as earlier, with no increase in inequality). People of all expenditure classes are voluntarily diversifying their diets away from cereals. The only reason that farmers continue to produce more cereals than demanded, and hence big stocks build up, is because too much output has been encouraged by 'too high' administered, minimum support prices of cereals. So MSP should be cut, cereals output in excess of what is demanded at present should be discouraged and the output pattern in agriculture should be diversified to more commercial export crops under the aegis of agro-businesses.

This analysis is completely incorrect and is inconsistent with the hard facts of rising unemployment, falling output growth, immiserization of farmers in debt and land loss, and resulting deep agrarian distress. It is dangerous in reaching policy conclusions which are the opposite of those required, and which if implemented will reduce food security further and pauperize even more farmers.

To give an analogy, albeit an imperfect one, suppose that a patient has been wrongly diagnosed by a doctor and loses weight rapidly to the extent of 30 kg. The doctor then blames the tailor for making the clothes of the patient too big and advises that the old clothes should be thrown away and new ones sewn to fit his wasted body. Such advice will certainly alarm the patient for it shows that an abnormal situation is being rationalized as normal and no treatment to restore the patient to health will be followed. The official position on food grains output and food security, regrettably shared by many academics who seem not to have applied their minds to the matter, is indicative of such illogical reasoning and is alarming indeed for farmers and labourers in distress. The official prescription of reducing MSP, ending open-ended procurement and cutting back on output will worsen food deprivation and deepen poverty for the millions of farmers and labourers already in deep distress. The idea that price fall benefits 'the consumer' ignores the fact that three-fifths of consumers in a poor country are themselves rural producers or dependent for jobs on producers, and deflation harms their incomes.

It is an alarming scenario too for the farmers of Northern India who over the last four decades have been asked to specialize in food grains production, and have performed magnificently, selling their rising surpluses uncomplainingly to the Food Corporation of India even when the domestic procurement price was far below world price in the 1970s and again in the decade up to the late 1990s. They have ensured cheap food to urban areas and food deficit regions by not seeking to maximize their own incomes. Today, as a result of the official embracing and putting into practice of mindless deflationary policies which have reduced mass purchasing power, they have lost internal grain markets to the tune of 26 million tonnes and are being given the irresponsible advice to 'diversify' and export to world markets even though these continue to be in recession, and even though all international organizations predict continuing fall in agricultural terms of trade up to 2009-10. Calculations by FAO shows that the terms of trade for agriculture globally, with 1990-91 as base year equal to 100, was about 50 by 2001, compared to over 200 in the 1970s. All projections up to 2009-10 by international bodies, show continued absolute price fall and further decline in terms of trade.

The question that is neither raised nor answered in official publications like the *Economic Survey* and the Reserve Bank of India's *Report on Currency and Finance* which articulate the fairy tale of voluntary diversification, is: How can people suffering employment loss and facing unprecedented crop price declines, be inferred to be better off and be voluntarily reducing cereals demand, and how is it that the current reduced level of total absorption of food grains per head of 155 kg. per annum, is not seen in any country except the least developed and sub-Saharan African countries? The observed falling share of food expenditure in total expenditure for almost every expenditure group, is officially cited as proof of every income segment including the poorest diversifying diets and becoming better off, and seems to have persuaded some academics. No attention is paid to steadily falling average calorie intake in rural India as 'diversification' proceeds. The argument is quite fallacious and is based on a simple confusion between the necessary and sufficient conditions for improvement.

A falling share of food expenditure in total expenditure, as a well as a falling share of grain expenditure in food expenditure, are necessary, but not sufficient indices of the consumer becoming better off, particularly when we are considering, not an advanced country rich population, but a population already at a low standard of life. The food spending share of total spending can fall and is actually observed to fall, when people are getting worse off because their real income is constant or falling, since owing to greater monetization of the economy and higher cost of utilities, they are forced to spend more on the bare minimum of non-food essentials. Thus even when price-index adjusted income is unchanged over time, some food expenditure has to be sacrificed at the later date to buy fuel (which is jointly demanded with food grains and is no longer available from common property resources), incur higher transport costs in search of work, incur higher health costs and so on. Since the overwhelmingly large part of food expenditure itself is on staple grains, it is this which falls when food expenditure is cut. Data for sub-Saharan African countries show dietary 'diversification' as per capita income declines. We observe a falling share of calories from cereals and rising share from animal products, even as, with the large decline in cereal intake absolute calorie intake is seen to decline quite steeply (see Patnaik 2003b and Essay 4 in this book for a discussion). In effect, a Sub-Saharan Africa already exists in rural India today.

The official solution is inhumane in rationalizing increasing hunger as voluntary choice, basing its prescriptions on bad theory and fallacious reasoning. The only solution which is both humane and is based on sound economic theory, is to restore lost internal purchasing power through a *universal* Employment Guarantee and to revert to a universal Public Distribution System. The Finance Minister unwisely cut rural development expenditures drastically to only Rs.13.5 thousand crores last year – the same absolute sum as was spent fifteen years earlier in 1989-90. Rs. 13.5 thousand crores is an all-time low of only 0.6 percent of NNP and this

Table 7
Summary of Annual *per capita* Foodgrains Output and Availability in India in the Nineties (Three Year Average)

Three-yr. Period Ending in	Average Population million	Net output per Head Cereals Kg.	Net output per Head Food-grains Kg.	Net Availability per Head Cereals Kg.	Net Availability per Head Pulses Kg.	Net Availability per Head Foodgrains Kg./ Year	Net Availability per Head Foodgrains Gms / day
1991-92	850.70	163.43	178.77	162.8	14.2	177.0	485
1994-95	901.02	166.74	181.59	160.8	13.5	174.3	478
1997-98	953.07	162.98	176.81	161.6	12.6	174.2	477
2000-01	1008.14	164.84	177.71	151.7	11.5	163.2	447
2002-03	1050.67	153.85	164.09	142.91	10.12	153.0	419
Individual Year							
2003-04*	1087.6	158.33	170.83	n.a	n.a.	n.a	n.a.
2004-05*	1107.0	151.21	162.35	n.a.	n.a.	n.a.	n.a.

Change in Per Capita Availability of Foodgrains, %
Triennium ending 1991-92 to Triennium ending 1997-98   - 1.6
Triennium ending 1997-98 to triiennium ending 2002-03   - 12.2
Total Change, 1991-92 to 2002-03.   - 13.6

Source: For output, trade and stocks, Reserve Bank of India, *Report on Currency and Finance*, various years; and Govt.of India, Ministry of Finance, *Economic Survey*, various years. For population, the annual compound growth rate of 1.89 % has been derived from the Census population totals for 1991 and 2001 and used to interpolate for inter-censal years. Before 1991 and from 2001 onwards, the population figures given in the *Economic Survey* have been used. This Table updates Table 4 on p.129.
* indicates provisional.

gratuitous act of deflation in the face of farm crisis, has worsened the problems of unemployment and hunger. It may be compared to the Rs, 51,000 crores spent by the NDA in 2003-04 in the aftermath of drought, which sum itself was inadequate at 2.5 percent of NNP, substantially lower than the pre-Reform 7th Plan outlays of nearly 4% of NNP.

To meet the 10th Plan budget estimates of outlays on rural development, the government now needs to spend at least Rs. 100,000 crores during fiscal 2005-06 and 2006-07, of which up to Rs.30,000 crores should be on the national rural employment guarantee, and the remainder on the urgent and neglected needs of agriculture, rural development, irrigation and village and small scale industry. Although one lakh crores may sound a large sum it is still less than 4 percent of anticipated NNP in the next two years and inadequate for the needs of 700 million people, three fifths of the nation, whose fate depends on the government's policy.

The bizarre official efforts to re-invent increasing hunger as free choice, are buttressed by spurious estimates of the population in poverty, discussed in the last section.

4. Alternative Measures of Head-Count Poverty: or,
How to Count the Poor Correctly versus Illogical Official Procedures

Poverty studies in India since the early 1970s, have been based on the use of a 'poverty line' expenditure level, defined as that level of expenditure per capita per month on all goods and services, whose food expenditure component provided an energy intake of 2400 kcal per capita in rural areas and 2100 kcal per capita in urban areas. All persons spending below the poverty line expenditure are considered to be poor. The required daily allowance (RDA) of energy was specified by the Indian Council for Medical Research and recommended by the Nutrition Expert Group to the Planning Commission in 1969. This is obviously a very minimalist definition of poverty, since no norms are set for essential non-food items of spending such as on fuel for cooking and lighting, clothing, shelter, transport, medical care or education.

The data base for estimating poverty has been the National Sample Survey Rounds on Consumption Expenditure which take the household as the sampling unit. These surveys present the distribution of persons by monthly per capita expenditure groups, and since the quantities of foods consumed and their calorie equivalents are available, they also present the calorie intake per capita per diem by expenditure groups. That particular expenditure group whose food expenditure met the calorie requirement in 1973-74, was identified and the relevant expenditure was defined as the poverty line expenditure (often this is mis-labelled as poverty line *income*, but we have no information on income). Large sample surveys are carried out at five-yearly intervals, the latest available data being from the 55th Round relating to 1999-2000, from which the relevant data for All-India is reproduced in Table 8 using two published Reports of the NSS.

A good idea of the current magnitude of head-count poverty can be obtained by the non-expert without doing any calculations, simply by inspecting the data in Table 8. Looking at the first, third and fifth columns, 69.7 percent or say seven-tenths of the rural population of India, spending less than Rs.525 per month per person, was below the average calorie level of 2403 (nearly the same as the 2400 norm), which was obtained only by the next higher spending group of Rs. 525-615. Since persons in the lower part of this group also obtained below 2400 calories, the poverty percentage is a bit higher than seven-tenths, and on plotting the data on a graph we obtain the more exact figure of 74.5 percent below Rs.565, the expenditure required to access the energy norm.[10] But, the official Planning Commission figure of rural head-count poverty from the same data is only 27.4 percent! The difference between the estimate obtained by direct inspection of the latest data and the figure as given by the Planning Commission is 47 percent, so nearly half of the actually poor rural population, about 350 million persons, are excluded from the set of the officially poor.

Again, from direct inspection we see that about two-fifths of the urban population spending below Rs.575 per capita per month obtained less than 2091 calories (very close to the 2100 urban norm) which was the average for the next higher spending group. The exact percentage in urban poverty on plotting the graph, is 44 percent. The Planning Commission figure for urban poverty for the same year is only 23.5 percent. What explains this big difference?

The Planning Commission has never officially given up the nutritional norm of 2400 calories. The majority of economists in India believe that this norm is still being followed. The reality is that the actual estimation procedure followed by the Planning Commission has de-linked its poverty estimates completely from the nutrition norm. The poverty line was obtained following the norm only in the year 1973-74 using the 28th Round NSS data, a date three decades in the past. For that year at prices then prevailing, the rural and urban poverty lines were Rs.49.09 and Rs. 56.64 per capita per month, since at these expenditures the 2400 rural and 2100 urban calorie intake norms were satisfied. It was found that 56.4 percent of the rural and 49 percent of the urban population were below these poverty lines.[11]

For later years, strange though it may seem, no use was made of a single iota of the actual consumption data and calorie equivalents, thrown up by as many as five successive large-sample surveys (in 1977-8, 1983, 1988-9, 1993-4, and 1999-2000). There was no official attempt to update the poverty lines on the basis of the available current information on what expenditure was actually required to meet the nutrition norm. Rather, the three decade old poverty lines (Rs 49.1 and Rs.56.6, rural and urban), were simply adjusted upwards by using a price-index, while assuming an invariant 1973-74 consumption basket. The adjusted poverty line was then applied to the cumulative distribution of persons by expenditure groups in current NSS data to obtain the 'poverty percentage'. Thus the current data were, and are being used selectively, with only the distribution of persons by expenditure classes being used, and the associated energy intake part being ignored completely. The declining energy intake corresponding to official poverty estimates are never mentioned, nor do academics following the same method ever mention the lowered calorie intake corresponding to their estimates (vide the papers in *Economic and Political Weekly*, 2003, special number tendentiously titled 'Poverty reduction in the 1990s'). The credibility of official and similar academic poverty estimates would certainly come into question if the educated public at large was informed how far below RDA (Required Daily Allowance)the consumption standard has been continuously pushed down, by the official method.

For example the official price-index adjusted poverty line for 1999-2000 was Rs.328 only (about 6.7 times Rs. 49) and this has been applied to the first and last columns of Table 8 to read the population below this line which came to 27%. *No attention was paid to the fact that at this expenditure a person could access at most only 1890 calories, over 500 calories per day below the RDA and nor is this fact ever mentioned to the public when poverty estimates are quoted by the Planning Commission.* This amounts to suppression of information and is not an academically acceptable procedure. The same applies to the academics who follow the official method and who never allude to the lower and lower calorie intake inherent in their price index- adjusted poverty lines over time.

Academics writing earlier (R. Nayyar 1991) however, had estimated poverty both by direct inspection of current data and by the official price-index adjustment to a base year method. Nayyar had explicitly noted that the poverty figures estimated by the official method, diverged more and more over time from the much higher poverty percentages yielded by directly using current data. As the base year of the official method gets further back in time the divergence has assumed absurd proportions. For 1993-4 the official price index adjustment method gave a rural poverty line of only Rs.205, and 37.3 % were below it in the 50th Round distribution of persons by expenditure groups, and so deemed to be 'in poverty', but the fact that at this poverty line only 1,970 calories per diem could be accessed (over 400 calories below the RDA) was never mentioned to the public. Inspecting the same current 50th Round data showed that 74.5% of persons or double the official estimate, had an intake below the RDA of 2400 calories, because their monthly expenditure was below Rs.325, the realistic poverty line at which the nutrition RDA could be accessed.

Mehta and Venkataraman (2000) in a short but significant paper, later also pointed out for the 50th Round data, this large divergence between the results of applying the official definition, and following the official price-adjustment procedure. They do not refer to the earlier discussion by Nayyar (1991) who had already pointed out the divergence for earlier Rounds and had also analysed state-wise divergence.

In 1999-2000 as we have already noted the official estimate gives only 27.4 percent in poverty because these are the persons spending below the price-index adjusted official poverty line of Rs.328, but again the further lowering of the associated energy intake standard to 1890 calories, over

500 calories per day below RDA, is never mentioned. The same current 55th Round data shown in Table 8 continue to give 74.5percent of persons actually in poverty, namely with intake below 2400 calories because their expenditure was below the Rs.565 actually required to access the RDA. (However greater poverty depth is seen by 1999-2000, with more of the population moving below 1800 calories as compared to 1993-94). Thus in 1993-4 the official method had left out 37.2 percent of the total rural population who were actually poor, while by 1999-2000 the official method was leaving out 47.1 of the total rural population or around 350 million persons who were actually poor. Table 9 summarizes the official poverty lines, poverty percentages and the falling calorie intakes at poverty lines, and it gives the true poverty lines required to access the RDA, along with the true poverty percentages.

There is no theoretically acceptable basis to the official claims of poverty reduction in the 1990s. *The basic point is that the method of comparison over time is not logically valid when the consumption standard is being altered, as is being done in the indirect estimates.* The consumption standard in 1973-74 was 2400 calories at which 56% was in poverty, by 1983 the official estimate of 45.7 % in poverty corresponded to 2060 calories intake, by 1993-94 the standard implicit in the official estimate (37% in poverty) was down further to 1970 calories, and in 1999-2000 for the official estimate (27.4 %) it was even lower at 1890 calories. By the 60th Round, 2004-05 it is likely to be below 1800 calories and correspond to less than one-fifth of rural population. We will once more hear spurious claims of further 'poverty reduction' without any mention of the lowering of the energy intake. All this has been happening because the price-adjustment to a base-year poverty line does not capture the actual current cost of accessing the minimum nutrition, and this failure becomes more acute as the base year recedes further into the past.

How can anyone say how 'poverty' has changed over time using the above method? To give an analogy, when a set of runners are lined up in a row on a circular race track for a long-distance race, if the person in the inner-most circle crosses the finishing rope first, it cannot be validly inferred

Table 8
Percentage Distribution of Persons by Monthly per Capita Expenditure
(MPCE) Groups and Average Calorie Intake per Diem, 1999-2000, All-India

RURAL

Monthly per capita Expenditure Rupees	Average MPCE Rupees	Calorie Intake per diem per Capita	Per cent of Persons %	Cumulative per cent of Persons %
Below 225	191	1383	5.1	5.1
225- 255	242	1609	5.0	10.1
255- 300	279	1733	10.1	20.2
300- 340	321	1868	10.0	30.2
340- 380	361	1957	10.3	40.5
380- 420	400	2054	9.7	50.2
420- 470	445	2173	10.2	60.4
470- 525	497	2289	9.3	69.7
525- 615	**567**	**2403**	**10.3**	**80.0**
615- 775	686	2581	9.9	89.9
775- 950	851	2735	5.0	94.9
950 & more	1344	3178	5.0	99.9
All	**486**	**2149**	**99.9**	

Summary

470- 525 and less		2289 and less	69.7	
525- 615		2403	10.3	
615-775 and more		2581 and more	19.9	

continued

URBAN Monthly per capita Expenditure Rupees	Calorie Intake per diem per Capita	Per cent of Persons %	Cumulative Percent of Persons %
Below 300	1398	5.0	5.0
300- 350	1654	5.1	10.1
350- 425	1729	9.6	19.7
425- 500	1912	10.1	29.8
500- 575	1968	9.9	39.7
575- 665	2091	10.0	49.7
665- 775	2187	10.1	59.8
775-915	2297	10.0	69.8
915-1120	2467	10.0	79.8
1120-1500	2536	10.1	89.9
1500- 1925	2736	5.0	94.9
1925 & more	2938	5.0	100
All	2156	99.9	
Summary 500- 575 and less	1968 and less	39.7	
575- 665	2091	10.0	
665- 775 and more	2187 and more	50.2	

Source: National Sample Survey Organization (55th Round, 1999-2000) Report No. 471, *Nutritional Intake in India* for calorie intake data by expenditure groups and Report No. 454, *Household Consumer Expenditure in India – Key Results* for the distribution of persons. The calorie intake data refers to the 30 day recall so the distribution of persons by the same recall period is taken above.

Note: This Table gives the same data as Table 5 in 'The Republic of Hunger' but is retained owing to more detailed discussion in the text.

Table 9
The Rural Poor as Percent of Rural Population in India

	Percent of Persons in Poverty					MPCE (Poverty Line) Rs				
	1973	1983	1993	1999	2004	1973	1983	1993	1999	2004
	-74		-94	-00		-74		-94	-00	
NSS ROUND:	28th	38th	50th	55th	60th	28th	38th	50th	55th	60th
Using Official Definition (< MPCE Giving 2400 cals)	**56.4**	**70.0**	**74.5**	**74.5**	n.a	**49**	**120**	**325**	**565**	n.a
Official Estimates and Implied Calorie 'Norm'	56.4	45.7	37.3	27.4	20.3*	49	86	206	328	354*
	2400	2060	1970	1890	n.a	(1.0)	(1.4)	(1.6)	(1.7)	n.a.

Source: First line calculated from NSS Reports on Consumer Expenditure, 50th Round 1993-4 and 55th Round 1999-00. MPCE is Monthly Per Capita Expenditure. Note that base year 1973-74 is the only year the official definition was correctly applied – in all later years the nutrition norm is continuously diluted. The same exercise can be carried out for urban India. (Figures in parentheses are the ratio of the expenditure actually required to access the calorie RDA, to the official poverty line).
* Provisional estimate, applying official poverty line of Rs.354 for 2004, to the ogive of persons by expenditure levels from NSS 60th Round, January – June 2004, Report No. 505 *Household Consumer Expenditure in India*, Statement 3.2 R. Note that 60th Round is a thin sample.

that he has won the race: for the distance run by him is much less than that run by others. For a valid comparison of the runners' performance, the distance run has to be the same standardized distance for all the runners, and this is done by staggering the runners. Similarly, in the official method the percent of persons below the same, standardized consumption level or levels, need to be compared but this is not the case in the indirect method. Rather, the method used implies that the percentages below un-standardized and changing consumption levels are sought to be compared over time (see Table 9).[12] This is not legitimate, and any statement about decline (or change generally) is not valid. Present day heated debates between the estimators about whether poverty has 'declined' by ten points or seven points, when poverty has not declined at all, can be likened to debates over whether the inner-circle runner has 'won' by one metre or two metres, when the fact of the matter is that he has not 'won' at all, because the premise for valid comparison is violated.

The official rural monthly poverty line expenditure for year 2004 (obtained by updating the 1999-2000 poverty line of Rs.328, using the CPIAL), is Rs.354 or Rs11.8 daily, equivalent to 26 US cents at the prevailing exchange rate. This paltry amount will actually buy at most one bottle of water, but it is supposed to cover all expenditure on food, fuel, clothing, shelter, transport, health and education – in short all daily spending on goods and services for one person! Estimates of Indian poverty for 1999-2000, 55th Round, by some individual academics like A.Deaton (2003b, 367) and S.Bhalla (2003) are even lower and imply a poverty-line of 20 US cents or less expenditure per day, one-fifth of the World Bank's dollar-a-day measure. There is no logic in arguing that purchasing power parity should be considered and instead of one dollar therefore around one third of that should be taken as the local poverty line, for the comparison is not between advanced and developing countries at all but between developing and other developing countries. A quarter U.S dollar in India purchases exactly as much as Rs.11 does, at the prevailing exchange rate, and a quarter US dollar purchases exactly as much as 2 yuan does in China (whose current rural poverty line is also far too low at 2.2 yuan per day). Poverty level incomes in the USA are not set three times higher than the Chinese or Indian one, but are at least thirty times higher.

Obviously, it is not difficult for either the Planning Commission or the individual academics to 'adjust' Indian poverty figures downwards when the consumption level embodied in the rural poverty line is depressed to such sub-human levels as Rs11 or less per day. Few people can actually survive long below these levels – those who are there today are on their way to early death. The poverty estimators should try a test on themselves. Let them be handed the weekly equivalent of their own estimated monthly poverty line – they need not even exert themselves to earn it as the poor are obliged to do – and let them spend only one week in a village living on that amount, which would range from Rs. 60 to Rs. 80. Since they will not be confident of drinking the local water all they would be able to buy would be a bottle of water a day and no food leave alone other necessities. What they would undoubtedly gain from their one-week stay, would be weight loss. Urban poverty lines are almost equally unrealistic.

Sometimes to justify the indirect method it is argued that the original rural consumption norm of 2400 was 'too high'. First, it is not 'too high' because the average intake of those below it works out to about 1950 calories which is lower than in any other country in the world except the least developed countries. Second, even if it is accepted for the sake of argument that it was 'too high' it does not justify comparing 1999-2000 'poverty' figures which are all those persons below 1890 calories intake, to those persons below 1970 calories intake in 1993-94 and those persons below 2400 calories intake in 1973-74.

By all means, let us consider lower norms, in fact take several alternative norms including 2400, but when comparing over time, compare the proportion of population under the same norm at the two or more points of time – for only then will the comparison be valid. The indirect estimates fail on this simple but essential criterion of comparability over time and those who nevertheless undertake such comparison are committing a logical fallacy – *the fallacy of equivocation*. This a well known type of verbal fallacy, in which the same term is used with two completely different meanings in the course of the argument, so the inference is not true. In this case, 'poverty line' was defined and initially calculated with respect to a nutrition norm, while 'poverty line' as actually calculated is de-linked from the norm, so the inference regarding change (whether rise, fall or constancy) is not true. [13]

Not only is the official comparison of poverty percentages, and claims of poverty reduction over time, quite spurious; the comparison of the poverty levels of states at a given point of time is equally invalid. As Table 10 shows, we have a bizarre picture when we calculate the maximum calorie intake levels below which people are designated as 'poor' by the official method in the different states of India. The calorie intake corresponding to the official state-wise poverty lines – from which the state poverty percentage have been officially derived – for the year 1999-2000, varies from 1440 only in Kerala, nearly a thousand calories below RDA, to 2120 in Orissa, less than 300 calories below RDA.

The fact is that the official method in India today adheres to no nutrition norm at all. Nutrition has dropped out of the picture completely in the indirect method, nor is there any lower bound which is set, to the extent of decline in the calorie intake corresponding to whatever the price-adjusted poverty line happens to be. That is why we find states with 1500 calories or less intake corresponding to their official poverty lines in 1999-2000. In as many as 9 states, the calorie intake associated with the official poverty lines was below 1800 calories in the 55th Round, while in four states it was 1600 calories or less (see Table 10). None of this is mentioned when poverty estimates are quoted by those making them.

Not even the late P.V. Sukhatme, who was a consistent critic of the 2400 calorie RDA being too high, would have accepted 1800 calories as a reasonable norm for estimating who the poor are – leave alone 1600 calories or less. He had used a norm of 2200 calories in one of his own estimates (Sukhatme 1977). By 2004-05 the All-India official poverty line itself will correspond to an intake of 1800 calories or less, and at least eight states will have a 1600 or less calorie intake corresponding to the state-specific official poverty lines.

The fact that comparability conditions are blatantly violated, is obvious. Officially it is inferred that poverty is much higher, for example, in Orissa at 48 percent, than in neighbouring Andhra Pradesh at only 11 percent. But how can we possibly infer that Orissa is 'poorer' than Andhra, when the 'officially poor' are those persons with below 2120 calories intake in Orissa but the 'officially poor' are those persons with below 1600 calories intake in Andhra? (As a matter of fact the below 2400 and below 2100 calories poverty percentages are both higher in Andhra than in Orissa as the same Table shows in the last two columns). Similarly, how can it be inferred that rural Gujarat with only 13 percent officially in poverty, is much better off than West Bengal with 33 percent officially poor, when the associated calorie 'norm' in Gujarat has been pushed down to only 1680 compared to 1900 in West Bengal? As a matter of fact the below 2400 calories poverty percentage is marginally lower for W.Bengal compared to Gujarat and the below 2100 calories percentage is substantially lower for W.Bengal. And so the anomalies can be multiplied. Further, how can , for each state, the official estimate in 1999-2000 be compared with that in 1993-94 and inference about 'decline' be drawn, when the associated calorie intake has been lowered in each state? (Except only one, Gujarat).

As a teacher if I were to follow the illogical procedure of saying that student A who has 53 percent marks is 'better' than student B who has 59 percent marks, because I apply a 50 out of 100 marks standard to student A and apply a different, 60 marks out of 100 standard to student B, I would rightly face a court case. Yet our Planning Commission and individual academics have been allowed to get away with making patently illogical and untrue statements on poverty. The Deputy Chairman of the Planning Commission recently congratulated the Andhra Pradesh government on its success in reducing poverty. This 'reduction' was solely the effect of applying an extraordinarily low price-adjusted poverty line of Rs. 262 per month in 1999-2000, or less than Rs.9 per day, at which less than 1600 calories could be accessed (See Table 10). Looking directly at nutrition poverty, on the other hand, we find that the proportion of persons below 1800 calories intake in that state has doubled to 40% by 1999-2000 compared to 1983 (Table 11). To complete the story, the proportion below 2100 calories has risen to 62% at the later date, compared to 56 % only five years earlier in 1993-4, and 44% in 1983.

What is the reason, the reader might ask, for the official method producing consistently lower estimates than the direct method, and why has the divergence been growing until now; the indirect estimate gives only 27 percent compared to nearly 75 percent by the direct estimate. It is not primarily a matter of the price index used : different price indices (different in terms of the extent of price rise, but all with the same base year quantity weights) do give different results but this accounts for difference of at most 10 percent or so of population in poverty, not the difference of over 47 percent of population which is actually observed. The basic reason for the large and increasing difference, *is the assumption of an invariant consumption basket in the indirect method, held unchanged for three decades.* In effect the official estimators are saying – if a person in a village consumed the same quantities of foods and other goods and services as 32 years ago, then Rs. 328 per month is enough to access these quantities in 1999-2000 and Rs. 354 per month is enough in 2004. If you do not get the calorie standard, it is the result of your free choice which has led you to consume in a different pattern.

This is not however a reasonable position to adopt. It is as unreasonable as telling a 32 year old man, that the one metre of cloth which was enough to clothe him when he was one month old, and which cost say Rs. 10 at that time, can be bought after price-index adjustment for Rs. 70 today, and if this expenditure leaves him semi-naked today, then it is his problem of free choice to be in that state. Such a position ignores the irreversible structural changes the person has undergone which means his set of choices has altered over time. Of course, this is only an analogy – we are not arguing that the proportion of adults in the population has risen! We wish through the analogy, to drive home the point that over the last three decades certain irreversible structural changes have taken place in the economy. There has been increasing monetization of the economy and disappearance of common property resources, along with higher cost of utilities and health care. With a given real income people have to spend relatively more on essential non-food requirements, overcoming illness and earning a living. The actual current rural consumption basket which satisfies the nutrition norm, and to which the total monthly expenditure on all goods and services corresponds, costs almost double the price-adjusted poverty line (from Table 8 summarized in Table 9, at least Rs. 570 is required compared to the official Rs. 328). The official poverty lines are simply far too low and are getting further lowered as the base year becomes more remote.

Rohini Nayyar (1991) in her careful doctoral study, had estimated poverty using both methods and had noted the widening divergence in the results between 1961-2 and 1977-8. She had taken some solace from the fact that though poverty levels estimated by the two different methods were drawing apart quite fast, at least they did seem to *move in the same direction* over time. The ranking of the states of India according to their poverty levels estimated using the two methods, was highly correlated: Nayyar found that Spearman's rank correlation coefficient worked out to 0.89 and 0.84 (using the official estimate on the one hand, and two different direct estimate norms of 2200 and 2000 calories) and was significant at the 1% level .

But in the 1990s this conclusion no longer holds. The poverty levels calculated by the two methods are moving fast in opposite directions and the rank correlation may soon become negative. Spearman's rank correlation taking the poverty ranks of the states by the official indirect method, and by the direct method for 1999-2000, 55th Round data, works out to only 0.236 and 0.075 (using the same two direct estimate norms) and neither is statistically significant at the 1% level. [14] Inspection of Table 10 will tell the reader why this is the case: some of the states with the lowest official poverty, such as Andhra Pradesh, a by-word for agrarian distress, have some of the highest actual poverty. In general the official method produces the largest divergence from the direct method, in the case of the southern and eastern states.

The rot in poverty studies discussions seems to have set in with neo-liberal reforms in India, particularly in the late 1990s. The Indian Government was eager to claim success for the economic reforms and the pro-reform economists were eager to see poverty reduction in the data. In such a milieu, the inconvenient direct estimates showing high and in some states, increasing levels of poverty were swept under the carpet. Discussion of direct estimation of poverty virtually disappeared from the literature. The dominant trend of discussion focussed on the official indirect method, which, to the great satisfaction of the pro-reform academics and the World Bank estimators, not only showed very low 'poverty' levels but actual decline in these levels. Not one of the authors using the official indirect method, alluded to the nutritional implications of their own estimates. This meant that they were using and presenting the NSS data selectively, taking only the distribution of persons by expenditure classes to read off the poverty proportion corresponding to their indirect poverty line, while ignoring the associated energy intake figures completely. Such lack of transparency and selective use of data, is not acceptable academic procedure. Owing to this lack of transparency, to this day most economists in India not directly working with the data, and including even those examining research theses on poverty, are not aware that drastically lowered consumption levels over time and arbitrary variation of consumption levels across states, are the necessary implications of following the indirect method and arriving at low poverty estimates. They assume that the original norms are being followed when this is not true.

There is a debate among the academics following the official, indirect method, that owing to change in the recall period during the 55th round, 1999-2000 compared to earlier Rounds, actual expenditure is slightly overstated in every expenditure class, and hence the distribution of persons by expenditure classes has been affected. Making the required adjustment for comparability alters this distribution slightly and raises the 27 percent below the Rs. 328 official price-adjusted poverty line, by another 2 to 3 percent (Sundaram and Tendulkar, 2003, Deaton, 2003a, Sen and Himanshu 2004-2005). If these adjustments are correct, quite obviously, the percentage of persons below the directly observed poverty line of Rs. 570 would rise to an even greater extent than 2 to 3, since a higher proportion of people than before would also come into the expenditure interval Rs. 328 to Rs. 570, and thus the difference between official estimate and the direct estimate would increase further. Thus all those with less than 2400 calories intake per diem, in 1999-2000 would be more than 74.5 + 3 = 77.5 percent of rural population, which is a rise compared to 74.5 percent in the 50th Round, 1993-94. Similarly those below 2100 calories would rise from 49.5 percent to more than 52.5 percent. [15]

However we have chosen to give the direct estimate for 1999-2000 unadjusted for recall period in all our tables, since the main point being made in this section is the type of mistake involved in the indirect method itself which leaves out nearly half the rural poor, *and this basic problem with all indirect estimates not only remains but gets further aggravated whenever adjustments are made by the estimators on account of altered recall period.* It may be noted that with the adjustment for recall period, they are leaving out more than 47 percent of the actually poor rural population from their set of 'the poor', while without the adjustment they were leaving out exactly 47 percent of the population.

Some economists who are critical of the official price-adjustment method which de-links the estimates from nutrition, have correctly put nutrition back at the centre of their own analysis, but they have followed another direct poverty estimation route, as compared to inspecting current NSS data – the method we have followed. They have estimated the minimum cost of accessing the calorie RDA on the basis of *current* nutrient prices, and thus have obtained a normative food expenditure. By comparing with the actual expenditure on food in the NSS, they arrive at the percentage of persons failing to reach the RDA and this is 66 percent at the All-India level for the 55th Round (See Coondoo, Majumdar, Lancaster and Ray 2004, Ray and Lancaster 2005). Subramanian (2005) has used indirect method base years closer to the present, as well as the direct method we use, to see how the trends in poverty behave under alternative scenarios.

Many critical voices (Suryanarayana 1996, Mehta and Venkataraman 2000, Swaminathan 1999, 2002) which had continued to draw attention to the high prevalence of undernutrition and malnutrition, to the secular decline in average rural calorie intake, to high direct poverty estimates using reasonable calorie norms and which criticized the indirect estimates, have been sought to be silenced by the pro-reform economists, by the simple expedient of ignoring them altogether. Not one critical author is referred to in the articles by those presenting their indirect estimates at a Conference and later collecting them in a special issue of *The Economic and Political Weekly* tendentiously titled 'Poverty Reduction in the 1990s' (Deaton 2003a and 2003b, Tendulkar and Sundaram 2003 etc.). The only article on energy intake while juxtaposing the official and direct estimates does so somewhat uncritically.[16] The critical writers on the other hand, have given cogent arguments to suggest why per capita calorie intake should be involuntarily declining in the lower expenditure classes over time. (It is also declining in

Table 10
Official Poverty Percentage by States and Associated Calorie 'Norm'

STATE	1993-94 Official Poverty percentage	Implied Calorie 'Norm'	1999-2000 Official Poverty Percentage	Implied Calorie 'Norm'	Direct Estimates, 1999-2000 < 2400 cal Poverty Percentage	< 2100 cal Poverty Percentage
Andhra Pradesh	15.92	1700	11.05	1590	84.0	62.0
Assam	45.01	1960	40.04	1790	91.0	71.0
Bihar	58.21	2275	44.30	2010	77.0	53.5
Gujarat	22.18	1650	13.17	1680	83.0	68.5
Haryana	28.02	1970	8.27	1720	47.5	30.5
Karnataka	29.88	1800	17.30	1600	82.0	50.0
Kerala	25.76	1630	9.38	1440	82.5	52.5
Madhya Pradesh	40.64	1970	37.06	1850	78.5	55.0
Maharashtra	37.93	1780	23.72	1760	92.0	55.0
Orissa	49.72	2150	48.01	2120	79.0	45.5
Punjab	11.95	1810	6.35	1710	47.5	36.5
Rajasthan	26.46	2130	13.74	1925	53.5	27.5
Tamilnadu	32.48	1650	20.55	1510	94.5	76.0
Uttar Pradesh	48.28	2220	31.22	2040	61.0	37.5
West Bengal	40.80	2080	31.85	1900	81.0	55.0
ALL INDIA	37.27	1970	27.09	1890	74.5	49.5

Source: As Table 8. From the basic data by states, the ogive or cumulative frequency distribution of persons below specified per capita expenditure levels was plotted, and on the same graph the relation of per capita expenditure and per capita calorie intake was plotted. Calorie intake corresponding to the official estimates was then obtained from the graphs. Note that for 1993-94 the mid-point value of each expenditure class has been plotted against the per capita calorie intake as the arithmetic average was not available in the published tables. For 1999-2000 it was available and has been used in deriving the figures for 1999-2000. We find that for several expenditure classes the mid-point value coincided with the arithmetic mean, and for the others the difference of mid-point value from mean was very small, suggesting that the same would be true for 1993-4.

higher expenditure classes but the problems of the initially over-fed who may be reducing intake, do not concern us at present). They have pointed out that there has been substantial monetization of the economy over the last three decades. Wages which used to be paid in kind as grain or meals,

Table 11

States which have seen rise in the percentage of persons with less than 1800 calories intake per day during period 1983 to 1999-2000, and states with over one-third of population below 1800 calories intake at either date

	RURAL *38th Round, 1983* *< 1800 calories percent of total Persons*	RURAL *55th Round, 1999-2000* *< 1800 calories percent of total Persons*
Andhra Pradesh	19.0	40.0
Assam	28.5	41.0
Haryana	8.5	10.5
Karnataka	24.5	35.5
Kerala	50.0	41.0
Madhya Pradesh	18.5	32.5
Maharashtra	20.5	28.0
Tamilnadu	54.0	50.0
West Bengal	38.0	22.5

Source: Abstracted from estimates for all states, using NSS Reports No.471 and 454 for 55th round, and Report Nos.387 and 353 for 38th Round. Estimation method as in note to Table 10. Note that in 1983 only 3 states – Kerala, Tamilnadu and West Bengal had more than one-third of rural population below 1800 calories intake. By 1999-2000 all three states had improved, West Bengal substantially, while Andhra Pradesh, Assam, Karnataka, Madhya Pradesh and Maharashtra saw worsening. Thus by 1999-2000, five states had more than one third of population below 1800 calories intake (six if we include the borderline Madhya Pradesh).

valued at low farm-gate prices in earlier NSS Rounds, are now paid in cash which the labourer has to exchange for food at higher retail prices, and so can buy less of it for a given real income. Common property resources have disappeared over the last three decades: fuel wood and fodder, earlier gleaned and gathered (and not fully valued in the NSS data), now have to be purchased, restricting the ability of the poorer population to satisfy basic food needs out of a given real income and leading to the observed energy intake decline. Staple grains and fuelwood or other fuels are obviously jointly demanded since no-one can eat raw grain, and with a given real income a part of expenditure on grain has to be enforcedly reduced to purchase fuel. To this we have to add higher medical, transport and education costs as state funding is reduced and some services are privatized. The correct thrust of these arguments is that under-nutrition and poverty are very high, affecting three-quarters of the rural population by now, and observed calorie intake decline for the lower fractiles is non-voluntary. By 1999-2000 for the first time average calorie intake in rural India has fallen below average urban calorie intake.

Concluding Remarks

This paper has embarked on a brief but sharp critique of the prevalent analysis and prescriptions regarding food security and poverty because of two reasons. First, the agrarian crisis is serious and widespread, and has been created by public policies which have been deflationary, combined with trade liberalization when world primary prices have been declining. It is manifesting itself in slowing output growth, rising unemployment, unprecedented income deflation for the majority of cultivators and labourers, enmeshing of cultivators in unrepayable debt, and loss of assets including land, to creditors. Kidney sales and nine thousand recorded farmer suicides are only the tip of the iceberg of increasing deprivation, a crucial index of which is an unprecedented fall in foodgrains absorption to levels prevalent 50 years ago, and decline in average calorie intake in rural India.

Second, the prevalent analysis by policy makers, the Planning Commission and the government, however, can be summed up as an obdurate refusal to face the facts, and an attempt to construct a counter-factual fairy story which is illogical and in patent contradiction with the trends in the economy. "We must learn truth from facts" (Mao ZeDong) "or the facts will punish us" (added by Deng Hsiao Ping) is a dictum that our policy makers would do well to bear in mind. Their theorization interprets severe loss of purchasing power and enforced decline in effective demand for food grains as its very opposite, as 'over-production' in relation to an allegedly voluntary reduction of foodgrains intake by all segments of the population, and reaches the dangerous inference that foodgrains output should be cut back. It refuses to recognize that, while in developed societies, consumers can be separated from a minority who are agricultural producers, in a poor country like India the majority of consumers are themselves rural and directly involved in production as cultivators and labourers, so deflationary policies hit them hard in both these roles of producers and consumers. Price deflation does not benefit even landless labourers since it is part of a process of income deflation which raises unemployment faster than prices fall. Our economists estimating poverty by the indirect method are still caught in the old conceptual trap of equating relative food price decline with declining poverty, without understanding that the adverse unemployment effects of deflation can swamp out any benefit of food price fall: they should study the economics of the Great Depression for some insights into how deflationary processes actually operate.

As Table 11 shows, by 1999-2000 as many as five states had one-third or more of rural population with less than 1800 calories intake, and in another three states the percentage of persons with below 1800 calories intake had risen between 1983 and 1999-2000, though not exceeding one-third at the latter date. (Note that Meenakshi and Viswanathan, 2003, obtain a larger number than we do, eight states with more than one-third of population below 1800 calories in the 55th Round – but their use of kernel density functions to obtain the calorie distribution ogive is perhaps overestimating the nutrition poverty figures, since their method includes all high income but calorie deficient people as well).

Despite this worsening situation at the ground level being reflected in the nutrition data, it would be very sad indeed if the present Planning Commission is tempted to make further spurious claims of 'poverty reduction' as the previous ones had done, the moment the next large-sample NSS data on consumption becomes available. Their indirect method - which selectively uses the data by ignoring the nutrition part of it - is bound to show a further steep and spurious 'decline' in rural poverty by 2005-06, to around 18-19 percent of rural population from 27.4 percent in 1999-2000. This is because, owing to the unprecedented income deflationary situation itself, the rise in prices has been at a historic low between 2000 to date. The CPIAL actually declined in 2000-01 compared to the previous year, and rose only 1 percent the next year. With low inflation, the CPIAL-adjusted official poverty line for 2004 works out to only Rs. 354, a mere Rs. 26 or 8% more than the Rs. 328 of 1999-2000. (By contrast the CPIAL had risen 60% between 1993-4 and 1999-2000).

It comes as no surprise that the recently released 60th Round NSS data relating to January- June 2004 shows that only 22 percent of all –India rural population is below Rs. 354, the official price-adjusted poverty line, if schedule 1 is used, and only 17.5 percent is below it if schedule 2 is used.[17] This is a share which is falling every year, solely because few persons can survive below such low spending levels – indeed it is amazing that there are people surviving at all on less than Rs. 12 per day. One can imagine how adverse their height, weight, morbidity rates and life expectancy would be relative to the average.

Of course, this alleged 'decline in poverty' will be necessarily associated with a further fall in the calorie intake level corresponding to the official poverty line, from 1890 calories to somewhere around or below 1800 calories, in short at least 600 calories below RDA. This information of declining nutrition standard associated with the official estimate is likely to be quietly suppressed as it has been in the past. The Government should bear in mind however, that any claims of 'poverty reduction' it might be misguided enough to make, will no longer carry credibility since the arbitrary and illogical nature of its method of calculation is today much better understood, and the contrast of any such claims, with all other adverse trends in the rural economy is too glaring to be ignored.

Since such a large fraction of the population is already at very low energy intake levels, they have been trying to maintain consumption by liquidating assets against debt. Thus there are not only adverse flow adjustment (lowered nutrition levels) but also stock adjustments going on, reflected in the emerging recent data on rising landlessness. We may expect to see rise in the already high concentration of assets in rural areas. In such a scenario labour bondedness against debt is also likely to be increasing.

The official refusal to recognize the seriousness of the crisis at the theoretical level, the consequent refusal to restore lost purchasing power through an immediately implemented universal employment guarantee, and the refusal to extend effective support to producers through continuing open-ended procurement at reasonable prices, all bode ill for the agrarian crisis, which is not being addressed. In fact the deflationary hammer has been applied once more on the rural population by the Finance Minister in the very first budget of the UPA government. The Tenth Plan, 1992 to 1997 sets out that Rs. 300, 000 crores are to be spent by the Centre on Rural Development Expenditures (adding up as before five items).[18] Three years of the Plan or two-thirds of the period is over: Rs. 100,000 crores or only one-third of the planned outlays have been spent, of which Rs. 85,000 crores spending was during the last two years of NDA rule, mid-2002 to mid-2004, while there was a sharp cut-back to Rs. 15,000 crores only in 2004-05. As in 1991, the first years after a general election are being used by the neo-liberal lobby in the new government which controls finance to apply mindless deflation, although unlike 1991 there is deep agrarian crisis today. This cynical move to cut rural development expenditures in the face of rising unemployment and agrarian distress can only be in order to please international financial institutions and meet the arbitrary provisions of the FRBM Act.

To achieve the 10th Plan target now at least Rs.100,000 crores must be spent both in 2005-06 and 2006-07, of which about 25 to 30 thousand crores should be on universal employment guarantee and 70 to 75 thousand crores on rural development expenditures. This level of planned spending would total only about 2.5 percent of NNP and it needs to be stepped up steadily in later years to reach the 4 percent of NNP which prevailed in the late 1980s during 7th Plan before economic reforms began.

The entire false analysis which re-invents increasing hunger as voluntary choice, is today sought to be re-inforced by bogus poverty estimates and invalid claims of decline in poverty. In such a situation it is the duty of all academics and activists who have not lost their sanity, to critique the official analysis and prescriptions, which if carried through will worsen immeasurably the already pitiable condition of the majority of the rural population.

Notes

[1] National Nutrition Monitoring Bureau, 25 Years of NNMB (Delhi 1997). Emphasis added.

[2] See Baker, Epstein and Pollin 1998, Halevy and Fontaine 1998. Patnaik 2000.

[3] In Infrastructure we are including the expenditures on Energy and Transport.

[4] A rising contribution of services to GDP from an initial situation of a high share of industry to GDP has been typical for advanced economies. India however is seeing a fast shift to services from a relatively low initial share of manufacturing and mining output, less than 30% of GDP, which is now down to about one-fifth. This shift to services reflects de-industrialization and worsening income distribution.

[5] Patnaik 2005, 'Ricardo's Fallacy'. A shorter version is available in Patnaik 2003a.

[6] See my discussion in Patnaik 1996, 2003c.

[7] I have discussed this in more detail in Patnaik 2003b, 2004.

[8] The official practice for 50 years, which I have followed in Table 7, is to deduct 12.5 percent from gross output in tonnes of foodgrains (cereals plus pulses) on account of seed, feed and wastage, and to the net ouput so obtained, add net imports and deduct net addition to public stocks.

[9] Rising inequality is not necessary because we can have fall in grain absorption when all incomes are falling and inequality is unchanged. It is not sufficient because if with increasing inequality all incomes are rising, grain absorption will not fall.

[10] The required graphs are 1) the ogive of cumulative percentage of persons below specified expenditure levels, and 2) the relation between per capita expenditure in each expenditure group and the per capita calorie intake for each expenditure group. With two relations and three variables – calorie intake, percentage of persons, and per capita expenditure – knowing the value of any one variable determines the other two.

[11] It is a curious matter of chance that poverty lines were Rs. 49.1 and Rs. 56.6 while the corresponding poverty percentages were 56.4 and 49.

[12] The analogy can be carried a little further. If the race is a short one over a straight segment of the course, lining the runners up in a straight line at the starting point is okay. Similarly if the base year of the price index is very close, say two to three years, then comparison over time can be made using the official method - which ignores every non-base year actual calorie intake - without leading to too much inaccuracy. But for a

long race (a base year further back in time) absence of standardization will arise and make comparison invalid.

[13] I have discussed the fallacy of equivocation involved in the indirect estimates, in Patnaik 2005b.

[14] 'Poverty Estimates in India: A Critical Appraisal', Ramanand Ram, M.Phil Dissertation submitted in JNU, 2004.

[15] We could easily find out how much higher the direct estimate would be than 74.5 percent, if those making the adjustment to the distribution of persons by expenditure class had bothered to present the associated average calorie intake by expenditure class. As usual however they ignore the nutrition part completely in their papers.

[16] Meenakshi and Viswanathan 2003 present 'calorie deprivation' as though it is an independent topic, not essentially related to official poverty estimates, and although they usefully juxtapose their estimates of population below differing calorie norms, and the official estimates, they do not refer to the falling energy equivalent of the official or individual poverty lines over time which affects comparability. Their method of estimating the calorie distribution ogives using kernel density functions, gives higher estimates of population below various calorie norms, than our estimates using the grouped data and the simple method described in the note to Table 10. This is probably because their estimate includes all well-to-do persons who have lower calorie intake than RDA. There is no reason however to consider rich race jockeys, super models or anorexic people as part of the poor.

[17] Two schedules were canvassed for the first time for different sets of households in the 60th Round. Schedule 2 departs from schedule 1 because it uses a recall period of 7 days and not 30 days, for a range of consumer items.

[18] Namely agriculture, rural development, irrigation and flood control, special areas programmes, village and small scale industry.

References

Baker D., G.Epstein and R. Pollin (Eds.). 1998. *Globalization and Progressive Economic Policy* (Cambridge: Cambridge University Press).

Coondoo, D., A. Majumdar, G.Lancaster and R.Ray. 2004. 'Alternative Approaches to Measuring Temporal Changes in Poverty with Application to India', Working Paper, December.

Cornia G. A., R. Jolly and F. Stewart (Eds.). 1987. *Adjustment with a Human Face Vol.1* (Oxford: Clarendon Press).

Deaton, A. 2003a. 'Adjusted Indian Poverty Estimates for 1999-2000'.

———. 2003b. 'Prices and Poverty 1987-2000'. Both papers in *Economic and Political Weekly*, Vol.38, January 25-31.

Halevy J. and J-M. Fontaine (Eds.). 1998. *Restoring Demand in the World Economy* (Cheltenham, UK: Edward Elgar).

Kindleberger, C.P. 1987. *The World in Depression 1929-1939* (Pelican Books).

Meenakshi J.V. and B. Viswanathan. 2003. 'Calorie Deprivation in Rural India', *Economic and Political Weekly*, Vo.38, Jan.25-31.

Mehta, J., and S. Venkataraman. 2000. 'Poverty Statistics – Bermicide's Feast', *Economic and Political Weekly*, Vol. 35, July 1.

Nayyar, R. 1991. *Rural Poverty in India* (Oxford University Press).

Patnaik P. and C. P. Chandrasekhar. 1995. 'The Indian Economy under Structural Adjustment', *Economic and Political Weekly*, November 25.

Patnaik, P. 1999. 'Capitalism in Asia at the end of the Millennium', *Monthly Review* 51, 3, July-August, Special number.

———. 2000. 'The Humbug of Finance', *Chintan Memorial Lecture*, delivered on Jan. 8, 2000 at Chennai, India. Available on website (www.macroscan.org), also included in P. Patnaik, *The Retreat to Unfreedom* (Delhi: Tulika 2003).

Patnaik, U. 1996. 'Export-Oriented Agriculture and Food Security in Developing Countries and India', *Economic and Political Weekly*, Vol.31, Nos.35-37, Special Number 1996, reprinted in *The Long Transition – Essays on Political Economy* (Delhi: Tulika, 1999).

———. 2002. 'Deflation and Deja-Vu', in Madhura Swaminathan and V.K. Ramchandran (Eds.), *Agrarian Studies – Essays on Agrarian Relations in Less Developed Countries* (Delhi: Tulika).

———. 2003a. 'On the Inverse Relation between Primary Exports and Domestic Food Absorption under Liberalized Trade Regimes', in J.Ghosh and C. P. Chandrasekhar (Eds.) *Work and Welfare in the Age of Finance* (Delhi: Tulika).

———. 2003b. 'Food Stocks and Hunger – Causes of Agrarian Distress', *Social Scientist*, Vol.31, Nos.7-8, July-August .

——. 2003c. 'Global Capitalism, Deflation and Agrarian Crisis in Developing Countries', Social Policy and Development Programme Paper Number 13, United Nations Research Institute for Social Development (UNRISD), October 2003.

——. 2004a. 'The Republic of Hunger', *Social Scientist,* Vol.32, Nos.9-10, Sept.-Oct.

——. 2004b. 'Alternative ways of Measuring Poverty and Implications for Policy – A Critical Appraisal from the Indian Experience', Draft paper presented at Conference on "The Agrarian Constraint and Poverty Reduction – Macroeconomic Lessons for Africa", Addis Ababa December 17-19, organized by The Ethiopian Economic Association and International Development Economics Associates. www.networkideas.org

——. 2005a. 'Ricardo's Fallacy', in K.S.Jomo (Ed.), *Pioneers of Development Economics* (Delhi:Tulika and London & New York: Zed).

——. 2005b. 'The Nature of Fallacies in Economic Theory', Satyendranath Sen Memorial Lecture delivered at The Asiatic Society, Kolkata, August 10 2004, forthcoming in the Journal of the Asiatic Society.

Ram, R. 2004.'Poverty Estimates in India: A Critical Appraisal' M.Phil Dissertation submitted to Jawaharlal Nehru University, July.

Ray, R. and G. Lancaster. 2005. 'On Setting the Poverty Line Based on Estimated Nutrient Prices: Condition of Socially Disadvantaged Groups During the Reform Period', *Economic and Political Weekly,* Vol.XL, No.1, January 1-7.

Sen, A. and Himanshu. 2004.'Poverty and Inequality in India: Getting Closer to the Truth', *Economic and Political Weekly,* January.

Subramanian, S. 2005.'Unraveling a Conceptual Muddle – India's Poverty Statistics in the Light of Basic Demand Theory', *Economic and Political Weekly,* Vol.XL, No.1, Jan.1-7.

Sukhatme, P.V. 1977 .'Incidence of Undernutrition', *Indian Journal of Agricultural Economics,* July-Sept.

Sundaram, K.and S.D.Tendulkar. 2003. 'Poverty *Has* Declined in the 1990s – A Resolution of Comparability Problems in NSS Consumer Expenditure Data', *Economic and Political Weekly,* Vol. XL, No.1, Jan.1-7.

Swaminathan, M. 1999. *Weakening Welfare – the Public Distribution of Food in India* (Delhi: Leftword Books).

——. 2002.'Excluding the Needy – the Public Provisioning of Food in India', *Social Scientist,* Vol.30, Nos. 3-4, March-April.

IT IS TIME FOR KUMBHAKARNA TO WAKE UP

The arguments for a universal, not targeted National Rural Employment Guarantee Act, as well as for a universal Public Distribution System (PDS), are far stronger than most people realize. Rural India is in deep and continuing distress. Unemployment continues to rise. Output growth continues to fall; last year's gross foodgrains output was 205 million tonnes, or only 162 kg. net output per head of population. Loss of purchasing power owing to drastic reductions in the State's spending on rural development during the last decade continues, and is reflected in a steep fall in per head foodgrains absorption which is now one of the lowest in the world at around 154 kg. for all-India, 20 kg. lower than a mere six years ago, and it is lower still in village India where calorie intake per head continues to decline. For comparison, China's per head annual foodgrains absorption is over 300 kg. Forty years of successful effort in India to raise foodgrains absorption through Green Revolution and planned expansionary policies has been wiped out in a single decade of deflationary economic reforms and India is back to the food grains availability level of fifty years ago. The farmers of Punjab and Haryana are in crisis for they have lost internal markets to the tune of 26 million tonnes of food grains – for if grain absorption had been maintained at least at the 1991 level of 178 kg per head instead of falling, the internal demand would have been 26 million tones higher than it actually is today.

While in the early 1990s when economic reforms started there were three states which had one-third or more of rural population below 1800 calories daily energy intake, the latest NSS data show five additional major states to have declined to that position. There is already a sub-Saharan Africa within India – half of our rural population or over 350 million people are below the average food energy intake of SSA countries. Of the rural population 75 percent was actually poor in 1999-2000, being below 2400 calories required daily intake, but the Planning Commission gave us an unrealistic estimate of only 27 percent by applying a poverty line which is far too low at less than Rs.11 per day, at which less than 1900 calories could be accessed.

Farmers exposed by trade openness to falling global prices, even as input costs and credit cost rose, have descended into deepening indebtedness and are losing assets including land. From 1998 to date over nine thousand farmers have committed suicide. These desperate acts of self-destruction continue unabated – there were 780 recorded suicides during the last year in Andhra Pradesh after the Congress came to power, and over the last three years, new centres of crisis have emerged in Karnataka and Vidarbha, while nearly 1300 suicides have been recorded in Kerala in Wyanad district alone. International bodies project continuing fall in real prices of primary products up to 2010, so there is no solace in trying to access external markets. The cornering of purchases of tea, coffee and spices by Transnational Corporations, following the downgrading of State marketing boards, has driven producer prices to levels far below global prices.

Rural India is crying out for work and food. The NDA government had exported a record 17 million tonnes of foodgrains out of stocks from June 2002 to October 2003, despite the worst drought in fifteen years. Rather than start food-for-work on a larger scale to generate employment, it used exports and open market sales to get rid of most of the 40 million tonnes of excess stocks, which had built up owing to more and more empty stomachs over four preceding years, as falling purchasing power prevented the poor from buying enough food, and as the actually poor were denied BPL cards because they were not officially deemed to be poor. This experience has shown that more exports are easy – simply let your own population go hungry by following income-deflating macro policies and by 'targeting' the PDS, and apparent 'surplus' for export automatically emerges. The exports were at below BPL price and were mostly used as animal feed abroad.

It was the agrarian crisis and the utterly callous policies of the NDA which led to its trouncing in the 2004 elections and the catapulting to power of the Congress on the promise of providing a rural employment guarantee. But the euphoria has been short-lived. As far back as the 7th Plan, 1985-90, the average share of rural development expenditures in Net National Product (NNP) had been raised to nearly 4 percent, with very positive effects by way of rising employment and rising real wages. In rural development expenditures I include five heads – agriculture, rural development, special areas programmes, irrigation and flood control, and village and small scale industry.

It might interest Sonia Gandhi to know that in the first year of UPA rule, rural development expenditures taking these same heads, have been slashed to an all-time low of 0.6 per cent of NNP. The absolute outlay (budgetary estimate) was a paltry Rupees 13.5 thousand crores as anyone may check from the latest *Economic Survey 2004-05,* and this sum is exactly the same, even without any adjustment for price rise, as that spent fifteen years ago in 1990-91. This brutal contraction in spending last year has added to the present continuing crisis of jobs and has increased hunger. Very seldom has a newly elected government administered such a slap in the face to its own constituents. Facing drought, under the same heads the NDA had spent Rs. 42,000 crores in 2002-03 fiscal and increased it to Rs.51,000 crores in 2003-04, the latter sum still amounting to less than 2.5 percent of NNP. Who could have imagined that the new government formed as a result of the peoples' agony, would slash budgeted rural development expenditures to less than a third of the already inadequate spending by the NDA.

Union Finance Minister P. Chidambaram has acted as though the agrarian crisis simply did not exist and has pulled the same trick Manmohan Singh had done as Finance Minister in 1991 - used the initial year in power to cut development expenditures sharply and deflate the economy, a prescription without any rational basis but always dogmatically urged by global financial interests. He has signalled clearly that his priority is to appease finance and adhere to the arbitrary spending cuts spelt out in the Fiscal Responsibility and Budgetary Management Act, and not to address rising unemployment and hunger. The contrast could not be more marked, with the recent actions of the governments of France and Germany, which have relaxed fiscal austerity norms to deal with much milder unemployment problems than we face today in India.

But those in charge of the nation's finances should remember that 2005 is not 1991. Rural India is in acute distress and the distress is bound to turn to turmoil if its crisis is not addressed. It is not too late. The need of the hour is to implement immediately and with sincerity a demand driven, universal employment guarantee and at the same time to abolish the arbitrary division between the 'above' and 'below' poverty line population to allow the poor to access affordable food. The Standing Committee of Parliament on the NREG Bill has submitted a very positive report supporting a universal, non-targeted Act and Sonia Gandhi's recent assurance that the NREG Act when passed will be applicable without targeting, is also heartening.

Any argument that may be put forward that the resources are not there, is simply untrue. The total budgeted outlays on rural development over the entire 10th Plan, 2002 to 2007, is a bit over Rupees 300,000 crores. Three years of the Plan period are over, and only one-third of this, or about Rs.100,000 crores have been spent, 87 percent by the NDA and 13 percent by the UPA last year. To meet the overall 10th Plan spending target, during each of the remaining two years, fiscal 2005-6 and 2006-7, at least Rs.100,000 crores have to be spent. Of this up to thirty thousand crores should be on the NREG and the remainder on the urgent development requirements of agriculture, rural development, irrigation and village industry. Large though the sum of Rs.100,000 crores per year may sound, it is less than 4 per cent of projected NNP and far too small for the needs of 700 million people.

Although they may not yet be aware of it, the Prime Minister and Finance Minister today have a historic choice before them. How will history remember them: will they take the disastrous path of Bruning's deflation, or the virtuous path of Roosevelt's New Deal? Chancellor Heinrich Brüning of Germany, nicknamed the 'Hunger Chancellor', had continued to follow deflationary policies even when unemployment was already high, in order to appease international financial interests. The resulting even higher unemployment discredited the Weimar Republic and made the rise to power of fascism a certainty. President Roosevelt, on the other hand, following what came to be known as Keynesian policies, offered expansionary macroeconomic measures to lift the USA out of depression. What India needs today is a genuine new deal for the rural poor. All those who understand the urgency of the issue of agrarian distress in this country today would wish to convey a sense of that urgency to the government. It is time for Kumbhakarna to wake up.

The Hindu August 5, 2005

AGRARIAN CRISIS IN THE ERA OF THE NEW IMPERIALISM AND THE ROLE OF PEASANT RESISTANCE

Introduction

It is truly a great honour to be asked to deliver this lecture in memory of Comrade A.K. Gopalan on the occasion of his birth centenary. Com. Gopalan's life reflected every phase of our country's social movements and its struggle for freedom from imperialism. Wherever people were engaged in struggle Com. Gopalan would always be there – starting in the early years with the famous temple entry agitation at Guruvayur to his activities in the Congress Socialist Party in Kerala, to his transition to dedicated work as a Communist. If Com. Gopalan had been alive today, he would surely be shocked and very angry that the independence from imperialism that he along with his comrades had struggled so hard to achieve, is being betrayed by the new compradors who lead this country in this age of the new imperialism.

Comrade A.K.Gopalan Centenary Memorial Lecture organized by Jansanskriti, Delhi, July 13, 2005.

During the last fifteen years, our economy and society have been subjected to the forces of so-called 'globalisation', which is but a euphemism for the attempted re-colonization of the developing world by the advanced countries, using new forms of control through the global financial institutions, through a new global trade and investment 'discipline' and through intellectual hegemonization. These forces of imperialist globalization have introduced a process of rapid alteration in the nature of the contradictions in Indian economy and society. This paper will focus mainly on the question of the changing contradictions in the agrarian sphere, which has been perhaps the most severely affected. Today we see that there is a pervasive agrarian crisis: the reasons for such an unprecedented crisis, not seen before since Independence, cannot be understood without an understanding of the question of changing contradictions in the agrarian economy.

For Marxists, the concept of 'contradiction' is an essential analytical tool for understanding the changing nature of social reality. At any given moment of time in a social formation there will be a multiplicity, indeed a bewildering multiplicity of both class contradictions and contradictions between varying levels of development of productive forces with respect to varying relations of production. Particularly in a vast and regionally diverse land like India, it is all too easy to lose the focus of analysis and be submerged in descriptive detail. Empiricism, or looking at 'facts' alone will not do: in fact, empiricism can lead to ignoring the most crucial 'facts' and to a wholly incorrect understanding of the prevailing crisis and therefore to an incorrect idea of how to carry forward the struggle against imperialist globalisation. To be able to pick out and analyse from the welter of numerous contradictions, what is it that constitutes the *principal contradiction*, to pin point the secondary contradictions and how they relate to and affect the principal contradiction, is important for obtaining an idea of the correct course of struggle and political action in the interests of the exploited classes.

Our understanding of what is meant by the concept of 'principal contradiction' in the agrarian sphere can be enhanced through a study of the writings of V. I. Lenin and Mao Zedong. While analysing the nature of classes in the agrarian economy of Russia at the turn of the 19th-20th centuries, Lenin while not explicitly using the term 'contradiction' in every case, nevertheless provided a very clear idea of the changing nature of contradictions. In *The Development of Capitalism in Russia* he argued that although the remnants of the old feudal lord-serf economy were still strong, the agrarian sphere was being rapidly penetrated and altered by forces leading to the growth of capitalist relations both as regards the economy of the peasantry and as regards the economy of the lords. The stress on the development of capitalist relations as the dominant tendency led to the stress in the RSDLP's agrarian programme, of *nationalisation of the land* 'in the event of the victorious development of the revolution'. Soon practical experience as regards the nature of the principal contradiction was provided by the 1905-07 Revolution in Russia, in the course of which the revolutionary peasantry attacked feudal landed property with the aim of seizing the feudal estates and redistributing land to the peasantry.

It is significant that Lenin at this point, learning from the experience of what the peasantry itself wanted, which was land as their private holdings, modified his own earlier analysis in *The Development of Capitalism in Russia*. In an important passage he said while his earlier analysis of the capitalist development of agriculture had correctly captured 'the trend' of change in production relations, it did not mean that 'the moment' of production relations had altered. I have interpreted this in my previous writings on the subject to mean that, while the dominant trend was indeed towards developing capitalist relations and the growing contradiction between wage labour and capital in Russian agriculture, it remained a secondary contradiction and had not yet supplanted the principal contradiction which remained that between the ex-serf peasantry as a whole and the ex-feudal nobility and lords. The idea of the worker-peasant alliance, a most crucial innovation in Marxist theory, was developed by Lenin on the basis of his analysis of developing relations of production in Russian agriculture on the one hand, and the practical experience of the First Russian Revolution (1905-07) on the other. It is on the basis of this understanding of 'trend' versus 'moment', the direction of change in contradiction versus the nature of the principal contradiction, that the actual programme of the RSDLP was changed during the 1917 Revolution from the nationalisation of the land, to the redistribution to the peasantry of the confiscated feudal estates.

With Mao Zedong, we come to an explicit discussion of contradictions in the famous essay titled *On Contradiction* written in 1937. "There are many contradictions in the process of development of a complex thing, and one of them is necessarily the principal contradiction whose existence and development determines and influences the existence and development of all other contradictions." He pointed out that what constitutes the principal contradiction at one point of time, such as the contradiction between 'feudal system and the great masses of the people', can move to a secondary position when there is a direct imperialist attack. "At such a time, the contradiction between imperialism and the country concerned becomes the principal contradiction, while all the contradictions among the various classes within the country (including what was the principal contradiction, between the feudal system and the great masses of the people) are temporarily relegated to a secondary and subordinate position."

Mao Zedong also explained the concept of the 'principal aspect of a contradiction' in the sense that, of the two contradictory elements (whether in a principal or in a secondary contradiction) one is dominant at a given point of time but can change to a subordinate position: thus with the victorious development of the peoples' struggles this aspect becomes dominant over the aspect of imperialism which might have been dominant earlier. A concrete application of the idea of changing contradictions can be seen in his essay *On New Democracy,* where the broadest unity of the 'proletariat, the peasantry, the intelligentsia and the petty bourgeoisie' was envisaged and the role of the Communist Party was 'to lead the people in overthrowing imperialism and the forces of feudalism'.

Principal Contradiction in India before and following Independence

The principal contradiction in the colonial period, was between the Indian people as a whole, and imperialism and its local comprador allies. After Independence, the principal contradiction changed to the contradiction between the mass of the working peasantry and labourers on the one hand, and the minority of landlords, traders and moneylenders who monopolized control over land and money-capital, thereby exploiting the peasantry through rent, interest and exorbitant traders' margins. While imperialism was by no means dead, it was on the retreat in the context of the post-War shambles that was the advanced world, and decolonisation allowed space for third world countries like India to try to de-link from the earlier international division of labour under which they had been completely open and liberalised economies geared to metropolitan growth, not national growth. They could now protect their economies and undertake state intervention in the interests of national development - in which they were helped by the existence and aid of the socialist camp. The old liberalisers were silenced, while the new liberalisers had not yet appeared.

In the agrarian sphere in India the resolution of the principal contradiction, namely that between the landlords and the mass of the peasantry, was tied up closely with the solution of a number of other important secondary economic and social contradictions. The principal contradiction implied that the need of the times was to break land monopoly by measures of effectively re-distributing land from the landlords to the land-poor and landless, to break the monopoly of credit and marketing through co-operative institutions of the peasants themselves on the one hand, and state intervention in channelling credit to the credit-starved and setting up non-profit marketing institutions between producer and consumer with the aim of stabilising prices for both. It was essential that the principal contradiction should be tackled boldly in order to resolve the other important and related contradictions.

These other important, related contradictions whose resolution depended on how the principal contradiction was dealt with, were many. There was the contradiction between the paucity of productive investment and hence the low level of productive forces in agriculture on the one hand - not because economic surplus was inadequate but because it was used unproductively - and the imperative need to increase the total grain output for feeding the rural population itself at higher levels, and at the same time to increase the commoditised portion of grain needed as wage-goods for the new industrial thrust, on the other. There was similarly the contradiction between the inadequate growth of raw materials and the need to continue some exports on the one hand, and the raw materials needs of growing domestic industry. There was the contradiction between the deep poverty - overwhelmingly rural in nature - and low standards of material life in the villages on the one hand, and the need to expand the internal mass market and make industrial expansion and overall development self-sustaining, on the other, which was only possible through measures increasing mass purchasing power.

There was the contradiction between the continuing caste, class, gender and other social types of oppression in a particularly intense form in rural areas on the one hand, and the very constitutional basis of the Indian polity which considered every citizen to be equal and to have equal opportunities regardless of caste, class, gender and so on. The moment we spell out these contradictions we can see the multifarious links between the principal and other contradictions, between the agrarian question and the question of national development free of imperialist pressures.

The non-left political forces, economists and planners in India however have consistently underestimated the role of effective re-distributive land reforms for breaking the economic and social power of the rural landed minority, thereby widening the social base of rural investment, and raising the rate of growth of both retained and commoditised output. They have underestimated its importance for laying the precondition for measures of mass poverty reduction and for providing an expanding market for industry, and its importance for reducing the old class, caste and gender based forms of inequalities which express themselves in high levels of illiteracy, declining sex-ratios, atrocities against *dalits,* and the persistence of child labour. Only in the states where the Left movement has been influential were some measures of land reform undertaken, with a very positive impact despite their relatively limited nature.

While the achievements of forty years of planned development in India were in many ways substantial, its economic and social failures therefore have been equally glaring. These lay in the inability to substantially reduce mass poverty, which is particularly concentrated in rural areas; an insufficient growth of the internal mass market and hence the emergence of pressure to seek external sources of growth in collaboration with foreign capital.

International developments led to the re-emergence of finance capital as a dominating force over industrial capital in the advanced world from the late nineteen seventies. The relative political unity achieved by the national bases of this finance capital (by subordinating inter-imperialist rivalry, to common aims vis a vis the third world), the aggressive use by finance capital, of the supra-national Bretton Woods institutions (the International Monetary Fund and the World Bank) for implementing its aims, and the collapse of the Soviet Union, have together led to a highly favourable conjuncture for imperialism, which is once again aggressively trying to re-colonise the third world and has substantially succeeded in many smaller countries. In recent years however tendencies of resistance to the dominance of finance capital have also started emerging in varied ways.

The new liberalisers arrived on the scene in Latin America and Africa many years ago; they have been stridently pushing the theories and practice of the new liberalisation in India since the beginning of the nineties. The old imperialism was transparent because there was direct political control, while the new imperialism is less transparent and therefore in many ways, more dangerous. The new liberalisation differs from the old colonial liberalisation in at least two respects: it has a strategy of improving further the economic position of the third-world rich at the expense of their fellow-citizens, which has materially corrupted the elite of our country; and it has an ideological thrust in terms of wrong theories, which has intellectually suborned the same third world public figures and intellectuals who were earlier supporters of independent growth, but who now mindlessly parrot the *mantra* of liberalisation they have memorised from their advanced country mentors. The new compradors are following anti-national theories and policies no less than the old compradors had done. It is extremely important for those who are within the Left movement to fight the revisionist tendencies creeping into the movement which lead to a 'soft' stance on liberalisation. To support any aspect of liberalisation even for pragmatic reasons is equivalent to political liquidationism.

Origins and Features of the Agrarian Crisis in India

India has been following since 1991 exactly the same set of deflationary policies at the macroeconomic level, already followed in the 1980s by nearly 80 indebted countries under the guidance of the IMF. These macroeconomic deflationary policies have included reduction in Central and state government development expenditures, high real interest rates namely tight money, reduction of the ratio of budget deficit to GDP, caps on organised sector wages, and devaluation. (See Table I summarizing the policies, in "Theorizing Food Security and Poverty" in this volume).

The useful papers in the two volume study edited by Cornia, Jolly and Stewart, titled *Adjustment with a Human Face* (1987), have detailed the effects of the neo-liberal policy package in those developing countries which undertook these policies a decade or earlier compared to India. The picture which emerged was alarming indeed: reduction in investment rates, reduction in growth rates, and absolute decline in output and income in a number of cases, a reversal of progress on the fronts of literacy, infant mortality rates and other health indicators, sharp cuts in wages and employment, and rise in poverty. All this was exactly as sensible macroeconomic theory would predict: if deflationary and contractionary policies are consistently followed, the results are bound to be as observed, and only those people can ever think otherwise, who adhere to a logically incorrect theory serving the narrow interests of finance capital.

The fact that neo-liberal policies represent an attack on the forces of production in developing countries is still neither understood nor believed by most people despite the overwhelming theoretical and empirical evidence which has emerged in favour of this conclusion during the last quarter century. Many persons are misled by the assertion that India has the second highest GDP growth rate in the world after China, namely 7 to 8 percent annually, into thinking that the growth is taking place in every sector. On the contrary, from the mid-1990s in particular, both the material productive sectors – industry and agriculture – have been in decline with agriculture being more severely affected than industry. The only sector which has expanded fast is the services sector. There has been a perverse structural shift in the economy even before any substantial industrial growth has taken place.

The policies followed by countries in the 1980s under IMF guidance included reduction in public expenditure, tight money, fiscal contraction, caps on wages and devaluation. These clearly add up to a policy package which is strongly expenditure-deflating. Since neo-liberal policies in India have also been expenditure deflating as regards the material productive sectors, and strongly so with respect to agriculture, it is not surprising that we see an agrarian crisis unfolding, while every indication is that absolute poverty is rising.

There have been more marked changes during the fifteen years of reforms, in the composition of GDP and of employment by the major economic sectors, than during the preceding thirty years. During the 1980s, the contribution of the secondary sector to the nation's income had risen, but under economic reforms it has stagnated at around a quarter during the 1990s and up to 2003-4. The share of agriculture in GDP which was declining slowly in the 1980s, has fallen steeply from about 36 percent at the beginning of the 1990s to below 25 percent by the triennium ending 2003-04, while the share of services has risen correspondingly from around two-fifths to over one-half of GDP, the largest rise being in trade, hotels, transport and communications followed by finance, real estate and business services (Table 1).

It is a cause for concern that there is 'tertiarization' of the Indian economy even before it has undergone substantial industrial development. A similar shift towards services accompanied by decline in agriculture and stagnation in manufacturing, had been last seen in the colonial period during 1891 to 1931.

Table 1
Percentage Contribution of the Economic sectors to GDP at factor cost,
1980-81 to 2003-04 (Taking constant values at 1993-94 prices)

Three year average centred on the year	Agriculture, forestry, fishing, mining & quarrying	Manufac- turing, construc- tion, utilities	All Services	Trade, hotels, transport & comm- unication	Finance, real estate & business services
1.	2.	3.	4.	5.	6.
(Pre-reform)					
1987-8	36.4	23.2	40.3	19.2	8.8
(Post reform)					
1993-4	33.5	23.9	42.5	19.4	11.2
1996-7	30.2	25.4	44.5	21.1	11.6
1999-0	27.5	24.6	47.9	22.3	12.5
2002-3	24.7	24.6	50.6	24.6	12.8
Percent change 2000-03 over 1987-8	-11.7	1.4	10.3	5.4	4.0

Source: Govt. of India, Ministry of Finance, *Economic Survey 2005-06*. Calculated from annual constant value data. (Current values show a steeper fall in the share of agriculture owing to crop prices declining faster than other prices). Note that cols. 2, 3 and 4 add to 100 while cols. 5 and 6 relate to sub-sectors of All Services.

Table 2
Distribution of Workers by Activities

	Agriculture and Allied Activities	Mining and Manufac- turing	Utilities, Construc- tion	Trade, Hotels, transport	Other Services	All
Rural						
Male						
1987-8	74.5	8.1	4.0	7.1	6.2	100
1993-4	74.1	7.7	3.5	7.7	7.0	100
1999-00	71.4	7.9	4.7	10.0	6.2	100
Female						
1987-8	84.5	7.3	2.7	2.2	3.0	100
1993-4	86.2	7.4	1.0	2.2	3.4	100
1999-00	85.4	7.9	1.1	2.1	3.7	100
Urban						
Male						
1987-8	9.1	27.0	7.0	31.2	25.2	100
1993-4	9.0	24.8	8.1	31.6	26.4	100
1999-00	6.6	23.3	9.5	39.8	21.0	100
Female						
1987-8	29.4	27.8	3.9	10.7	27.8	100
1993-4	24.7	24.7	4.4	11.3	35.0	100
1999-00	17.7	24.4	5.0	18.7	34.2	100

Source: NSSO, large sample Rounds. Note that figures may not add exactly to 100 owing to rounding.

The occupational distribution of the workforce shows that the share of agriculture in the male rural workforce has declined very little, from 74.5 percent to 71.4 percent comparing 1999-2000 with 1987-88 even though the share of agriculture in GDP has declined by 11 percentage points over that period, while for the rural female workforce dependence on agriculture has slightly risen over this period from 84.5 to 85.4 percent. This indicates that real output per head in agriculture has been falling under economic reforms and trade liberalization. The share of male urban workforce dependent on mining, manufacturing and utilities which was 29.5 percent in 1977-78 and had fallen slightly by one point by 1987-88, shows a steep decline from that date to only 24.1 percent by 1999-2000 while urban female workers similarly register a declining share in these activities, from 28 to 24.6 percent. The share of employment in all services taken together register a large rise in urban areas for both males and females but more so for the latter. These data relate to number of workers and do not reflect the reduction in days worked per worker which is an important dimension of unemployment. On the employment criterion one can definitely say that there has been significant de-industrialization over the reform period combined with tertiarization of the economy.

The disturbing feature underlying these relative shifts is that from the mid-1990s, there has been is *absolute decline* in numbers of workers employed as well as days of employment in agriculture, mining and quarrying, and in public utilities. The share of organized industry (where work conditions are better) in total manufacturing employment, has also declined. Employment growth in rural India at 2.4 percent, was robust in the 1980s, while it has collapsed in the reform period to only 0.7 percent. This collapse of rural employment is particularly significant as seven-tenths of the total population is dependent on rural livelihoods.

The only sector of the economy which has registered rapid expansion is the services sector, of which a small segment is high-income generating IT- enabled services and financial services, both of which have been growing fast. The bulk of services remain low-income provision of personal and catering services to the small minority of rich Indians, one sixth or so of

Table 3
Employment Trends by Economic Sectors

Change in Number of Employed workers, millions

Sector	1983 to 93-4	1993-4 to 99-0	Annual Growth Rate, %		Elasticity of Employ -ment w.r.t. GDP	
	Period 1	Period 2	Period 1	Period 2	Period 1	Period 2
1. Agriculture	35.23	- 4.90	1.51	-0.34	0.5	0.00
2. Mining & Quarrying	0.94	-0.43	4.16	-2.85	0.69	0.00
3. Manufacturing	8.47	5.51	2.14	2.05	0.33	0.26
4. Electricity, Gas &water	0.50	-0.07	4.50	-0.88	0.52	0.00
5. Construction	4.90	5.54	5.32	7.09	1.00	1.00
6. Trade, Hotels etc	8.56	9.54	3.57	5.04	0.63	0.55
7. Transport, Storage & Communications	2.94	4.36	3.24	6.04	0.49	0.69
8. Financial & business	1.82	1.53	7.18	6.20	0.92	0.73
9. Community, Social & Personal	8.33	1.07	2.90	0.55	0.50	0.07
10. ALL	71.69	22.55	2.04	0.98	0.41	0.15

continued

Absolute No. of Employed Workers in millions

	1983	1993-4	1999-00
1. Agriculture	207.23	242.46	237.56
2 +3. Mining, quarrying & manufacture	35.79	45.20	50.28
4. Utilities	0.85	1.35	1.28
5+6+7. Construction. trade, hotels, transport, storage, communications	33.39	49.79	69.63
8. Financial& business Services	1.70	3.52	5.05
9. Community, social & personal services	23.80	32.13	33.20
All	**302.76**	**374.45**	**397.0**

Source: Planning Commission, 2002.

the total population, who have enjoyed a rapid rise in their real incomes under economic reforms. National Income was already highly unequally distributed in the 1990s, but there has been further rise in income inequality of a very specific and disturbing kind, namely an absolute decline of real income for the vast majority of the population, combined with a very rapid rise in real incomes for a small minority. This has meant, on the one hand, a very visible real estate and building boom in urban areas, a fast growing market for high-end consumer durables and electronic goods on account of the old rich plus the burgeoning new-rich minority which is seeking to emulate Northern life styles. On the other hand, for the majority of the population it has meant higher unemployment, indebtedness, asset loss and hunger, in short growing immiserization.

A New Phase of Attacks on the Land, Forest and Water Resources of Small Scale Producers

The agenda of economic reforms and privatization is being pushed by the State with continual pressure from the international financial institutions, and it is reflected in a new round of attacks in recent years, both on the small-scale property of the peasantry and on the common property resources of tribal populations, in the name of 'development' and the corporate take-over of land and water resources. At the same time, the agenda of globalization is meeting increasing resistance: the polarization of Indian society is setting up new patterns of class re-alignments, in which a picture which is both complex but in a sense increasingly clear, is emerging.

Karl Marx had pointed out while discussing ground rent in *Capital*, that in all 'civilised' capitalist societies the ruling classes ruthlessly dispossessed vast numbers of small producers from the crop land and natural resources from which they derived their livelihoods, merely to establish large country houses; they planted arable land for forests and stocked them with deer for hunting and reserved streams for exclusive fishing, sports they engaged in only for a few weeks in the year. The attempt of the Indian ruling classes especially the corporate sector and the rich, to attain this type of 'civilised' status is visible today as they blatantly set out to grab the land, forest and water resources of small producers dependent on farming, fishing or forest produce, all in the name of 'development' – which is more correctly to be read as the further enrichment and enjoyment of the rich, at the expense of the right to work and right to food of the poor. For 'country houses and deer forests' read farm houses, sea-side resorts, theme parks, luxury housing estates and golf courses, and the situation today is the same as that described by Marx. There is an additional element however in our case as in all other developing countries, that of the entry of the foreign TNCs which represents the attempt to subordinate small producers to global capital whether through contracting or through direct acquisition of local land and water resources. The objective is not merely individual corporate profits – in its totality the system serves to maintain high living standards at the core countries of capitalism at the expense of a squeeze on the living standards of local populations. This too leads to displacement of producers as the labour intensity of such production is lower than in previous producing regimes, and land is also acquired directly by corporates. The question of displacement of small producers has come to the forefront as never before owing to the sustained and increasingly widespread attacks on the property rights of small producers.

Most projects proposed by domestic and foreign corporates in which land is being taken over for a pittance from farmers by the government or directly by the corporates with facilitation by the government, although claimed to be for setting up industries which will generate employment, in reality represent nothing but real estate speculation. The same is true of the hundreds of 'special economic zones' which are being indiscriminately set up often on prime agricultural land, where the moneyed are rushing to enjoy tax bonanzas and speculate in real estate catering to the urban rich.

What the policy makers in the Indian government pushing these policies and the economists justifying them in an opportunistic manner, choose to forget is that the lakhs of European small producers who were displaced over the years by similar land-grabbing in the Northern heartland of capitalism during the phase of primitive accumulation in the 18th and 19th centuries, were exported abroad along with the potentially explosive social and political problems that their dispossession created. Fifty million Europeans migrated in the latter century alone and settled on vast land areas that had been seized from the indigenous inhabitants in the Americas and in other continents. If our small producers are displaced today they have nowhere to go, and displacement will simply create social and political turmoil. The 21st century is not the 19th, and attacks on small scale production should and will generate bitter resistance. It is interesting to note that in one recent episode in Maharashtra of proposed take-over of agricultural land by a corporate group, the resisting villagers promised that they would now engage not in self-killing, or suicide (*atmahatya*) but in killing (*hatya*).

More than five thousand indebted farmers, mainly cotton farmers, have committed suicide in Andhra Pradesh alone since 1998 as its government which had entered into a state-level Structural Adjustment Programme with the World Bank, raised power tariff five times even as cotton price fell by half. Over a thousand farmer suicides have also taken place in Punjab, and a similar number in the Vidarbha region of Maharashtra where suicides continue at present. During the four years from 2001, over 1,250 suicides are recorded in Wynad and Palakkad in Kerala as prices to the local growers of coffee, tea and spices have nose-dived even more steeply than global prices once large companies have taken over purchase and marketing. Thus by 2003 the price of coffee to the grower was only one-quarter and that of tea and pepper only one-third of the prices prevailing in 1999. The purchase price of paddy rice also fell.

The agrarian crisis was the main reason for the decisive mass rejection of neo-liberal policies and the May 2004 electoral defeat of the NDA coalition at the Centre as well as the TDP government in Andhra Pradesh. In recognition of the employment crisis the new United Progressive Alliance or UPA had promised to implement an Employment Guarantee Act which has been formulated, but which has been diluted already by not setting a time-frame for implementation throughout the country.

India has exported record volumes of wheat and rice during the last six years, and its share in global exports of rice and wheat has risen quite noticeably. Despite the drastic slowing down of output growth, India exported 22 million tonnes of foodgrains during the two years 2002 and 2003, and the share of grain exports in total exports has risen from under one-fifth to almost a quarter. There is higher global trade integration reflected in rising trade-GDP ratio. During the severe drought year starting from monsoon 2002, despite grain output being 30 million tonnes lower than in the previous year, from June 2002 to November 2003, a total of 17 million tonnes of foodgrains were exported by the NDA government. Superficially it looks as though policies of trade liberalization have 'worked'.

The crucial fact which is suppressed in official publications and in the writings of pro-reform economists, and this is true even after the elections and the change in government, is that the vastly increased grain exports have been coming out of more and more empty stomachs as millions of rural labourers and farmers have suffered job loss and income decline. Food grains absorption in India today has reached a historic low as a result of the massive decline in purchasing power especially in villages owing to the combination of rising unemployment, rising input and credit costs for farmers and exposure to global price declines. Loss of purchasing power is pervasive affecting both the 158 million wage-dependent workers as well as the 120 million cultivating workers and their families. Targeting the food subsidy from 1997-8 by restricting supply of cheaper grain to only those officially identified as 'below the poverty line' has also added to the institutional denial of affordable food grains to the poor, not merely owing to mistakes of wrong exclusion from the set of the officially poor, but also owing to the gross official underestimation of the numbers in actual poverty.

The actual rural population in poverty (applying the official definition of those with less than 2400 calories intake to NSS data) was 75 percent in 1993-4, increased to at least 78 percent by 1999-2000, and the depth of poverty also increased with more people moving below 1800 calories, the bare minimum for survival. In 1983 only in three states of India (West Bengal, Tamilnad and Kerala) one third or more of the rural population had an intake below 1800 calories. The 1999-2000 data show that West Bengal and Kerala have improved greatly, West Bengal sufficiently to move up out of this set, but four new major states (Andhra Pradesh, Assam, Karnataka and Madhya Pradesh) have seen sharp decline in nutrition and one-third or more of their population fell below 1800 calories intake. The situation after 1999-2000 to the present, would be worse still, since it is from 1998 that we see the steep fall in per capita foodgrains absorption to which I have repeatedly drawn attention. In fact the situation is even worse than the nutrition data indicate since the poor have been selling assets and losing land against debt in order to survive at these lower levels. (The Planning Commission estimates of 'falling' poverty are a fairy-tale since they have been obtained using a logically wrong procedure which entails continuous decline over time, of the consumption standard against which poverty is measured).

The per capita availability or absorption of food grains in India has fallen alarmingly during the decade of deflationary neo-liberal economic reforms, to only 153 kg. annually taking the three year average ending in 2002-03. This current level is the same as during the First Plan fifty years ago and is lower than the 157 kg. recorded during 1937-41 under colonialism. Thus the food security gains of the four decades of protectionism up to 1991 have been totally reversed. This important finding and the reasons for the present debacle have been discussed in greater detail in 'The Republic of Hunger' and in 'Theorizing Food Security and Poverty', both included in this volume, and in 'Food Stocks and Hunger – Causes of Agrarian Distress' published in *Social Scientist*, July-August 2003.

Summarizing the Discussion

To sum up, the origins of the agrarian crisis facing all developing countries lie in the following policy measures which they have adopted under the tutelage of the international *sahukars* and advanced country governments – policies which are strongly pushed by the International Monetary Fund, the World Bank, satellite banks like the Asian Development Bank, advanced country governments' aid packages with their own conditions, and the WTO discipline. These policies and their effects in India can be summed up as follows:

1. Income-deflating, contractionary policies are followed at the macroeconomic level. There are large cuts in government investment in irrigation and infrastructure, large cuts in public rural development expenditures including plant research and development. *This hits the forces of production directly* and leads to a slowing down of output growth and to rise in unemployment on this account. It also hits the livelihoods and incomes of farmers and labourers through another route, since every Rs.100 less spent by government on rural development leads to at least Rs.400 loss of incomes through multiplier

effects involving very large job losses. The two factors together have sharply reduced the purchasing power of farmers and labourers. *Increasing pauperization and deepening hunger are the outcome.* The annual absorption of foodgrains per head has fallen from 178 kg. in the three years ending in 1991, to 154 kg. by the three years ending in 2003. As mass purchasing power is reduced and the internal foodgrains market collapses, our land and resources are diverted from foodgrains to export production and foodgrains are also directly exported.

2. Subsidies are reduced, lowering the competitiveness of our farmers, while at the same time very large subsidies are maintained in advanced countries. *There is a systematic attack on subsidies on fertilisers and on power, an attack on affordable bank credit for farmers, and an attack on public procurement and marketing bodies. All this raises the cost structure for our farmers and makes them less competitive, which is in the interests of advanced countries trying to penetrate our markets.* At the same time these advanced countries maintain and increase the direct subsidies to their own farm and agro-business in order to dominate and control global markets.

3. Through the WTO, signatory developing countries are forced to remove quantitative restrictions on trade, to convert to tariffs and to lower tariffs to very low levels, thus allowing imports which undermine the livelihoods of our farmers. *Through the Agreement on Agriculture, provisions are made by rich industrialised countries to make large direct payments from their national budgets to their farm sector which accounts for less than 5 percent of their GDP and employment. This option is not open to developing countries like India which have large farm sectors contributing 60 percent of employment and a quarter of GDP, and have small budgetary resources.*

4. Exports of agricultural products needed by advanced countries are promoted and contract farming systems are introduced to subordinate

our farmers to the giant agro-business corporations. At the same time competitive devaluation of currencies and competitive deflations are encouraged among developing countries, so while *the quantum of their agricultural exports rises fast, the earnings from these exports do not rise and can even fall, because the unit dollar value falls continuously.*

5. The *public distribution system of food grains comes under attack* as it is in the interests of the developed countries to dismantle local food security systems so that they can export food grains to us. The food subsidy is first cut by raising the issue price of food grains from the ration shops which prices out poorer consumers. The deflationary policies at the same time by reducing purchasing power cause a drastic fall in sales from the ration shops. Food grain stocks build up raising the cost of holding the stocks. *Having themselves created the problem of falling purchasing power, increasing hunger and huge stocks, the neo-liberals then say the PDS is not working and demand its dismantling.*

6. Not only are the mass of ordinary small and poor peasants and labourers deeply affected by falling employment and incomes: the collapse of the internal rural market hits also the surplus foodgrains producers and induces a crisis in their productive system. In the case of India a crisis has been created in the agriculture of North India (Punjab and Haryana in particular) owing to the loss of internal markets to the tune of 26 million tonnes of foodgrains.

7. At the international level owing to the following of deflationary policies even developed countries face recession and unemployment. They turn prices against the developing countries: there has been continuous fall in prices of crops during the last ten years – from an index of 100 in 1993 it is now down to only 53 by 2004. This is as fast a rate of fall as during the Great Depression and it is a major component of agrarian crisis. More than 9,000 officially recorded farmer suicides owing to debt have taken place since 1998, actual numbers are more, and the suicides are continuing. Large scale land

loss by peasants to creditors has been taking place and the percentage of the landless has risen. The developed countries on the other hand, maintain their own global competitiveness when prices are falling, by giving billions of dollars of direct payments on an increasing basis to their farmers and agro-business concerns.

8. The varied plant and bio-genetic resources of developing countries are pirated without payment, and through the enactment of retrogressive Seed Acts and Patent Acts the monopoly of TNCs over the monetary benefits of research is ensured, depriving our farmers of their right to exchange seed and fully benefit from their traditional knowledge. Common water resources are appropriated by TNCs which also contribute to environmental pollution. *The privatisation of water resources is a major plank of the ongoing private appropriation of public resources.*

It is clear that the attack on third world peasantries is many-pronged, is systematic, and has the aim of the advanced countries and their TNCs acquiring control over our resources. Since the peasantry is seen as a barrier it is sought to be destroyed. This certainly represents a new phase of imperialism.

With these developments, in India the nature of the principal contradiction has changed in recent years, and it is once again moving rapidly towards the contradiction between the mass of the Indian people, and the new imperialism. In the agrarian sphere this new principal contradiction which is emerging, to be seen as a *process*, is now the contradiction *between all the peasant classes in rural areas on the one hand, and imperialism with its local landed collaborators on the other hand.* This does not mean that the earlier contradictions have ceased to be important but only that they have begun to move to a subordinate or secondary position, *in the sense that the nature of the emerging new contradiction determines the nature and path of the land question, and all other contradictions.* The way in which the principal contradiction is tackled by the progressive movement, is now crucial for deciding the course of the resolution of all the other contradictions.

The Land Question in the Present Conjuncture

When we argue that the principal contradiction is shifting rapidly in the agrarian sphere to that between the peasantry and workers on the one hand and imperialism with its local landlord and other collaborators on the other, many persons in the left movement who are not familiar with the idea or analysis of contradictions, feel alarmed because they think that 'the land question' is being put on the back burner. Nothing could be further from the case: they should remember that when the principal contradiction shifts to that between all the toiling masses and imperialism, it means that this contradiction is the one, "whose existence and development determines and influences the existence and development of all other contradictions" including what was earlier the principal contradiction.

This can be seen very clearly in our country today. As a result of imperialist globalisation, millions of peasants have got enmeshed in debt and have lost assets and land to their creditors, and there is already an onslaught of agro-business corporations, including foreign Transnational corporations, on peasant land and water resources, an onslaught which is likely to intensify further. The restrictions on landownership by non-cultivators where they existed have been removed by state governments, ceilings on landholdings have been rolled back in many states to facilitate the entry of agro-business corporations. The peasantry is losing land on a massive scale and despite asset loss is getting pushed further and further down into the mire of hunger. Even the former rich peasants and surplus producers are facing steeply falling profitability conditions and have started leasing out on hunger rents to dispossessed peasants. The earlier phase of capitalist development in agriculture marked by rise of capitalist farming from within the peasant classes, as well as the emergence of landlord capitalism, has virtually ended owing to the falling remunerativeness of direct capitalist cultivation. Reverting to extracting surplus through land rent and usurious interest is once again the order of the day, and peasant pauperisation is seen once more.

Virtually all the gains of previous land redistribution to land-poor and landless, have been reversed in many states. In such a situation, the struggle for land is inseparable from the struggle against imperialism. At the moment it is a defensive struggle which the poor and middle peasantry are losing because there is a lack of proper analysis of the ground-level reality regarding the agrarian crisis and land transfers. The level of complacence even among the progressive intelligentsia remains very high. Some vocal defenders of imperialist globalisation representing the Fund-Bank ideology claim to represent the interests of 'the farmers' and claim to be 'leaders' but in reality they are simply extremely reactionary ideologues without any social base : however, they often succeed in misleading even progressive elements of the intelligentsia and contribute to the latter's complacency since they deny the very existence of agrarian crisis.

What these self-styled leaders of farmers as well as members of the ruling classes advocate is the Fund-Bank line of the subjugation of our peasantry through debt-contract systems to foreign transnational corporations. The corporatization of agriculture which is sought to be promoted represents the control of transnational capital over our peasant production, and not 'the development of capitalism in agriculture' which has a completely different connotation in Marxist-Leninist literature. The 'development of capitalism in agriculture' took place when expansionary policies of autonomous national development were followed as during 1950 to 1990 in India, and it was geared to an expanding internal market. It led to some prosperity, though very unequally shared, in the agrarian sphere. By contrast the corporate subjugation of peasant production is nothing but the imperialist domination of our peasantry for the purpose of export production and it pauperises the peasantry and labourers.

When in general profitability is falling because prices on global markets are low, the giant transnational corporates entering agriculture today by tying peasants to contracts under debt on account of advances of high-tech GM (genetically modified) seeds and inputs, set the terms of contract in such a way as to grind the peasants down to sub-human levels of living because they ruth-lessly seek to maximize their own profits. The experience of other countries in Latin America and sub-Saharan Africa has demonstrated this clearly.

Thus the land question has now become one of defending the right of peasants including tribal peoples to their land and livelihoods. Not only can it never be separated from the fight against imperialist globalisation, this fight is a necessary condition for any advance on the land question. It is shameful that no resistance has been articulated by the liberal intelligentsia and political movements to the modification of ceiling laws or the permission for non-agriculturists to acquire land, all for the benefit of corporations. There is no outcry against blatant usury or land loss against debt, whereas even the colonial period had seen anti-usury laws and enactments against peasant land alienation owing to debt.

Some petty bourgeois intellectuals keep putting forward carping criticisms on how the left movement has 'not taken account of' caste, 'not taken account of the demands of the *dalits*' and so on. They are greatly impressed by the superficial parliamentary successes of identity politics, but fail to realize that the leaders of backward castes and *dalits* have been co-opted without exception into the exploitative ruling elites and have done nothing for their constituents except futile symbolic gestures. Nor are these opportunist leaders capable of doing anything for the exploited mass of the backward castes and the *dalits* of our society because their ideology itself is a backward one based on the same principles of exclusion that have been practiced against them, and thus merely represents an inverted form, not a transcendence, of these principles of exclusion. The paramount requirement however is the revolutionary mobilisation of the *dalits* who are in the main the poorest workers and peasants, along with all other exploited people and classes in a united fight against imperialism which necessarily includes the fight against all forms of social discrimination.

The clearest indicator that the principal contradiction is changing, is provided by the very fact of *the agrarian crisis* itself, which in its scale, generalised nature affecting all the peasantry, and in its depth, is quite unprecedented. This ongoing agrarian crisis is the direct outcome of the implementation of neo-liberal reform policies and trade liberalization detailed above, in short of *the impact of imperialist globalisation on our agriculture*. Moreover, the worst effects are yet to be seen, for there is a determined effort being made by the advanced countries today, supported by the local compradors, to acquire direct control over our land resources through contract farming and corporatization of agriculture, to enmesh our farmers in high-tech debt through GM seed and plants, and a direct effort to acquire control over the genetic basis of our bio-diversity. In this they are aided by the comprador elements in government placed in key decision making positions and they also have the support of comprador elements of the domestic landlords.

Our peasantry and labourers are reeling under the attacks on them and are struggling today merely to survive. Their agony is being turned destructively upon themselves in the form of suicides. The agony has to change to anger and be directed towards their oppressors. Only a fighting unity of all the peasant classes and workers against the onslaught of imperialism and its domestic collaborators including collaborating landlords, can now save the peasantry. In fact this unity is necessary for repulsing the imperialist attack in every sphere and not only in the agrarian sphere, for with its sheer weight of numbers the peasantry has the potential to act as a revolutionary force where the working class on its own cannot. Of course, it is only the working class ideology that can provide the basis for an effective anti-imperialist mobilisation. This fighting unity of peasants and workers will not come spontaneously and automatically from the millions facing increasing impoverishment, hunger and loss of assets. It has to be patiently but urgently forged by the left and progressive movement. For this a clear theoretical understanding on the nature of the principal contradiction combined with an awareness of the urgency of the present conjuncture, is required. Otherwise, imperialism will roll over our masses like a colossal tank and break the spines of our toiling millions, while intellectuals and activists impotently look on.

The most effective way of countering these attacks at the local level is for the small producers whether they are engaged in crop production or in livestock and other activities, to organize themselves into associations directly for the purpose of production and marketing. The last fifteen years' experience has shown that individual small farmers cannot cope with the lethal neo-liberal combination of attacks on subsidies, exposure to global price volatility, withdrawal of state purchasing, and in many places also attacks on their property rights. At the level of national policy making these mindless policies should and are being contested and the need for effective public intervention to stabilize prices is again making itself felt. But initiatives are also necessary at local level to overcome the agrarian crisis.

The small producer in this country is one of the lowest cost producers in the world, and there is a good prospect of small production stabilizing and facing international competition, *provided the advantages of large scale production are reaped through production associations*. While input and credit cooperatives in this country have a long history and their expansion is necessary, they can at best play a supportive role. They cannot address the present problem of overall decline in the incentive to produce and invest owing to the sharp decline in the profitability and viability of agricultural production itself. To redress this, the combination of the small producers in associations for directly carrying out productive activities is necessary.

There are a number of individual examples, though few and far between, in the country where voluntary associations of small farmers for production have been successful: they have purchased inputs in bulk more cheaply, have been able to avail of lower cost credit owing to joint responsibility, have been able to overcome labour supply problems through pooling the labour of many families during peak demand, they have got better terms for the sale of produce and have also engaged directly in some cases in marketing and in processing their produce. Associations of labourers too are on record, who have successfully pooled and jointly operated the small plots of ceiling-surplus land distributed to them. This can be generalized if already displaced landless small farmers and labourers jointly take land on lease from large owners who are increasingly finding it unprofitable to cultivate directly.

Where the state governments are progressive they can play an important supportive role and ensure the viability of the farmers by setting up systems of state contracting on longer term contracts of three to five years with farmers' groups and associations, where the contracts specify the quantum to be supplied voluntarily by the farmer and the price of the output. This is important for the food crops whose output has become stagnant over the last five years and it is particularly important for the export crops where exposure to price volatility has been playing havoc with viability and has been leading to declining output and farmer suicides. In periods of fast rising global prices the farmers on such contract will be foregoing windfall gains but equally, during the inevitable subsequent global price declines, they will be assured of a higher than global price and will not be ruined through cumulating debt as is the case at present.

Without urgent and active interventions of this nature, and active opposition to the attempts to subordinate peasant production to global capital, the trajectory of genuine development which benefits the people is bound to be replaced by the trajectory of so-called 'development' which is not development at all because it immiserizes the people in the interests of the local rich and the global market. Given the high degree of fragility already imparted to the agrarian economy by public policies in the last fifteen years, and the stagnation and contraction of effective demand for such a large mass of people, reflected in the alarming decline in per head food grains absorption to pre-World War II levels, it is entirely possible that any future shock to the system such as rapid inflation or prolonged drought will precipitate famine. The further re-colonization of the Indian economy must be prevented: if the rulers of this country are not capable of doing so and indeed are taking us towards destruction, then the people have to take a hand, and gently administer political euthanasia to the comatose comprador leaders.

Printed in the United Kingdom
by Lightning Source UK Ltd.
129793UK00001B/130-156/A